Public Policy in India

Public Policy in India

Editor
Dr. Furqan Ahmad

ADROIT

Adroit Publishers

NEW DELHI • KATHMANDU

ISBN : 978-81-87393-82-5

First Edition: 2026

Published by
ADROIT PUBLISHERS 4675/21, Ganpati Bhawan, Ansari Road, Daryaganj, New Delhi-110 002 Phone : 011-23266030
adroitpublishers@gmail.com

Typeset in Garamond Premier Pro by Arun, Akriti Graphic Solution, Delhi-110081 E-mail: arun263923@gmail.com,

Dedication

This book is dedicated to my students
of the Department of Political Science
Jamia Millia Islamia University
New Delhi

Preface

India is going through a time of significant change. Economic growth, technological advancements, rapid urbanization, a growing youth population, closing gender gap and escalating impacts of climate change are coming together to redefine India's role and mandates as a major world power. While these developments bring new opportunities, times of transition can be both creative and challenging. India could not achieve many Millennium Development Goals (MDGs) particularly in hunger, health, nutrition, gender and sanitation.

We need to revisit all our existing policies in every sector to see whether they will meet the requirements of our changed demography, fluctuating economy, rapid urbanization, and jobless growth resulting in differentiated citizen access to good education, housing, health care and jobs.

Post seminar publications are fairly common. Prelude volumes which precede a seminar are rare. The Department of Political Science decided to take on the more challenging task of publishing the full papers received by us to be presented in our International Seminar this year.

This enables all participants to have a look at the papers before the seminar and have a meaningful discussion in all the sessions. This prelude volume includes 16 papers submitted for presentation and discussion in the International seminar hosted by the Department of Political Science on 26th – 27th February 2020. Varied perspectives on Public Policy are present here and we invite readers to enjoy the flavour of each. I thank each individual contributor for having enriched this volume.

Dr. Furqan Ahmad
Head, Department of Political Science
Jamia Millia Islamia

Contents

Chapter One

Democracy and Development in Post-Colonial India Revisiting Policy-making During the Nehru Era

Surya Narayan Misra[1]

Abstract

India remained under British colonial rule for about 200 years and very colonial era experienced exploitation, under-development and drain of resources. The post-independence era had to meet (i) the challenges of feudal order (ii) lack of resources, (iii) cold war conflict (iv) illiteracy and poverty etc. After freedom, India became the largest democracy in the world with J. L. Nehru its first Prime minister responsible for 'Nation-building' and 'State-building. Being a Fabled in nature and democratic in approach, Nehru steered the nation as leader of both the government and the party i.e. the Indian National Congress. Nehru stood for (i) democracy, (ii) decentralization, (iii) planned economic development and (iv) secularism. Since both agriculture and industry suffered during the colonial era, Nehru's government launched five year plans for smooth economic development and consequently; removal of poverty and malnutrition. He remained contending elected for 17 years and was understood as an architect of many policies and three five year plans. He was a great nation-builder and attained an international image.

Keywords: *Colonialism (i.e. slavery), Mixed Economy, Socialist Pattern of Society, Nation-building, Five Year Plan, Community Development, Welfare State.*

A Conclusive View at a Glance

India achieved her freedom after a prolonged nationalist struggle for over a century and freedom ushered in the decolonization process in the Afro-Asian region. India then was an old civilization but it turned into a new nation. India awakened to life and freedom at the stroke of mid-night on 14 August, 1947. The untold story of India's pre-meditated partition was - to divide Hindu-

1. Formerly, Professor of Political Science, Utkal University, Bhubaneswar, Odisha

Muslim unity especially which was noticed during the great uprising of 1857. The monumental task before the new elites was how to govern the nation where- (i) poverty, illiteracy, (ii) ignorance, (iii) undevelopment, (iv) social unrest and (v) financial crises were most disturbing. Earlier on 5th of December, 1946; the constituent assembly had started the process of writing the new Constitution of India. The ideology of the constitution was - to be fine-tuned keeping in view the consensus developed during the freedom struggle and the values emerged during the post-war years enunciated at Atlantic Charter as- 'The Four Freedoms'. It is for the first time that Indians from the length and breadth of India-gathered at one place to write their own future amidst the daunting circumstances before them. The Objective Resolution moved by Jawaharlal Nehru accorded primacy to democracy, republicanism, justice and the spirit of the French Revolution i.e. (i) Liberty, (ii) Equality and (iii) Fraternity.

India remained under British colonial control as long as about two centuries. Indians were socio-culturally neglected yet economically exploited. India was drained of its vital resources. Rather it was turned into a market for sale of British products made out of Indian raw-materials. The British used several strategies to subjugate all Indians. It was one of the largest colonies under the control of one of the European powers.

Colonialism is the holding and ownership of colonies or the treating of another country as though - it was in fact a colony. Colonialism is a situation where one country's capital or economically dominant part is under the control of a foreign country. According to Robertson (1985: 53): for true colonialism to exist, two conditions are necessary:- (i) The land held as a colony must have no real political independence from the mother country and (ii) the relationship must be one of forthright exploitation. The entire reason for holding colonies is to - increase the wealth and welfare of the colonial power either by extracting resources, material or labour, from the colony more cheaply than could be bought on a free market or by ensuring a market for one's own goods at advantageous rates. In this way a set of colonies may be rather different from an empire. In the latter case, the far flung land that constitutes the empire; may be integrated equally in economic and political terms with the original home-land i.e. the motive for imperial expansion being the spreading of a way of life or of political design or merely the pushing away of borders and thus; military danger emerged from the heart-land.[1]

British colonialism in India was not intended to have a positive approach for holistic development of the subjects. The economic exploitation broke the back-bone of a stable traditional society and it initiated the process of underdevelopment. This led to the crystallisation of the colonial economic structure which generated poverty and dependence on and subordination to Britain.

Historian Bipin Chandra (2008: 11) observed that there were four basic features of the colonial structure in India.

1. Colonialism led to the complete but complex integration of Indian economy with the world capitalist system but in a subservient position. Since 1750s India's economic interests were wholly subordinated to those of Britain. This is a crucial aspect, for integration with the world economy was inevitable and was a characteristic of independent economies.
2. To suit British industry, a peculiar structure of production and international division of labour was forced upon India. It produced and exported food stuff and raw materials- cotton, jute, oil seeds, minerals- and imported manufactured products of British industry from biscuits and shoes to machinery, cars and railway engines.
3. Basic to the process of economic development is the size and utilization of the economic surplus or savings generated in the economy for investment and therefore expansion of the economy (the net savings in the Indian economy from 1914 to 1946 was only 2.75 percent of GNP).
4. Feature of colonialism in India was the crucial role played by the state in constructing, determining, and maintaining other aspects of the colonial structure. India's policies were determined in Britain and in the interest of the British economy and the British capitalist class. The state, unfortunately, didn't support industry and agriculture. Thus the obvious intention was to keep India subordinate to the British colonial design and it also lured the emerging elites to British educational and employment structure who in return stood and spoke for the colonial employer.[2]

Colonialism was a curse on the Indian economy. The most visible neglect was - for agriculture and industry. They became later on, the causes for poverty and unemployment. Between 1901 and 1941, the per capita agricultural production was reduced by 14 percent. The per capita food grain production was more alarming as it fell by 24 percent. Ever since Cornwallis system came in 1793 the agrarian structure was dominated by land lords, money lenders, merchants and the colonial state. The colonial state was more concerned with the extraction of revenue and they had no interest in the promotion of agriculture and improvement of the quality of life. The process created ambitious rich peasants and impoverished cultivators.

The state of agriculture which was the prime absorber was in bad shape. Commercialization of agriculture didn't lead to capitalist farming or improved technology. As a result despite better soil, abundance of water and the availability of other resources agricultural production initiative was diverted from food crops to commercial crops. This was the main reason for India's economic backwardness. Other than agriculture the next victim of the colonial state was industry. Because of competition between cheap market products by the colonial power the durable handloom, handicraft and other artisanal products lost their market and by this the indigenous products suffered leading to unemployment and the fall of ancillary workforce. The ruined artisans failed to get alternative employment. They shifted to non-profitable sector in agriculture as tenant, share-croppers as well as landless agricultural labourers. Besides flourishing industrial development due to industrial revolution in the West, India suffered a setback as the colonial state didn't evince interest in industry and industrial development.

Further major development, during the second decade of the twentieth century can be summed up as- (i) there was rise of a strong indigenous capitalist class with an independent economic and financial base. This private initiative without foreign assistance could help in the rise of an industrial base. Similar was the case with small scale industries. Within four decades, i.e by 1947 the Indian capital had made a headway in banking and insurance.

Bipan Chandra (2008) had observed as these positive features of the Indian economy to be seen in a wider historical context. He identified that the so-called industrial development was not a product of the industrial revolution. It operated within a colonial system. Hence, it had stunted growth. However, decline in the British economy due to two world wars, economic depression of 1930s and pressure of the nationalist movements urging for boycott of foreign goods, the entrepreneurial class progressed to protect their image and investment.[3]

India: 1947

Thus, by the time India became independent; steady pauperization of the people especially the peasantry and the artisans had already accused. Extreme and visible poverty, disease and hunger and - starvation because the lot or destiny of the ordinary people. Social development was something foreign to the colonial state. The social development indicators provide the picture of the colonial state. Health services were very poor. Although education was taken as a crucial input in economic development yet vast majority of Indians didn't have access to education. It was found that in 1951 only 16% were literate and it was 8% for women. For a vast country - there were 13, 590 middle schools and 17,288 high schools.

India became free on 15th August, 1947 and in fact, India became a major instrument resulted in decolonization. The European powers particularly Great Britain's economic compulsions urged the colonizers to have a second thought about the centuries long exploitation of Afro-Asian countries. The Asian Relations conference held during March, 1947 in New Delhi - can be taken as 'freedom from colonial bondage initiative'.

The Indian National Congress which led an organized nationalistic struggle against the British - was in fact the dominant political group controlling the constitution-making process for new India. Among others leaders, Sardar Patel and Pandit Nehru were the most prominent Congress leaders advocating the Congress view to tackle the problems of a post-colonial state which faced the problems of resource-crunch, poverty, illiteracy and communal hatred emanating from the British policy of divide and rule leading to Partition of India on the basis of religion. Pandit Nehru became the first Prime minister and Sardar Patel was his deputy with the home portfolio to take the job of integrating India into one sovereign republic. The constitution makers were aware of the Gandhian legacy which stood for Swaraj and Swadeshi. Further, the participation of the INC, particularly in the government making as per the 1935 act - was most visible in orchestrating and shaping of the new republic on parliamentary lines. The new constitution came out of the anvil of the Constituent Assembly pronouncing Justice, Liberty, Equality and Fraternity as goals of the constitution. Tragedy occurred when Gandhi was assassinated and Patel died on 15th Dec, 1950. Thus, for 'nation-building' and 'state-building' Nehru had to shoulder the responsibility of leading both the party and the government.

Pandit Nehru headed the interim government. The country was experiencing Congress and Muslim League differences over the issue of homeland for the Muslims. There was no sign of any accommodation and at that stage the

Constituent assembly was constituted. The League boycotted the Assembly and sharpened its demand for partition. British India suffering from poverty, illiteracy, and malnutrition, had thus, experienced a new kind of communal hatred milieu leading to the partition of India. So the nation-building of the newly liberated India became the responsibility of Nehru and his government. Democracy, development, communal harmony, secularism, socialism and non-alignment had runs, ultimately dominated Nehruvian policy-making.

Democracy & Development

Nehru believed in Parliamentary democracy. Democracy was not only a form of government, it was a way of life, a way of solving problems by arguments, discussions and persuasion. Democracy thus, involved tolerance and restraint (GHOSE: 1984: 290). The first general election held in 1951-52 with 173 million, registered voters and a new Universal Adult Suffrage was the first test for him. He believed in democracy as a participatory cult which imbibes self-discipline. He wasn't in favour of imposed discipline. For him democracy stood for tolerance, calmness and understanding. a post-colonial state where new citizens were neither politically literate, nor constitutionally placed in a sound and comfortable stage, thinking of self-discipline was a part of Nehruvian understanding which rejected the fascist approach.[4]

Amidst rising social conflict and religious strife Nehru, for the greater interest, for according democracy a rightful place in a post-colonial situation had to approve the introduction of Preventive Detention Act which was characterized by Kripalini as 'Lawless law'. But Nehru defended it on the ground of situational exigencies. He was firm on the view that merely agitational approach or excessive resort to direct action might weaken democratic structure.

Nehru had differences with Gandhi, Sardar Patel and Rajendra Prasad. But he could persuade all of them and initiate his democratic operations and push his development agenda. He thought that planning through application of science could be of help to solve national problems of post-colonial India. Economic planning was dear to his heart. He was overwhelmed by the plan-based development in USSR. The National Planning Committee was constituted in 1938 when Netaji Bose was the president of AICC and Nehru was its chairman. He was an avowed socialist. After independence over the economic policy, Nehru had to confront his opponents who had no trust upon the Soviet pattern of development. The Industrial Policy was announced in 1948 contemplating public ownership of munitions, atomic energy, railways and in certain other industries like coal, iron & steel, aircraft manufacturing, ship building, telephonic and telegraphic materials and minerals. The government reserved the exclusive right to start new ventures. The existing ones were spared from being nationalized for at least 10 years. The rest of the industrial field was let open for free enterprise.

Ghose (1984) said: "This policy contained no revolutionary programme and was welcomed by the business community, but was denounced by the leftists as a retreat from socialism. It represented a compromise between socialist Nehru and conservative Patel. It was a policy of the 'Socialization of the vacuum' as it envisaged that the state would invest its resources only in fields which were inadequately occupied or not occupied by the private enterprise".[5] This was called Mixed Economy. Nehru had seen the utter neglect of agriculture and industry during the colonial era causing widespread poverty and growing unemployment.

5 Year Plans

The Nehruvian Era had three Five Year Plans beginning from 1951. The timing of the plan was said - to keep the election cycle in consideration. The First Plan (1951-56) was a moderate one. Two third of the expenditure was allotted for the public sector to deal with agriculture, community development, irrigation, power projects, transport and communication. Only 10% of the allocation was for industrial development. In the Second Plan (1956-61) emphasis was given to industry so that India could attain economic self-confidence and develop along modern lines.

Before the Second Plan was introduced, Nehru had persuaded the AICC held in 1955 to accept the establishment of a socialistic pattern of society as its goal. In this, he was influenced by the Karachi resolution of 1931 and impressive visit to China. The Second Plan was designed to accelerate the economic growth and establish welfare state. Resource crunch and natural calamities forced the Planning Commission to prune the size of the plan leaving core areas like agriculture production, power projects and upcoming steel plants in collaboration with British, German and Russian support.

The Third Plan (1961-66) was more ambitious and it had a bigger target than its predecessor. Its objective was to take India to a stage where the national economy would become self-sustaining.

Ghose (1984) observed that by opting for a planned economy Nehru wanted to obviate the anomalies of the uncontrolled markets. The ' invisible hand' praised by Adam Smith didn't always allocate resources and commodities and manner conducive to the welfare of the majority.

Nehru defended planned approach by saying planning means a logical, scientific and organized approach to an objective while replying to questions why people oppose five year plan.[6]

People observed whether planning was possible under a democratic structure or not? The Prime minister was the Chairman of the Planning Commission. As the chairman of the Planning Commission Nehru said: "What is on the trial is, in the last analysis, whether democracy can solve the problem of mass poverty"(Planning Commission, 1958).

Mixed Economy

Planning under Nehru was based on the concept of the Mixed Economy. As per the Planning Commission (1952):

'In a planned economy the distinction between the public and the private sector is one of emphasis. The two sectors are and must function as parts of a single organism. But Nehru said that it was obvious that an undeveloped country like India couldn't progress except by enlarging the public sector and except by controlling the private sector at important points. The private sector would have to function under certain broad strategic control otherwise with freedom and initiative" (Nehru's Speeches, Vol 2). Further, Nehru didn't speak of the wholesale expropriation of private property or of the immediate socialization of the means of production. He wanted to follow the middle path. After the second plan was introduced Nehru said in 1958 that he didn't want State Socialism of that extreme kind in which the state was all powerful and governed practically all activities.

Hiren Mookherjee (1964: 176) had written critically on Nehru's economic policies. He described Nehru's Mixed Economy as confused economy, democratic socialism as adulterated socialism, and his pragmatic approach as - amounting to an inability to ride the waves of social revolution.[7]

Even the right wing politicians criticized Nehru. K. M. Munshi in 1959 claimed that it was not parliament but nominated super cabinet, Planning

Commission, that governed India. Shri Munshi was a great intellectual and a member of the Drafting Committee to write the new constitution of India.

Prof. D. R. Gadgil (1958) said that though the Planning Commission was established only to- (i) assess resources, (ii) formulate the plan, (iii) define its stages, (iv) apprise the progress and (v) make related recommendations on policy and administration; it misdirected itself in getting involved with the actual process of the formation of public policies and in matters other than development.[8]

M L Dantwala (1964) observed that "India's economic policy since independence has a fairly clear vision of the ultimate goal, its social and economic colour and content and the broad path to be followed in reaching it. Nehru was instrumental in imposing a socialistic pattern of society. Of course, he didn't subscribe to the Marxian path. The choices before him was to choose between democracy and socialism. He brilliantly made a combination of both."[9]

Dantwala futher stated that "Nehru's biggest contribution to economic strategy was in committing the nation to a policy of planned economic development. This was by no means, the easiest thing to do. Within the country, he had to contend with his Gandhian colleagues who saw in this imposition of centralized statism, while they were emotionally stood to bring village self-sufficiency. Planning was equally an anathena to western democracies whose financial aid was a critical factor in the task of development."[10]

The criticism of the Planning Commission - a product of parliamentary resolution with the Prime minister; its chairperson - was not accepted by many economic policy analysts. Country to it, other people opined that very constitution of the Planning Commission an important landmark in the economic policy and the development of the country.

Nehru was aware of the poor state of industrialization under the British colonial administration. During the Second plan, he took a bold step for modern type of industrialization namely, 'Mahalonabis Model'. It accorded emphasis on heavy industries. Even his detractors called the step as a 'Soviet Path' - leading to totalitarianism. Some called it un-Gandhian in approach owing to its less attention to agriculture and cottage industries.

Ghose (1984) observed " functioning within the institutional framework of a political democracy and a constitution which guaranteed property rights during the years of power Nehru chose the path of evolutionary rather than revolutionary socialism. He wanted to achieve socialism without violence or dictatorship."[11]

Nehru said " I believed more and more in Socialism, more and more even in some parts of Communism, not the action, but the theory part of it, a communist society somewhere in the future. But the method should be peaceful".[12] Nehru didn't accept Marxian dialectical materialism in its entirety and he never spoke much about the labour or surplus theory of value. He gave primacy to economic factors.

What is worth noticing here is that - Nehru accorded primacy to government by discussion- (i) development suitable for India to provide equity and social justice, (ii) non-alignment as a response to post-world war i.e. mischievous cold war and secularism which announced in 1931 Karachi AICC. Hence, all his attempts were directed towards- (i) planned economic development, (ii) community development and (iii) democratic decentralization. His policy-making laid emphasis on educational advancement as well as Science and Technology. There were only 17 universities at the time of independence and science education was not in proper shape. It was Nehru who gave a push and universities as well as IITs' rolled out of his futuristic goals. His emphasis on nuclear potential could bring laurels to the country later.

Nehru's socialism had an agrarian bias. Ghose (1984) said " he realized that an agricultural country, like India, development of peasant organization was essential. He said that the Indian Communists had associated mostly with the industrial workers in the big towns and they had little knowledge of or contact with the peasants."[13] In 1959, the Congress under his leadership had passed a resolution for co-operative farming in India.

Nehru denounced Capitalism and also Fascism. He looked upon the two as twin brothers which crossed freedom. This he had written in his work 'the Unity of India (1944)'. Nehru government promoted Indian brand of socialism had laid emphasis on the mixed economy, rapid industrialization and socio-economic justice. "Nehru took initiative through planning to build large river valley projects, hydroelectric power schemes, basic and heavy industries and to establish a welfare state preparatory to the establishment of a socialist state".[14]

In 1961, British economist Barbara Ward was surprised to see industrialization, food production and infrastructure development. The economist wrote that "from over 40 years of zero percent growth rate between 1900 and 1947, India saw the economy growth at the rate 4% per annum till 1962, and thus, being ahead of China, Japan and UK".[15]

It was Nehru's dedication, observed Cees Roffelsen (2016), to democracy and civil rights - that prevented India from experiencing large scale famine deaths. As a result of radical reforms, over 40 million people died in China during 1950s and 60s due to Mao's poor governance. The absence of free media in the People's Republic of China (PRC) left the Chinese powerless to inform each other about it, thus, giving incompetent officials free reign over the country".[16] In India, media reach was extraordinary and it was impossible for the government to hide the famine situation and thus, foreseeing the officials to be held accountable for inaction.

Nehruvian Policies: A review

Nehru's seventeen years as Prime Minister were quite rewarding for post-colonial India. It was the period of maturity and achievement. Very period was also that of high hopes and aspirations, optimism and confidence. Those seventeen years, experienced had the period of stability and economic development. People were enjoying their hard-earned freedom and were living in a secure and secular environment. Unlike other countries freed from the colonial bondage and subsequently, trapped under neo-colonial pressures; the case of India was different and it could become a vibrant democracy. By advocating equidistance from cold warriors India could pave the way for the emergence of a consolidated third world. Their voice could be heard on the floor of the UN General Assembly.

An Exception

But there are people who hold different opinions over the Nehru era. There was some discontent among citizens unhappy with the slow pace of development, rising poverty and unemployment including slow and unsatisfactory land reforms.

Historian Bipan Chandra (2008- 168) while acknowledging the short-comings, listed the laudable efforts of the Nehru government. They included- (i) the consolidation of the nation, (ii) solution of the language and the tribal problems, (iii) the initiation of the process of independent and planned economic development, (iv) the evolution of an independent and (v) innovative foreign policy, (vi) electoral democracy properly rooted, setting in place of an administrative structure, (vii) the development of science and technology and (viii) the beginning of a welfare state.

As an architect of modern India, Nehru's contribution will forever remain significant for democracy, development and secularism.

End Notes & References

1. Robertson, David, 1985, Dictionary of Politics, USA, Penguin
2. Chandra, Bipan et al, 2008, India Since Independence, Gurugaon, Penguin
3. Chandra, Bipan et al, 2008, India Since Independence, Gurugaon, Penguin
4. Ghose, Sankar, 1984, Modern Indian Political Thought, New Delhi, Allied
5. Ghose, Sankar, 1984, Modern Indian Political Thought, New Delhi, Allied
6. Ghose, Sankar, 1984, Modern Indian Political Thought, New Delhi, Allied
7. Mukherjee, Hiren, 1964, The Gentle Colossus – A Study of Jawaharlal Nehru
8. Gadgil, D.R., 1958, Indian Planning and Planning Commission
9. Dantewala, M.L., 1964, "Economic Ideology of J.L. Nehru", Economic and Political Weekly, Special Number, 1964
10. Dantewala, M.L., 1964, "Economic Ideology of J.L. Nehru", Economic and Political Weekly, Special Number, 1964
11. Ghose, Sankar, 1984, Modern Indian Political Thought, New Delhi, Allied
12. Excerpts from 'Conversation with Nehru', 1956, Planning Commission, PP-31-32
13. Ghose, Sankar, 1984, Modern Indian Political Thought, New Delhi, Allied
14. Ghose, Sankar, 1984, Modern Indian Political Thought, New Delhi, Allied
15. Barbara, Ward, 1961, India and the West, London, Hamish Hamilton
16. Cees, Roffelsen, 2016, How Nehru Shaped India's Development

+++

Chapter Two

Public Policy Actors In India Since The 1990s Changing Role

Minarul Islam Biswas[2]

Abstract

Significant changes in the public policy process took place in India since the 1990s. With the adoption of the New Economic Policy (NEP) in 1991, the LPG (Liberalisation, Privatisation and Globalisation) model has been followed in India. The monopoly of the state in the delivery of public goods and services has been a thing of the past as non-state actors have come to participate in the process of governance. The 73rd and the 74th Constitutional Amendments Acts came into force to ensure participation of local community in policy making. Thus, since the 1990s the public policy process involved three broad type of actors- state, market and society replacing the state as a single dominant actor. While the state agencies have been criticized due to their under-performance, the non-state agencies are also found lacking in many respects. This article attempts to study these changes and newer challenges in the public policy in India in the context of the changed scenario since the 1990s.

Keywords: *Public Policy, LPG, State, Society, Market*

Introduction

Adoption of New Economic Policy in the year 1991 and enactment of 73rd and 74th Amendment Acts in 1992, have brought about significant changes in Indian administration in general and in public policy in India in particular. Economic liberalization has brought India under the overall influence of the trinity of Liberalization, Privatization and Globalization (LPG), making the market forces, civil society organisations etc able to participate in the public policy process which hitherto remained the domain of the government and other public institutions. The establishment of Panchayati Raj Institutions (PRIs) and Urban

2. PhD Research Scholar, Department of Political Science, Jamia Millia Islamia, New Delhi

Local Bodies (ULBs) have promoted a decentralised and bottom-up approach of policy making. Thus, the policy making process which was, before 1990s, the monopoly of the public agencies including the government- has now been also contributed by the non-governmental actors, and has become less centralized. In today's model of governance, along with traditional public administration, business houses, civil society organisations including NGOs, and common people contribute in public policy making. With these non-governmental actors in public policy making, there arise a number of associated questions. The role of the state and its bureaucracy has been highly criticised, though keeping the private players in check and making them accountable to the people in tune with public interest, has also posed new challenges. Local governments are still grappling with many ills, making the goal of decentralized policy process yet to be substantiated. Therefore, the non-state actors in public policy making in the contemporary time, while being appreciated for their merits, must not go unquestioned too for their shortcomings. The government still has a greater role to play as a facilitator to other actors. The 1990s have created a new context for public policy making in India where new actors have emerged with new roles and the role of the state has changed.

The entities in the process of public policy making have been described in this article - as the actors of public policy. Two categories of these actors are state actors and non-state actors. Non-state actors have again been classified as – market and society. Thus, all the policy actors can also be divided into three types – (i) state, (ii) market and (iii) society. State and government have been interchangeably used. Market includes, as policy actors, private organisations, business houses, private enterprises etc. 'Society' has been used here to include civil society organisations, common people etc. NGOs are a part of civil society organisations. This article does study changes in public policy since the 1990s because the process of liberalisation, privatisation and globalisation (LPG) came into prominence in India in the 1990s, particularly, after the adoption of New Economic Policy by India in 1991. Since then, market forces have been started to be invited and embraced to compensate for the government's shortcomings. The state and its bureaucracy have been called to shrink and make room for private players who were fashionably glorified for their so-called efficiency and effectiveness. Another landmark in the 1990s is the constitutionalisation of the rural and urban government from 1992.

Understanding Public Policy

The term 'policy' simply means a plan of action. In this view, public policy is concerned with the public- made by the public or made for the public. Traditionally, public policy has been defined as the policy made by the state or its government. Thus, public policy is defined as a course of action adopted and pursued by government (Henry, 2013), and public policies emerge as instruments of state action (Mathur, 2013). Public policy refers to the action or decisional pattern by public administrators on a particular issue (Basu, 2004), and this issue is concerned with public interest. Thus, public policy refers to the allocation of values for the whole society by the government by taking the public interest into consideration (De, 2012).

But in today's globalised world, public policies are not limited to the public institutions only. In every stage of the policy process- (i) policy initiation, (ii) policy formulation, (iii) policy implementation, (iv) policy monitoring and (v) policy evaluation- (vi) the market and (vii) civil society organisations also play their role. Public policies are developed by governmental bodies and officials, though non-governmental actors and agencies may also exert direct or indirect pressure or influence in the policy-making process (Basu, 2004). While acknowledging the role of the non-state actors, Sapru (2017) attributes primacy to the government in the policy process, and he opines that although a public policy is made by the government in response to the public's problem and demand, it may be implemented by public or private actors or both, but public policy is ultimately made by the government even if the ideas or opinions come from the private actors or through the interaction between government and non-government forces [Sapru, 2017].

Public Policy is the sum, total of (i) the actions and (ii) broad guide to rules formulated by the government to satisfy public needs and wants (Sen, 2016). Public Policy is whatever governments choose to do or not to do (Dye: 1978). Guy Peters (1996) defines public policy as the 'sum of government activities'. But in today's world of increasing Privatisation, these definitions need to be revised because civil society organisations like the Non-Governmental Organisations (NGOs), private companies also take part in governance. Now, public policy is the outcome of the interaction among the state, the market and the society. In other words, public policy process refers to the (i) plan of action, (ii) its execution, monitoring and (iii) evaluation- which is jointly performed by the state, private companies and civil societies i.e. Non-Governmental Organisations (NGOs) for the purpose of fulfilling the needs and demands of the public.

Public Policy Making: Role of Multiple Actors

The model of Liberalisation, Privatisation and Globalisation is being followed in India since the 1990s. Under the model of governance since the beginning of the 1990s, public policy making process is also under change as the beginning of the 1990s has made the traditional structures and the process of the government obsolete (De, 2012). The 1990s, saw fundamental changes in the previous state policy (Ahmed, Kundu & Peet). "Globalization has made the process of policy-making more complex as it facilitated the entry of numerous players into the process of policy-making. Apart from this, the advent of information technology has complicated the process of policy-making as people can influence the process of policy formulation through the Internet." (De, 2012).

Policy-making is no longer, a mere state-driven endeavor but it has become a collaborative effort in which the role of non-state authorities does not seem to be less significant. That is why, attention is being directed towards improving the understanding of the wider public policy system in which the institutions of the government appear to be involved in the process of negotiation, bargaining, and compromise with a host of other actors (Mathur, 2019) "The introduction of liberal economic reforms in 1991 - signalled far-reaching changes in the government's economic policies and a change in the role of the state and the government. Policy and governance reforms were seen as efforts to create a favourable environment for the private sector to grow and invest in India's growth (Mathur, 2019). Unlike during the period of planning, business houses were no more seen as hostile actors to subvert the goals of the state, but as partners in achieving them, and the government's role is to provide a conducive atmosphere in which business could flourish and the government - began with initiating many policies that withdrew the controlling and regulating role of the state and then went on to establish institutional structures that provided a formal forum where the big businesses could participate in policymaking (Mathur, 2019). The entry of the private sector into the public policy institutional space is making the collaboration between the government and business more open and transparent; the era of clandestine lobbying is receding into the past (Mathur, 2019).

Before 1990s, it is the public sector - played the major role in public policy in India. But since the 1990s, other two sectors- (i) market and (ii) society have become important actors in the public policy process. Since then, both the market forces and citizens are becoming more assertive and participatory. The need was felt for setting - up new institutions that could improve delivery of public goods and services. An active partnership with private sector began in right earnest in the neo-liberal governance framework (Mathur, 2019). Therefore, business houses began to be incorporated in policy and advisory bodies, and new institutions began to be established to implement development programmes (Mathur, 2019). If it was a new role for the state, business was also carving out a new role for itself and it was no longer an agency reacting to government policy, but now actively involved in framing that policy (Mathur, 2019).For example, Public-Private Partnership (PPP) can be one such new institution for implementing development programmes. "PPPs are an arrangement between a government or statutory entity or government-owned entity, on one side, and a private-sector entity, on the other, for the provision of public assets and/or management undertaken by the private sector entity for a specified time period, where there is a substantial risk sharing with the private sector." (Mathur, 2019). In PPP model, the government works in partnership with the various private institutions, and the partnership among the three actors – state, market and civil society- began to be promoted as a strategy of good governance (Mathur, 2019).

In the context of the consolidation of liberalised, privatised, globalised regime in India, - policy-makers have provided a new direction to the making of public policies which were inconceivable in the erstwhile state-led planned economic development (Chakrabarty & Chand, 2016). Chakrabarty & Chand see the changes in public policy making in three ways: firsly, policy-making no longer remains a prerogative of either the bureaucrats or politicians with the gradual involvement of stakeholders from different walks of life, with the fact that in the changed milieu, the NGOs and civil society actors cannot be bypassed and their role is most critical in conceptualizing and also making of public policy. Secondly, the growing importance of the global or transcendental actors who may not be directly involved in the preparation of policies, but remain critical given their importance as donors; and thirdly, the rising importance of citizens in policy-making, which is no longer an exclusive domain of the politicians or bureaucrats, with an alert citizenry providing critical inputs to the making of policies that the state cannot afford to ignore because of the obvious adverse consequences. The global actors, whether the World Bank, IMF or foreign donors, have become part and parcel of policy activities which, in the past - remained an arena where the domestic players had the final say (Chakrabarty & Chand, 2016). As far as the role of NGOs is concerned, Globalisation has ushered in a change in the meaning and context of NGOs in terms of their increased role as service delivery institutions as well as implementation agencies of public policy (Ramadu, 2008). The contemporary model of governance pays equal attention to the multiple players, both domestic and global, who are critical in policy decisions in the changed environment of globalization(Chakrabarty & Chand, 2016).

World Bank's emphasis on governance reforms - has also accorded prominence to civil society organisations in the developmental process, as part of its Structural Adjustment Programme (SAP), and this provided a fertile ground for the NGOs to sprout and play - a vital role in the public policy of a country (Ramadu, 2008). The activities of NGOs related to public policy have been considered to be pivotal and proved to be quite effective in the last few decades, as they rigorously work as policy makers in their own style, as far as they attempt to incorporate their views and perspectives into the policy domain(Ramadu, 2008). After a policy is formulated, - they join the officers concerned for its execution, work towards enhancing responsiveness of the delivery system, so as to make it more effective in achieving goals of the concerned policy and also monitor implementation, processes and register difficulties, if any - and report them to the experts from time to time(Ramadu,2008). Thus, the NGOs take part in the entire policy process- policy initiation, policy formulation, policy implementation, policy monitoring and policy evaluation. NGOs mostly use the advocacy method to influence the public policy process and in this approach the NGOs make recommendations to the government on policymatters with respect to a variety of issues though the final authority lies with the policymakers whether to accept their recommendations or not (Ramadu, 2008). Thus, a new context has emerged in which a state no longer holds the hegemonic authority as in the past, but acts a coordinator while deciding policy preferences (Chakrabarty & Chand, 2016). Public policy-making, in the context of the emerging style of governance in India- is becoming complex as in addition to state institutions, the corporate sector and civil society organizations have begun to play an interactive role in producing public policy making a multi-layered governance structure replacing the all-familiar single focal point of government (Mathur, 2013). However, what needs to be stated unambiguously is that - globalisation does not necessarily mean the demise of the state or its bureaucracy, but may mandate their functions and role to be redefined and reinvented (Basu, 2008).

Despite the increasing importance of other agencies, the state still has to play a pre-eminent role as a regulator by setting parameters which are consistent with national priorities at a time when the market and the civil society seem to be equally important (Chakrabarty & Chand, 2016).

The new context post - 1990s and the advent of multiple of new actors have also created a need for the reorientation of the bureaucracy to live up-to the changes. Therefore, recognizing that the Indian administrators were nurtured in a policy environment of state intervention for public good, the government initiated several measures to reorient them to the new tasks of facilitating private sector to invest in development projects and be their partners and not their regulators, and the government has been keen to expose civil servants to the practices in the private sector and attune them to the liberal perspective(Mathur, 2019).

The 73rd and the 74th Constitutional Amendments Acts have constitutionally empowered the rural and urban local bodies for the formulation and implementation of public policies. Now the local problems faced by the local people are addressed by themselves. The interests and rights of individuals and groups which had so far been controlled by the bureaucracy are being taken care of by the people themselves. Thus, a bottom-up approach has been adopted where the community participates in the policy process. With the enactment of 73rd and 74th Amendment Acts in 1992 and consequently, the establishment of Panchayati Raj Institutions (PRIs) and Urban Local Bodies (ULBs), there has been adopted a decentralised and bottom-up approach of policy making through which people's participation is being encouraged. Now, everything is not imposed by the higher level on the lower level of governance. People at the grassroots are being empowered to take part in the policy process. These two amendment Acts aim to ensure the women participation in the policy making process, by reserving seats for the women at the local government. The reservation of seats for the Scheduled Tribes and Scheduled Castes also ensure representation of the people of marginalized sections in the policy-making. These are major shifts in public policy-making in India.

Challenges with Multiple Actors

With the increasing participation of non-state actors in the policy process, a number of new issues have posed new challenges. Questions are being raised regarding the transparency, accountability, credibility etc. of the market and civil society organisations. Regarding the PPP model, critics point out that these partnerships can be a strategy of the state to evade responsibility and a fear that partnerships can be used by the corporate sector to embellish their own power and resources is also expressed, and even there is no way of evaluating whether a project under PPP has been more efficiently or economically implemented than if it was under government (Mathur, 2019). Network governance obscures the process and accountability for public policy formulation, decision-making, execution, and the policy impact of such networks on socially and economically deprived groups - leads to their exclusion and not to the prophesized benefits from the market. It is because the private sector being hesitant to become partner with the government's non-profit schemes (Mathur, 2019). "New institutions that are being established rapidly to make delivery of public services and goods more efficient through the varying strategy of privatization bring in another set of challenges. In a parliamentary democracy, these challenges come in the form of accountability issues. How is this delivery accountable?" (Mathur, 2019). These accountability issues must be resolved.

Many NGOs have been running all over India dealing with different issues. But there are also such NGOs which run illegally. According to news published in The Hindu dated December 03, 2018, a certain NGO had been running illegal shelter homes. The Hindu (April 04, 2018) reported that at least fifteen NGOs from Arunachal Pradesh face scrutiny, and according to Intelligence reports, four of them were involved in religious conversions. There are fraud NGOs too spread in different parts of the country. In many instances, NGOs suffer from lack of professionalism, work in a variety of fields, but in many cases without technical know-how, the NGOs are criticised, as they tend to be elite and unaccountable - except to their donors (Ramadu, 2008). The non-state actors like the NGOs are critical of the highhandedness of the bureaucracy, but they themselves run in a bureaucratic way when their paid managers ultimately give a bureaucratic flavour to their activities (Ramadu, 2008). To an extent NGOs are concerned with accumulating funds rather than delivering social services as they are mostly run by the influential and elite classes only to amass wealth under the safety valve of social service (Ramadu, 2008). They do not appear to be democratic in their functioning and they are not accountable and transparent to anyone except their donors. But the need of the hour is that a healthy relationship among the policy makers and the NGOs is needed to produce better policies, so they should not be allowed to escape from the principles of good governance, particularly, accountability and transparency (Ramadu, 2008).

As far as decentralisation of power is concerned, theoretically; the people at the grass-roots have got the power. But in practice, the power has been captured by the local elite. It has been misused too by the local leaders for furtherance of the private interest instead of empowerment of the local people as a whole. Along with decentralisation of power, there has also been decentralisation of corruption (corruption has spread to a greater extent). The 73rd and 74th Constitutional Amendment Acts aimed for the empowerment of the women through reservation of seats at local level, and thus wanted to ensure women participation in the policy process, but many of the women leaders act as the proxy of their husbands or other family members thereby denying the purpose to some extent.

Conclusion

Thus, since the 1990s, multiple actors are working together in the public policy process. There has been a demand for a minimal role of the government agencies, and more space for non-governmental actors. While the government agencies have been criticized due to their under-performance, the non-governmental agencies are also found unsatisfactory in many respects. Therefore, while partnership model between the state actors and non-state actors can be adopted in policy making, the gaps in each of the actors need to be filled. Thus, even after the advent of multiple players in policy making, the role of the government agencies cannot be undermined. Now they mostly work as the facilitator in contrast to their earlier role as provider. The non-governmental actors have been working in collaboration with the government, but when the former are found lacking in their responsibilities, the latter have to play a decisive role. Thus, there have been changes in the actors and their roles vis-à-vis the public policy in India since the 1990s.

In fact, under the impact of LPG, certain changes have been made possible to improve and streamline the functions of the state. At the same time, it has been conspicuous that the private sector is not able to take up all the issues successfully, for example the welfare issues of the masses. Besides, the state must be there at-least to look after the new partners participating in the governance. So, the state machinery was very much there before the advent of LPG and still is there today but with a changed role.

In conclusion, firstly - many of the definitions, particularly the earlier definitions of public-policy need to be revisited, as public-policy is pursued today not only by the state agencies, but also the non-state agencies. Secondly, in public policy process, state is now mostly a facilitator and coordinator, in contrast to its earlier role of a provider and regulator. Thirdly, though the market, civil society and common citizens play important roles in public policy, they also suffer from many lacunas which must not be overlooked. Fourthly, the nature of the role of the state, has, no doubt got changed since the 1990s, but its role has not become less important. Today public policy process is an endeavour involving multiple actors with different roles to be complemented with each other.

References

1. Ahmed, Waquar., Amitabh Kundu & Richard Peet, 2011, India's New Economic Policy: A Critical Analysis, Jaipur, Rawat Publications
2. Basu, Rumki(Ed), 2008, Globalisation & the Changing Role of the State: Issues and Impacts, New Delhi, New Dawn
3. Basu, Rumki, 2004, Public Administration: Concepts and Theories, New Delhi, Sterling
4. Chakrabarty, Bidyut & Prakash Chand, 2016, Public Policy: Concept, Theory and Practice, New Delhi, Sage
5. De, Prabir Kumar (Ed), 2012, Public Policy and System, New Delhi, Pearson
6. Dye, Thomas R., 1981, Understanding Public Policy, New Jersey, Prentice-Hall
7. Henry, Nicholas, 2013, Public Administration and Public Affairs, New Delhi, PHI
8. Mathur, Kuldeep, 2013, Public Policy and Politics in India: How Institutions Matter, New Delhi, OUP
9. Mathur, Kuldeep, 2019, Recasting Public Administration: Reform, Rhetoric, and Neoliberalism, New Delhi, OUP
10. Peters, B. Guy, 1996, American Public Policy: Promise and Performance, New Jersey, Chatham House
11. Ramadu, Sreepati, Role of Non-governmental Organisations in Public Policy in the Era of Globalisation, in Basu, Rumki(Ed), 2008, Globalisation & the Changing Role of the State: Issues and Impacts, New Delhi, New Dawns
12. Sapru, Radhakrishnan, 2017, Public Policy: A Contemporary Perspective, New Delhi, Sage
13. Sen, Saugato, Public Policy: Concept and Approaches in Dhameja, Alka & Sweta Mishra (Eds), 2016, Public Administration: Approaches and Application, Chennai, Pearson

✦✦✦

Chapter Three

India's National Health Policy 2017 A Critical Review

Rumki Basu[3]*

Abstract

Public health outcomes in India are an odd mix of achievements and failures. Among peers in the developing world and neighbours in South Asia, India is among the low performers when it comes to the coverage and outcomes of its public health system. Besides achieving specific health goals, India faces a larger challenge of placing into operation a functioning system of Universal Healthcare (UHC). As India looks ahead and prepares itself for the 21st century, it will need to make room for a new India, and to think very differently than it has in the past with regard to health policy challenges for the future. The National Health Policy 2017 falls in line with the growing emphasis to provide universal access to primary healthcare, functioning as a "gatekeeping mechanism" and opening up secondary and tertiary levels of care to market-based reform. India is committed to achieve UHC as a signatory to the globally agreed Sustainable Development Goals (SDGs). The National Health Policy 2017 can prove a catalyst and a platform to prepare India for achieving that goal by 2030, which is the final deadline for implementation of SDGs by all signatory countries like India.

Keywords: *India's National Health Policy 2017, Universal Health Coverage*

Introduction

Public health outcomes in India are an odd mix of achievements and failures. Indians are healthier, live longer and better nourished today, than they were in 1947 when India started its journey as an independent state. In historical perspective, India has gone through its own "great escape", as Deaton (2013) aptly describes the unprecedented improvement of living standards that happened globally in the second half of the twentieth century.

3. *Professor of Public Administration, Jamia Millia University, New Delhi*

Among peers in the developing world and neighbours in South Asia, India is among the low performers when it comes to the coverage and outcomes of its public health system. Whether it is life expectancy, maternal or infant mortality. On most counts, India ranks below China, Brazil and Sri Lanka, just below Bangladesh and Nepal and in some cases, even Pakistan (Dreze 2017). Since independence, India has created a vast health infrastructure and personnel for primary, secondary and tertiary care in the public, voluntary and private sectors. India's per capita public spending on health is a meagre Rs. 2494 per annum (2019).

Besides achieving specific health goals, India faces a larger challenge of placing into operation - a functioning system of Universal Healthcare (UHC). The basic principle of UHC is that quality healthcare should be guaranteed "to all members of the community irrespective of their ability to pay". The principle of UHC is now well accepted in the developed world, with the notable exception of the United States. A growing number of developing countries (including Brazil, China, Mexico and Thailand) have also made great strides towards UHC in recent years. In India, however, UHC remains an elusive goal, not only because the health system is highly privatized but also because the very idea of UHC has made little headway in public policy debates in India so far. (World Bank, 2017)

There are some interesting developments in progress within India. In the early 21st century, extreme hunger and poverty have almost ceased to exist (Sustainable Development Goals 1 & 2) and with the total fertility rate nearing replacement rate, the population growth rate has slowed sharply and expected to fall below 1% per annum by 2025, with several states already showing negative rate of growth. Despite consistent food surpluses in the country, high levels of mal-nutrition among the population - exist as one of the paradoxes of our health sector.

Health challenges Ahead

As India looks ahead and prepares itself for the 21st century, it will need to make room for this new India, and to think very differently than it has in the past with regard to health policy challenges of the future.

This new India faces some very different challenges. There are very few people below the poverty line but close to 95% of the population are in the low-income category with over 50 million people sinking into poverty each year due to health shocks. Despite all this expenditure, a continuing burden of (i) maternal and child mortality and (ii) infectious diseases like dengue, malaria, tuberculosis alongside a rapidly rising burden of non-communicable diseases such as cancer, high blood pressure, diabetes, and mental illness which have a direct impact on the well-being and economic productivity of young Indians exist. To respond effectively to these new challenges, India will need to focus its attention and redirect its scarce tax resources towards building-up its human capital though relying more now on its well-functioning capital markets and private sector. This is does to address the more traditional challenges of the lack of adequate capital and infrastructure. (Mor, 2019)

Let us compare the health status of two comparable nations – China is the world's most populated and India has the second largest population in the world. In 1949, when the People's Republic of China was established, its health status was worse than that of India. Under-five mortality was 317 per 1000 births (India had 290) while infant mortality was 195 (India 164). China's public spending on health went consistently on the rise from 1.3% of GDP in 1960 to 3% in 1980, and has the remained the same. India's spending stands at 1.2% even today: China focused on health - promotion, inspection, disease surveillance and effective health campaigns e.g. on sanitation and health insurance. The results are there for everyone to see. China's IMR is as low as seven (India, it is 30). Its total fertility rate is down to 1.7, in India it is 2.2. The average Chinese citizen can expect to live till age 76, in India it is 69. Chinese men, on an average, even gained 3cm in height over Indian men. Absolute hunger may have become a distant memory but chronic anemia and malnutrition among children continues to be a recurring problem with the latest Global Hunger Index (GHI) ranking India at 102 out of 117 nations (National Nutrition survey CNNS 2016-18). At 20.8% India's child wasting ratio is the highest in the world. Almost a million children die in India before they reach their first birthday. Countries that have prioritized public health saw a corresponding rise in GDP, that is why China is way ahead of India.

Healthcare in India is a story of insufficient resources and poor outcomes. Investment is well below WHO guidelines in both qualitative and quantitative terms. Bed density is low (less than 1.5 beds per 1000 persons as compared to WHO guidelines of 3.5), doctors few (less than 1.8 per 1000 as compared to WHO guidelines of 2.5) and out of pocket spending high (62.6% as compared to an average of around 40% for low income countries). (WHO, 2010) India was ranked at 154 of 195 countries on health service delivery index in 2017 (Lancet Journal 2017).

Health infrastructure and human resources: There were 156,231 Sub Health Centres (SHCs), 25,650 Primary Health Centres (PHCs) and 5,624 Community Health Centres (CHCs) in India as on 31st March, 2017. However, most of these health centres suffer from poor infrastructure, under-staffing, lack of equipment and medicines. Only 11% of SHC, 16% of PHCs and 16% CHCs meet the Indian Public Health Standards (IPHS). There is a huge shortage of specialists and general physicians at all levels of the system. More specifically, SHCs, which are the first contact point between community and government health system, one-fifth were without regular water supply, one fourth without electricity, one in every ten without all-weather road, and over 6,000 did not have an Auxiliary Nurse Midwife/health worker (Government of India Reports, 2017).

Health financing: The high out of pocket expenditure on health at 62.6% of total health expenditure is a major health challenge in India. The out of pocket expenditure on health in India is one of the highest in the world and nearly thrice of global average of 20.5%. Part of the reason is poor government spending on health, at 1.15% of gross domestic product (GDP), which is one of the lowest in the world (National Health Accounts 2017).

Service Delivery: In the absence of well-functioning government facilities, people choose private providers. Nearly 75% of all out-patient consultations and 65% of all hospitalization in India happens in the private sector. Regular visits to out-patient consultation, preventive and promotive measures and regular medications cumulatively result in high cost interventions and is a major part of the private health expenses of citizens.

Intra-State Disparities

Within the country, disturbing disparities exist both in terms of health care as well as health outcomes among federated regions (hereinafter called 'states') Kerala's life expectancy at birth is about ten years more than that of Madhya Pradesh and Assam. Infant mortality ratio in Odisha is about five times than that of Kerala. The maternal mortality rate and death rates in Jharkhand and Chhattisgarh are about twice the crude death rates of Delhi and Nagaland.

While better health outcomes depend on multiple reasons, it appears that doctor to population ratio had a far higher impact on Infant Mortality Rate (IMR) or Maternal Mortality Rate (MMR) than better infrastructure. Tamil Nadu, that has fewer primary health centres (PHCs), one per lakh of population, as compared to Chhattisgarh and Odisha that have two PHCs is better placed in health outcomes.

Tamil Nadu has one doctor for 789 Patients and an infant mortality rate of 21 and maternal mortality of 97. In sharp comparison, Chhattisgarh has one doctor for 6221 patients and witnesses 47 infant deaths for every 1000 live births and 269 maternal deaths per 100000 live births. Odisha that has one doctor for 2500 patients, too, suffers from high infant and mother deaths. It has IMR of 53 and MMR of 258, respectively.

Increasingly, states like Andhra Pradesh, Goa, Karnataka, Kerala and Tamil Nadu alone account for 42% of all medical colleges in India thereby producing most of India's doctors. Not surprisingly, these states also have the best Doctor Population Ratio (DPR).

These states show no shortfall of doctors at PHC level and have already met the Millennium Development Goals (MDG). At least three of the five – Kerala, Goa and Tamil Nadu – have IMR below 21. Incidentally, West Bengal has one of the highest per capita coverage of primary health centres – nine per lakh population. However, it has just one doctor for 1508 patients and IMR of 32 while its MMR is 145.

In comparison, north Indian states of Madhya Pradesh, Bihar, Uttar Pradesh, Odisha and Chhattisgarh have very few medical colleges, a fact which reflects in their DPR. Unsurprisingly, most states with poor DPR also have a relatively high shortfall of doctors at the PHC level. For example a state like Bihar has one doctor for every 2785 persons. This translates to IMR of 43 and a MMR of 261. (MDGs in India Country Report, 2015)

The deteriorating public health scenario has come under policy attention since the launch of the National Rural Health Mission in 2005. While there is some degree of consensus on the fact that the current moribund public system cannot serve the health needs of our citizens in the 21st century, there is a major divergence in approach regarding the solutions offered. One school of thought would like to continue with the rapidly growing trend of privatization including the facilitation of the privatization processes of current public health institutions. Others argue that there is a case for strengthening existing public health infrastructure, coverage and services for an average citizen.

The concern for improving the public health system in India has not been a result of domestic compulsions alone. In 2005, WHO member states adopted a resolution encouraging countries to develop health financing systems aimed at providing Universal Health Coverage (UHC). This was defined as securing access for all to appropriate, preventive, curative and rehabilitative services at an affordable cost. UHC entails strengthening health systems for better outreach, apt governance and management including financial sufficiency and innovations in resource pooling and spending. Universal coverage provides an essential operational framework for actualizing "the Right to Health" for citizens.

The journey towards UHC

In India, from the Bhore Committee of 1946 on, there has been a series of committees – Sokhey sub-committee 1948, Mudaliar Committee 1962, Chaddha Committee 1963, Kartar Singh Committee 1974, Srivastava Committee 1975, ICMR-ICSSR Joint Panel 1980 – which have focused on different aspects of the UHC issue. (Bagchi & Soman 2005) There is a three tier system of health centres in public sector for primary, secondary and tertiary care. These have been complemented by two enunciations of the National Health Policy 1983 and 2002, a National Population Policy 2000, the Report of the National Commission on Macroeconomics and Health (NCHM 2005) and most recently the High Level Expert Group on Universal Health Coverage (HLEG 2011).

The Bhore Committee focus was on building a health infrastructure in the rural areas while enunciating the principle that nobody should be denied access to health services for his inability to pay. The Sokhey sub-committee of the National Planning Committee recommended one community health worker for every 1000 village population and reinforced the Bhore Committee's recommendations. The five year plans and the Mudaliar Committee focused on building infrastructure and launching vertical disease control programmes. The Alma Ata Declaration in 1978 and the Indian Council of Medical Research/ Indian Council of Social Science Research Joint Panel 1980 resulted in a National Health Policy that was approved by the Indian Parliament in 1983. The Alma Ata vision had comprehensive preventive and curative care as its ultimate goal. The 1990s saw tax and other incentives being given to private sector which led to an unregulated expansion of the private health sector. The Second National Health

Policy in 2002 began by acknowledging that 13 of the 17 goals of the first one had remained unfulfilled. The new policy argued for raising government health spending to 2% of GDP - chipping health goals more realistically to financial and administrative capacities and an enhanced role for the private sector.

National Rural Health Mission

With the establishment of the National Rural Health Mission (NRHM 2005) the focus shifted to the demand side, although supply side attempts to improve infrastructure, build the capacity of health personnel, create a cadre of accredited social health activists (ASHAs). Similarly, improvement of Health Management Information Systems (HMIS) were also given attention. (NIPFP 2017) Cash transfers have been part of the country's anti-poverty programmes for decades, but it is only with the Janani Suraksha Yojana (JSY) that they have been linked to health specific behavior for the first time. Two policy shifts are important to an understanding of our health policy-one, a very sharp reduction in the number of drugs on the controlled list, leading to significant increases in drug prices, and two, the introduction of user fees for the non BPL (Below Poverty Line) population in public hospitals.

India is called the world's pharmacy because it exports quality medicines to about 200 countries. It is the third largest drug producing country in the world. Yet ironically about 65% of Indian citizens do not have access to essential medicines though Indian drug prices are among the cheapest in the world. Currently, the per capita public expenditure on medicine in different states of India, range from Rs. 2 to Rs. 22 per annum.

Recommendations of HLEG

It is clear from the above discussion that any policy movement towards Universal Health Coverage (UHC) addresses the questions of access and affordability. This in turn means addressing in a central way, the questions of financing, the respective roles of the public and the private sectors and of Public Private Partnerships, the cost and availability of drugs and diagnostics, and of health promotion and prevention of illness. It also requires meeting the challenges of accountability of citizens and ensuring that the people's "Right to Health" is effectively guaranteed. The High Level Expert Group (HLEG) on UHC with Srinath Reddy as Chairperson was set up by the Planning Commission of India in October, 2010 whose express purpose was to develop a blue print and investment plan for meeting the human resource requirements to achieve the goal of Health for all by 2020.

The HLEG held extensive discussions with a range of stakeholders – public, private, civil society, national and international – before finalizing its report. Some of its key recommendations were as follows:-

The HLEG has called for provision of universal financial protection and access to good health care without involving insurance companies or any independent agencies to purchase health care services on behalf of the government. Instead, the HLEG proposes general taxation as the principle source of health care financing complemented by additional mandatory deductions from salaried individuals and tax payers, either as a proportion of taxable income or as a proportion of salary. Government funded health insurance schemes should be integrated into the UHC system and government expenditure on health should rise from the current 1.4% of GDP to at-least 3% of GDP by 2022. Public spending on generic drug procurement should rise to 0.5% of GDP from the current 0.1% and thus, ensure availability of free essential medicines.

Even assuming the total spending on health remains at the current level of 1.15% of GDP the HLEG hopes there will be a sharp decline in the proportion of private out-of-pocket spending on health from 67% to 33% by 2020. There should be no sector specific taxes for health financing. However, specific purpose transfers will equalize levels of per capita public spending on health by different states to mobilize resources to ensure all citizens an uniform level of essential health care. States can have flexible and differential norms for financing, but there will be no user fees for UHC services, primary health care and health promotion targeted towards specific risk factors, and should account for 70% of all government healthcare expenditure.

National Policy 2017 and Ayushman Bharat Program (ABP)

In this background, when Ayushman Bharat Program (ABP) was announced in India's Union Budget 2018-19, it received wide public attention. This paper reviews the key health sector related announcements in the union budget 2018-19, critically analyzes its components, and suggests a few strategies to strengthen implementation and accelerate India's journey towards UHC.

The Government of India's union budget, for the financial year 2018-19, was presented to the Parliament of India on 1st February, 2018. The Ministry of

Health and Family Welfare received an allocation of Rs. 54,800 Crore (approx. US $ 8.4 billion), an increase of nearly 11.5 percent over the budget of the earlier year. Though in nominal terms, the budgetary allocation to health sector has multiplied in the last decade as proportion of gross domestic product (GDP), it has changed marginally from 1.1% to 1.15%.

A key announcement in the union budget 2018-19 has been the Ayushman Bharat Program (ABP). This program has two components: (*a*) delivering comprehensive primary health care by establishing 150,000 health and wellness centres (HWCs) by year 2022, and (*b*) Providing financial protection for secondary and tertiary level hospitalization as part of the National Health Protection Scheme (NHPS). The ABP with two components intends to provide services with continuum across three levels of care and brings back the attention on delivery of entire range of preventive, promotive, curative, diagnostic, rehabilitative and palliative care services.

One of the two initiatives in ABP is to upgrade 150,000 (of the existing 180,000) Sub health centres (SHCs) and Primary health centres (PHCs) in India, to the HWCs by December, 2022. The scope of services from existing SHCs and PHCs is proposed to be broadened from current range of services, and implements the national health programs to a broad package of 12 services. This intends to make comprehensive primary healthcare accessible by the community within 30 minutes of walking distance. A total of 11,000 and 16,000 HWCs are proposed to be made functional in financial years (FY) 2018-19 and 2019-20, respectively. This includes upgrading all 4,000 primary health centres in urban areas to the HWCs by March, 2020.

The second initiative in ABP is NHPS which has been referred as "the world's largest government-funded healthcare (insurance) program". The NHPS aims to provide a coverage of up to Indian Rs. 500,000 (or US$ 7,700) per family per year for expenses related to secondary- and tertiary-level hospitalization. The AB-NHPM, after the launch would sub-sume Rashtriya Swasthya Bima Yojana (RSBY), and the Senior Citizen Health Insurance Scheme (SCHIS) (Union Budget 2017). RSBY was providing insurance coverage of Rs. 30,000 (US$ 470) for up to 5 members of a family per annum, for a target beneficiary base of 60 million families. The target beneficiary in NHPS has increased to 107.4 million families, and estimated 535 million people, equivalent to 40% of the Indian population, *the largest government funded scheme so far*.

First 100 days of Ayushman Bharat

A little under 700,000 people have so far been treated free in various empanelled hospitals across India under the Narendra Modi government's flagship health insurance scheme, Ayushman Bharat- Pradhan Mantri Jan Aarogya Yojna (AB-PMJAY), which was launched on September 23, 2018.

The scheme, billed as the world's biggest public health scheme, provides annual health cover of ₹5 lakh per family to 107.4 million poor and vulnerable families (around 500 million people) listed in the socio-economic caste census data for secondary and tertiary care hospitalisation through a network of empanelled hospitals. In the first 100 days, 685,000 people had availed of the scheme.

How Ayushman Bharat fared since implementation?

The ambitious Pradhan Mantri Jan Aarogya Yojna, which aims at providing free healthcare, was launched on Sep 23, 2018

The Scheme Rs. 10,000 cr Budget for 2 years 6.85 lakh: No of people treated	**Beneficiary Entitlement** 5 lakh: Per family annual health insurance cover
800 crores: Amount spent on secondary, tertiary care treatment	107.4 million : Poor families covered
297 crores: Amount spent on angioplasty, Coronary Artery Bypass graft and Valve replacement	500 million: People coverd
40.38 lakh: Number of beneficiary e-cards generated	1,350: Disease packages
16,134 : Govt hospitals empanelled	Family size: No Cap Mode: Cashless
8,807: Private hospitals empanelled	Aadhar : Not mandatory
3,500: Common Service Centres engaged for beneficiary verification	Covered : Cost of all secondary and tertiary care hospitalizations

Some treatements covered: Cancer surgeries; radiation therapy; chemotherapy; cardiac surgeries; stenting; neuro (brain) surgeries, spine surgeries; dental surgeries; eye surgeries; specialised tests such as MRI, CT Scans etc.

Monitoring mechanism: Complaint – and grievance-redressal mechanism using mobile phone, internet etc.

Source : Times of India, 2.1.2019

Many people from weaker sections avoided hospital treatment in order to avoid the burden of out-of-pocket medical expenses. Today, 40% of India's population is assured of a treatment in a hospital at public cost. This scheme also supports the hospitals by ensuring patients for them and it will lead to better equipped hospitals especially in smaller cities and towns of India. Health sector jobs are set to increase. It is also hoped that this scheme will help create an accountable health system because beneficiary feedback is an integral part of its implementation.

Those involved in implementation of Ayushman Bharat say that it has been received well and that the number of beneficiaries is rising rapidly.

While the number of hospital admissions under the scheme is rising, it's the relatively less expensive medical fields such as obstetrics and gynaecology, general medicine and ophthalmology that have seen the most demand for treatment under the scheme, highlighting the need for more super-speciality hospitals to be empanelled for treatment.

One of the major challenges in implementing the scheme has been the reluctance of big corporate hospitals to come on board, largely for financial reasons. The problem here is that in the insurance model, you cannot have two separate rates for the same procedure. The rates in this scheme are - lower than CGHS (Central government health scheme) rates. The medical industry proposed CGHS rates plus 10%; and if not that then at least CGHS rates.

Union ministry of health provides comprehensive medical facilities to the current and retired employees of the central government and their dependents in their empaneled hospitals at subsidised rates that are fixed by the ministry.

At least 50% of the hospitals empanelled under the scheme are - privately run but the big ones seem to be reluctant as their cost structure is too high because of the kind of salaries they pay and other costs involved.

2017 Policy – A Review

The National Health Policy, developed after extensive consulations with state governments and other stakeholders, aims to shape the health system in all its dimensions – by investment in prevention of diseases and promotion of good health; by access to technologies; developing human resources; encouraging medical pluralism; and by building knowledge for better health, financial protection and regulation. The Policy is aimed at reaching healthcare in an assured manner to all, particularly to the under-served and under-privileged.

The need is also to shift from selective primary healthcare services to assured comprehensive primary healthcare with two way referrals i.e. (i) care for major non-communicable diseases (NCDs) (ii) mental health, geriatric care, palliative care and rehabilitative care. As a critical element, the Policy proposes to raise public health expenditure to 2.5% of the GDP in a time-bound manner with allocation of major proportion (two-third or more) of resources to primary care.

The second critical focus of this Policy is to strengthen and design our health systems affordable healthcare for all. It is through free access to universal comprehensive primary healthcare, free drugs, diagnostics and essential emergency services in government hospitals as well as "strategic purchasing" through government financed insurance programmes. To facilitate access within the "golden hour", the Policy aims to ensure availability of 2,000 beds per million population across all geographies.

The Policy recommends establishing mechanisms for speedy resolution of disputes, and of National Healthcare Standards Organization to develop evidence-based standard guidelines for care. Resource allocation to government hospitals will be made responsive to quantity, diversity and quality of case-loads.

The Policy recommends establishing federated national health information architecture, consistent with Metadata and Data Standards (MDDS), introduces use of Electronic Health Records (HER), use of digital tools for AYUSH services by AYUSH practitioners, for traditional community level healthcare providers and for household level preventive, promotive and curative practices.

Additionally, to address the shortage of specialized care especially in some states, besides upgrading district hospitals to medical colleges, use of technology to scale initiatives such as tele-consultation, which will link tertiary care institutions (medical colleges) to district and sub-district hospitals with secondary care facilities, will ensure that excellent medical care reaches the remotest locations.

UHC as a Goal and a Challenge

There is sufficient evidence available that strengthening of primary healthcare is the most appropriate approach to achieve UHC. Investment on comprehensive primary healthcare system is a practical and affordable solution for India. Health services are human resource intensive and India has plenty of potentially trainable human resources available at a low cost. The successful engagement of nearly 1 million Accredited Social Health Activists (ASHA) under the National Health Mission (NHM) in India is - a proof of the potential and effectiveness of community health workers. More of appropriately skilled workforce such as Mid-Level Healthcare Providers (MLHP) as part of HWCs would be affordable, efficient and effective. In the process, *India might end up building a low cost, high impact model of primary healthcare.* Many countries such as Chile, Costa Rica and Thailand have succeeded through their own context-specific model for primary healthcare at low cost, and achieved comparable health outcomes as to high-income countries. (Rasanathan et al, 2012)

The global evidence on effectiveness of government funded and Social Health Insurance (SHI) in reducing out of pocket expenditure is however limited. (Ghosh 2017) Still there is enough evidence to conclude that if implemented well and at-scale, insurance schemes increase access to health services, and improve financial affordability. It is this emerging evidence to make health services affordable to poor people, that many state governments in India launched publically funded health insurance schemes, mostly in the last decade. There is evidence that such schemes can prove an effective tool to improve quality of health services through differentiated rates and incentives if providers meet certain quality standards, and have accreditation; increased adherence to Standard Treatment Guidelines (STGs), and provider's willingness to accept slightly higher regulation, amongst other approaches. (Sood - 2014)

Implementation challenges in ABP

Successful outcomes in the health sector requires appropriate and context specific design and implementation. In setting up HWCs, recruiting Community Health Officers (CHO), one each for 150,000 HWCs should be a good idea. This is an opportunity to innovate and explore solutions for recruitment of additional cadre of public health personnel.

There is limited capacity amongst Indian state governments in identification and enrolment of beneficiaries, designing the benefit package, fixing the package rate, empanelment of facilities, monitoring and regulation and fraud detection. *Many of these are 'sine qua non' for success of a health insurance scheme.* The insurance schemes require a state level authority with sufficiently trained staff, and a well-functioning Information technology (IT) system to implement the program. The success of Ayushman Bharat would also be dependent upon how the supply-deficient Indian states such as Uttar Pradesh, Bihar and the Northeastern states take up and implement the scheme. A well-functioning IT platform would be essential to meet diverse needs of different stakeholders including patients, service providers and program managers. The implementation would benefit from generating real time data and then use of data for action.

The ABP success on advancing health and achieving UHC in India would be dependent upon the response and leadership of 29 Indian states. In India, over the past 15 years, contracting in healthcare has emerged. These are of different kinds such as service contracts, management and operation contracts, and build, manage, operate and transfer (BMOT/BOT) contracts. Shift to the Public Private Partnership (PPP) model requires huge amount of consistent data work to draw up successful purchase of services. Drawing up healthcare packages and flexibility within it is - crucial with an increasing population suffering from complex needs (communicable/non-communicable diseases and disabilities). Contracts with an appropriate service mix will remain a continuous challenge in this context.

With ushering of market through "strategic purchasing," the policy calls for the role of stewardship as incumbent on the government. It is the central, state or local level government money that will be entrusted to purchase services. The effect of purchasing will depend on - how well the purchaser can plan the population health needs annually and long-term for the quantity of services required, quality standards, and budget estimates? Its impact will also become dependent on how well the providers meet the contract objectives. PPP at all levels (centre/state/local) of healthcare services demands administrative reforms and strengthening of purchaser capacity.

An Urgent Need for Public Health Management Cadre

In view of expanding the primary healthcare services, reaching out to the community, and increased administrative role with strategic purchasing in the hospitals, the NHP 2017 suggests revival of the need to a start a Public Health Management Cadre.

Strengthening health care systems in India

As per the principle of National Health Policy 2017, public health is back on the *national policy priority agenda* and should be used as a catalyst for decisive and broader health system re-designing and strengthening. Here are a few suggestions to implement health related goals in India.

- *Need to increase government investment on health*: In the years ahead, the universal implementation of two components of 'Ayushman Bharat Program' would require approx. Rs. 70-100 thousand Crore (US$ 11.5 - 15.5 billion) per annum. This increased investment in health would be in alignment with NHP-2017 target of government spending 2.5% of GDP on health by year 2025. This would require an annual increase of 20-25% in budgetary allocation by both national and state governments. The UHC is about universalising health goals for all citizens and therefore the mechanisms for financial protection beyond targeted 40% families, should be explored and linkage between primary and secondary/tertiary care strengthened. Ayushman Bharat caters only to the poor, out of pocket payments remain high, with only around 20% of the population covered by health insurance. The government thinks tank Niti Aayog has suggested "consolidation" of healthcare services and providers to reduce health expenditure and improve access. In a new report on building a 21st century health system for India, the Aayog proposed "strategic purchasing" of services "risk-pooling" and "digitisation" of health records for transformation of the healthcare sector. The Aayog is mulling building up a healthcare system for the middle class which is still not covered under any public healthcare system. This should be part of mid-term roadmap and "progressive universalization" of the Right to Health for all citizens of India.
- *Catalyse for systematic health reforms in India*: The success of ABP would be in bringing the shift from the traditional approach of disease specific and targeted initiatives to focus on people-centered integrated services and financial protection. The health system strengthening does not appear to be an explicit focus in ABP in India. In due course, it would be beneficial to converge the ABP and NHPS to improve both supply- and demand-side issues and achieve a stronger health system infrastructure in all states of India. (Lahariya 2018)

Concluding Observations

Universal healthcare by extending access to healthcare as widely as possible and providing quality care through minimum standards entitles every citizen with the Right to Health. Soviet Union implemented it in 1937 followed by UK nearly a decade later. Most nations have funded it through general taxation, as supplement it by specific levies and private payments.

India's central government needs to play a leadership role. By focusing on universal healthcare as a long term journey, with consensus on political backing and hard choices along with secured long term funding, *universal coverage for good quality healthcare can be achieved* in India to hugely empower its 1.3 billion population. By building an effective regulatory framework and consistent policies across states and the Centre, workforce shortages can be overcome a strong Public Health Management Cadre can be built along with integrating healthcare facilities across the villages, towns and districts.

Private sector can help improve India's healthcare infrastructure:- However, without faster accreditation; few private players will gain credibility, or raise standards, resulting in low customer satisfaction, lower hospital stays and poor governance. The National Accreditation Board for Hospitals and Healthcare Providers needs to roll out incentives encouraging accreditation making it a mandatory process.

Public-private partnerships, or build-operate-transfer, or operations and maintenance contracting schemes can utilize private capital for provisioning healthcare services. Insurance coverage is also limited in India, with just around 25% of the population covered. To achieve universal access, a coverage ratio of around 75% (publicly funded) needs to be targeted, with the remainder offered access through privately funded schemes.

Social insurance schemes really need to be rolled out at scale, with the government deploying a greater share of healthcare funds. Pilot programmes launched at regional levels can help us determine the best model for the Indian market because there cannot always be "one size fit all" schemes for large countries like India.

India has shown that in the health arena, it can accomplish great feats with the requisite leadership commitment and support. Polio and small pox eradication efforts of the most innovative kind –has been successfully undertaken in India. The government of India deserves international acclaim for engineering this success. The country turned the tide on HIV epidemic, cutting new infections by more than half in just a decade and averting the disaster that many had predicted.

The improvement in child mortality is less recognized but just as impressive. The number of children under five years of age who die every year has gone down by 60% since 1990 – and that number will keep decreasing even faster as a result of the government's decision to introduce new vaccines to its immunization system.

Moreover, India has the schemes in place to drive rapid improvements in health. The National Rural Health Mission (NRHM) was created in 2005 and provides a framework by which the government can support the health goals outlined at the sub-district, district and state levels.

Sustainable Development Health Goals are entirely achievable with an efficient and monitored public health system, if the declining infant and maternal mortality ratios are sustained and improved and a significant effort at fighting malnutrition are adopted. By a small increase in public expenditure on health to a little above 1% GDP, the gains of the National Rural Health Mission are perceptible. Therefore, it is clearly understood why a 3% public expenditure on health is required for universal health coverage. There can be partnerships with the non-governmental sector but they should be within a framework of a credible public system with public accountability.

Significantly, innovations in the health sector are also coming in from other states in India as well e.g. innovations and partnerships for emergency transport, diagnostics, drug availability, recruitment and training of new health workers. The Janani Suraksha Yojna (JSY) has brought women to health facilities for institutional deliveries on an unprecedented scale, taking the national coverage to over 70% from a low of 44% just five years ago. Besides, the thrust on decentralized planning enhanced political will and need based provision of human resources created confidence in the failing public systems to start delivering quality services.

While the HLEG has clearly recognized an important role for the private sector in the provision of health services, it has insisted that a strong regulatory frame work is essential and an effective process for building in accountability to the country's citizens is equally important.

As per the Fourteenth Finance Commission's (FFC) recommendation in 2015-16, the share of tax pool to the states increased, but majority states used it for other sectors and not on health and education. Post the FFC recommendation, only Sikkim, Mizoram, Goa, Meghalaya, Himachal Pradesh,

Jammu and Kashmir. Worth noticing is that Kerala invested more on health (Scroll 2016). A recent study on the relationship between different types of tax and varied health indicators shows that direct tax can be linked to better health outcomes and increased levels of health spending (Reeves et al 2015). Therefore, it is critical for countries like India to pay greater emphasis on public finance, and how and where they can be optimally used.

World leaders adopted a high level UN political Declaration on Universal Health coverage at the UN general Assembly in 2019, making it the most comprehensive set of health commitments ever adopted. India made a financial and political commitment at the UN to accelerate progress towards universal health coverage by scaling up essential health services, affording financial risk protection and access to safe, quality effective and affordable medicines and vaccines for all. (Times of India, September 2019).

Overall the NHP 2017 falls in line with the growing emphasis to provide universal access to primary healthcare, functioning as a "gatekeeping mechanism" and opening up secondary and tertiary levels of care to market-based reform. India is committed to achieve UHC as a signatory to the globally agreed Sustainable Development Goals (SDGs) and the National Health Policy 2017 can prove a catalyst and a platform to prepare India for achieving that goal by 2030, which is the final deadline for implementation of SDGs by all signatory countries like India.

References

1. Bagchi A K and Krishan Soman (eds) 2005, Maladies, Preventives and Curatives: Debates in Public Health in India. New Delhi: Tulika Books, pp. 79-95.
2. Deaton Angus, 2013, The Great Escope: Health Wealth and the Origins of Inequality, Prinnceton University.
3. Dreze Jean (eds) 2017, Social Policy, New Delhi Orient Black swan
4. Ghosh S, Gupta ND., 2017: Targeting and Effects of Rashtriya Swasthya Bima Yojana on Access to Care and Financial Protection. Economic & Political Weekly
5. Government of India. India Budget 2018-19 and Budget Speech. Ministry of Finance, New Delhi. Available from: http://www.indiabudget.gov.in/. Accessed February 12, 2018.
6. Government of India. Millennium development Goals, India Country Report 2015. Minsitry of Statistics, Planning and Implementation. Govt of India, New Delhi. 2016. Available from: http://mospi.nic.in/sites/default/files/publication_reports/mdg_2july15_1.pdf. Accessed March 03, 2018.
7. Government of India. National Health Policy 2017. Ministry of Health and Family Welfare, Nirman Bhawan, New Delhi, 2017. p. 1-32.

8. Government of India. Report of the Task force on Primary Health Care in India. Ministry of Health and Family Welfare, Nirman Bhawan, New Delhi, 2017. p. 1-60.
9. Government of India. Rural Health Statistics 2017. Ministry of Health and Family Welfare, Nirman Bhawan, New Delhi, 2017.
10. Health in India, 2017. Lancet. 2017; 389:127.
11. HLEG 2011 High Level Expert Group Report on Universal Health Coverage for India. Planning Commission of India, New Delhi at http://www.Planningcommission.nic.in/ reports/genrep /rep _uhc /2011. pdf
12. K Rasanathan, et al, 2012: Healthy public policy: the first National Health Assembly in Thailand. Health Expectations
13. Lahariya Chandrakant, 2018, Ayushman Bharat Program and Universal Health Coverage in India, Indian Pediatrics, Vol 55, June 15
14. Mor Nachiket, January 2019, Health sector needs new ideas , New Delhi, Hindustan Times,
15. National Commission on Macro-economics and Health (NCMH). 2005. Report of the National Commission on Macroeconomics and Health. New Delhi : Ministry of Health and Family Welfare, Government of India.
16. National Health Systems Resource Centre. National Health Accounts 2014-15. Ministry of Health and Family Welfare, Nirman Bhawan, New Delhi, 2017. p 1-74.
17. National Institute of Public Finance and Policy. Report on Utilisation, Fund Flows and Public Financial Management under the National Health Mission: A Study of Selected States, NIPFP; 2017.
18. Reeves R, et al, 2015: Financing Universal Health Coverage-Effects of Alternative Tax Structures on Public Health Systems. Cross-national Modelling in 89 Low-income and Middle-income Countries, Lancet, 386 (9990): 274-80.
19. Scroll, 2016: It is not Just the central Spending on Health that is Appalling-The States Too are giving up, Scroll, 3 May, https:scroll.in/pulse/807433/it-is-not-just-the-central-spending-on-health-that-is-appalling-the-states-too-are-giving-up.
20. Sood N, et al 2014, Government health insurance for people below poverty line in India: Quasi-experimental evaluation of insurance and health outcomes. BMJ
21. World Health Organization and International Bank for Reconstruction and Development / The World Bank. Tracking Universal Health Coverage: 2017 Global Monito-ring Report. Available from: http://www.who.int/health info/universal_health_coverage/report/2017 _global_ monitoring_ report.pdf. Accessed February 15, 2018.
22. World Health Organization. World Health Report 2010: Health Financing for Universal Coverage. Geneva: WHO, 2010.
23. World Health Organization. World Health Statistics 2017: Geneva: WHO. 2017. Available from: http://www.who.int/gho/ publications/world_health_statistics/2017/en/. Accessed Febuary 04, 2018.

+++

Chapter Four

Redesigning India's Rural Economy by Rural Road Connectivity by Pradhan Mantri Gram Sadak Yojna

Pooja Paswan[4]

Abstract

Development Administration in a welfare state has been considered as an important instrument to expedite the process of change through planned development and positive intervention. The main aim of development is to increase the per capita income, to raise the standard of living of the people and to secure justice, equality, freedom and security of life in the society. The primary concern of planned development is the removal of infrastructural obstacles that restrict the capability and deny the opportunities for participation in social activities. These activities include access to education (attending school at primary level), having access to primary health care facilities, sanitation and drinking water as well as an assured gainful employment. People have to participate in the growth process and share its benefits collectively. The total well being of any country is measured in terms of the facilities and services that are available to the people. Connectivity and mobility is the key to reaching out and opening up new opportunities. With the construction of village roads, rural India is rapidly transforming. Wherever the roads network has come up the rural economy and quality of life has improved.

Keywords: Development Administration, planned change, infrastructure facilities, rural road connectivity

Significance of Rural Road connectivity

Rural Road connectivity is a key component of rural development, since it promotes access to economic and social services, thereby generating increased agricultural productivity, non-agricultural employment as well as non-agricultural productivity, which in turn expands rural growth oppsortunities and real income through which poverty can be reduced.

4. Assistant Professor, Department of Political Science, Jamia Millia Islamia, New Delhi

A study (Fan et al. 1999) carried out by the International Food Policy Research Institute on linkages between government expenditure and poverty in rural India has revealed that an investment of Rs 1 crore in roads lifts 1650 poor persons above the poverty line. Public investment on roads - impacts rural poverty through its effect on improved agricultural productivity, higher non-farm employment opportunities and increased rural wages. Improvement in agricultural productivity not only reduces rural poverty directly by increasing income of poor households, it also causes decline in poverty indirectly by raising agricultural wages and lowering food prices (since poor households are net buyers of foodgrains). Similarly, increased non-farm employment and higher rural wages also enhance incomes of the rural poor and consequently, reduce rural poverty. This study estimated that while the 'productivity effect' of government spending on rural roads accounts for 24 per cent of total impact on poverty, increased non-farm employment accounts for 55 per cent and higher rural wages accounts for the remaining 31 per cent. Further, of the total productivity effect on poverty, 75 per cent arises from the direct impact of roads in increasing incomes, while the remaining 25 per cent arises from lower food prices (15 per cent) and increased wages (10 per cent). Similar results are found in other developing countries. The study by the same institute (Fan et al. 2000)) in China revealed that with every 10,000 Yuan (about $1200) spent on rural roads eleven persons are lifted above the poverty line. Living Standard Survey in Vietnam in 2002 showed that populations living within 2 km of all-weather roads have lower poverty rates as noted in the draft Vision Document for Rural Roads, 2006 (MoRD, 2006). Statistical evidence apart, the link between poverty and lack of accessibility is quite apparent. Nearer home, a household survey (APERP, 1997) conducted in the state of Andhra Pradesh indicated that the rural road improvements lead to substantial reduction in freight charges, increase in household income, more employment opportunities, and expansion of cultivated land.

Conceptual Framework

A new, all-weather rural road will bring various benefits to the villagers along its route. As producers, they will enjoy higher net prices for their marketed surpluses as consumers, they will pay less for urban goods. If there is no school in the village itself, those children who already attend one elsewhere will spend less time travelling to and fro, and those who did not attend earlier may do so now. If there is a village school, it is the teachers themselves who may appear more regularly. Much the same holds for medical treatment. Children and those adults with chronic ailments are more likely to make regular visits to the clinic; and in an emergency, those in need of medical attention will be able to reach the clinic sooner, which may make the difference between life and death.

A robust and efficient infrastructure network is a sine qua non for a vigorous and inclusive growth of any economy. The economy is able to attain high levels of efficiency and is able to compete in the global market only if there is an adequate infrastructural support. The state government has taken various steps in the recent past to accelerate the pace of development and reduce the deficit in infrastructure sector.

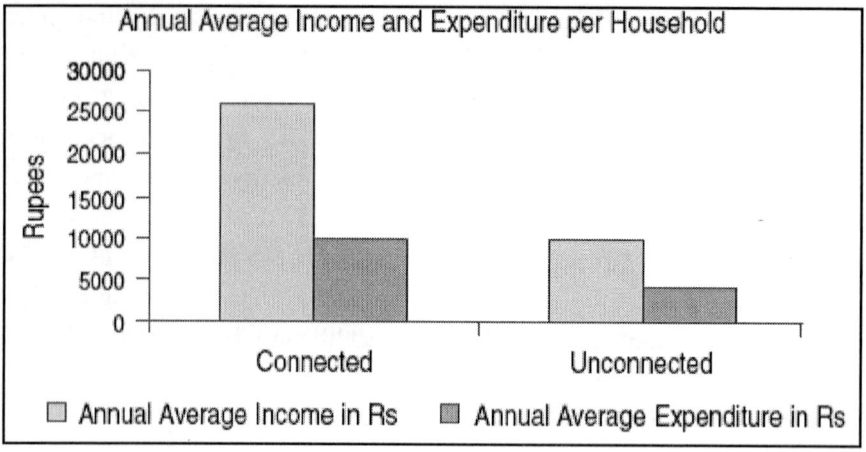

Figure 1.1 Comparative average income and expenditure of connected and unconnected villages

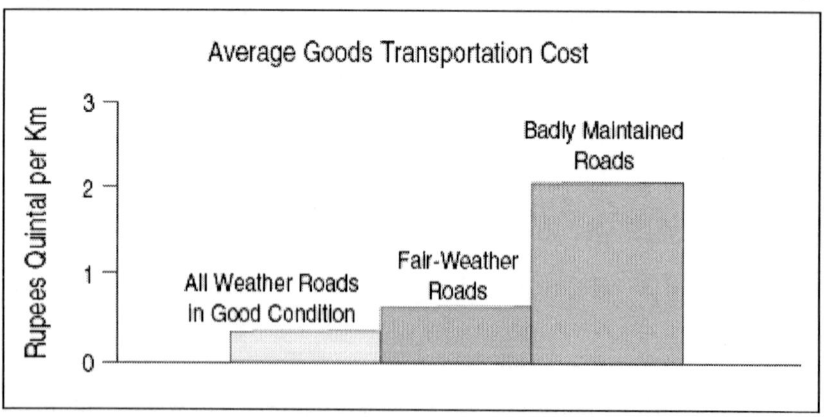

Figure1.2 Goods transportation costs on different types of roads.

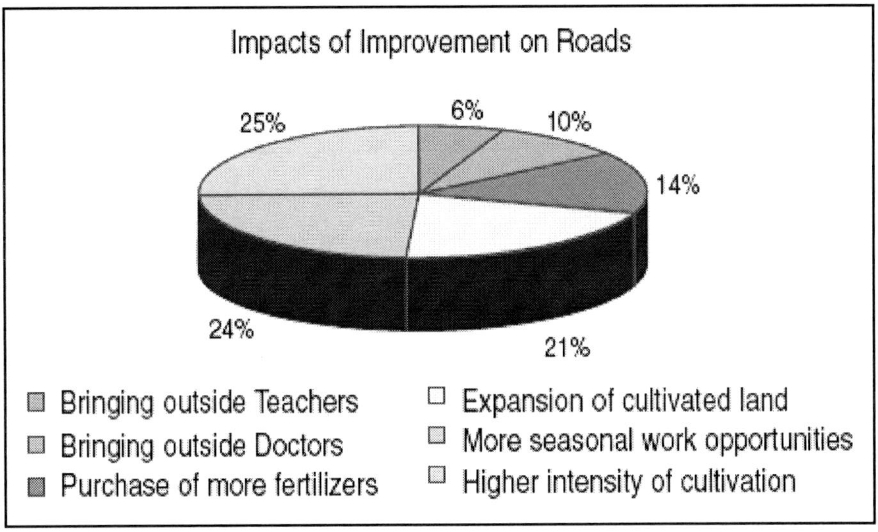

Figure 1.3Impact on Standard of Living from Improvement on roads.

Status of Rural Roads in India

Roads are classified under a time-honoured system into National Highways (NHs), State Highways (SHs), Major District Roads (MDRs), Other District Roads (ODRs), and Village Roads (VRs), with well-recognized standards for construction and maintenance laid out in respect of each category. Generally speaking, there are clearly understood demarcations of responsibility in terms of governmental offices expected to deal with each category. However, while the activity mapping with respect to NHs and SHs is clear cut, with respect to MDRs, ODRs, and VRs, these distinctions are blurred.

In many states, though PRIs are assigned responsibilities with respect to ODRs and VRs, a plethora of agencies and line departments undertake formation and repairs of roads. These include the state government's PWD wing, the Agricultural Produce Marketing Committees (APMCs), parallel bodies created by multilateral agencies, Forest department, Development authorities and so on. There are several general funds that are used for roads, apart from special schemes tied to specific road projects. Thus roads are repaired using Sampoorna Grameen Rozgar Yojana (SGRY), scarcity relief funds, and untied funds devolved by States. Consequently, it is difficult, if not impossible, to assess the exact amount that is being spent for the maintenance and construction of ODRs and VRs. The overlapping of responsibilities and the fragmentation of funds between agencies for maintenance and development of roads is a source of inefficiency and confusion. Quite often, the only point where all these responsibilities and funds converge is at the level of the local implementing officer, the Assistant Executive Engineer, who is used by all agencies (named above) for implementation. This thinly spread management structure is inefficient; it does not ensure good monitoring or downward accountability and unnecessarily complicates planning.

India has a rural road network of about 2.7 million km developed with an investment of almost Rs 35,000 crore, estimated to have a replacement value of about Rs 180,000 crore. This constitutes over 80 per cent of the total road network, however, about a million km length of the road does not meet the technical standards required. According to government statistics, by year 2000, India had connectivity to almost all villages with populations of over 1500, 86 per cent with 1000 to 1500 inhabitants, and 43 per cent of villages with less than 1000 population.

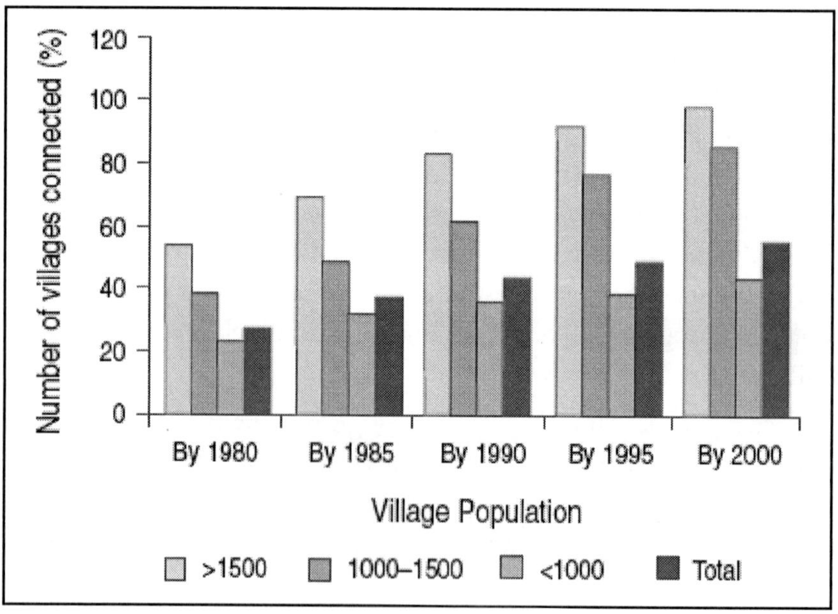

Figure 1.4 Connectivity Status

A Watch Word: Successive plans aimed at achieving higher road densities and managed to over achieve it.

Table 1.1 Basis for assessment, assessed targets and expected densities in the Road Development Plan.

Basis for assessment, assessed targets and expected densities in the Road Development Plans.

Name of the Plan	Basis of fixation of targets	Targets km	Achievement km	Target density (All roads)
Nagpur Plan (1943–61)	Length of ODRs + VRs assessed on the basis of number of villages with population 500 and less, 501–1000, 1001–2000, and 2001–5000.	332,335	500,802	0.32 km per sq km
Bombay Plan (1961–81)	Length based on the number of villages with population less than 500, 500–1000, 1000–2000, and 2000–5000	651,780	912,684	0.46 km per sq km
Lucknow Plan (1981–01)	Length assessed on the basis of number of villages and towns.	2,189,000	2,994,000	0.82 km per sq km

Even though, the total length of rural roads targeted at the end of the Lucknow Plan appeared to be large, it must be noted that almost 100,000 km of the roads were constructed under different employment generation schemes and poverty alleviation programmes such as Food for Work, National Rural Employment Programme and Jawahar Rojgar Yojana. The roads were of indifferent quality constructed by unskilled labour. The objective of these programmes was provision of sustenance support to the rural people. The technical standards of asset quality were not insisted upon and construction was often restricted to earthen tracks with no provision even for cross drainage or side drainage. Since water is the main enemy of the sustainability of roads, roads constructed under such employment generation schemes were often not durable. Rural roads have suffered greatly due to lack of systematic planning. While rural road development plans provided for a network structure and target lengths of different types of roads, specific connectivity requirements of individual settlements (villages/habitation) and issues of regional imbalances were not adequately addressed. This led to more than one connection for the same village resulting in redundancy and development of a large unmanageable network. While constructing rural roads, adequate care was not taken in adopting need based designs, parameters for pavement construction, quality assurance, and quality control. Multiplicity of organizations involved in the rural roads development led to uncoordinated efforts, adhoc decisions, and a lopsided network structure.

Selection of Indicators

The basic purpose of development is the well being of the people. The main aim of any development project is to make an attempt to eradicate the human suffering and restructure the orientation of lives of the people in such a manner that it leads to the enhancement of human capabilities by extending the availability choices and opportunities and thus enabling them to lead a life of respect and value.

The three basic components of development at all levels essential for people to lead a long and healthy life, to be acknowledged and to have access to the minimum resources need for minimum standard of living. This study has evaluated all the three basic components of development, explored to what extent the state has been successful in enhancing the development of the concerned population. The list of variables used in the study are as follows:

1. **Indicator of educational development**
    a) Percentage of literacy
    b) Female literacy rate
    c) Gross enrollment ratio
2. **Health Indicator**
    a) Availability of health centers.
    b) Availability of health facilities.
3. **Indicator of Basic Income**
    a) Income from agriculture
    b) Income from auxiliary sources such as handicrafts, tourism etc.

Setting standards across the country

Prior to unveiling the PMGSY program, the Central Government was responsible for only National Highways. It was for State Governments to plan, fund, construct and maintain rural roads. There was no national level consensus or coordination on rural roads.

The PMGSY initiated a paradigm shift in the way rural roads are mapped, designed, monitored, and built. At the initiative of the MoRD, NRRDA prepared an operational manual to systematize the process of road building, to be uniformly applied throughout the country. For the first time, nationwide operational standards have been adopted in the area of institutional structures, planning, design, reporting systems, procurement, contract management, financial and accounting systems, manpower skills and safety measures. Monitoring of the quality of works and materials by third parties has become mandatory. Guidelines on acceptable standards with desired specifications have also been put in place - in order to cut down on subjective evaluations.

World Bank partners PMGSY

The World Bank, a partner with the Government of India to build rural infrastructure, alleviate poverty and improve rural livelihood, is supporting the PMGSY program. The Bank's Rural Road Project1 (RRP) is being implemented in select districts of Jharkhand, Himachal Pradesh (HP), Rajasthan and Uttar Pradesh (UP).Since the inception of the PMGSY, the World Bank has provided technical support to the Ministry of Rural Development in formulating the operational guidelines of the program. It includes setting up the Core Road Network approach to prioritize the selection of habitations. A highlight of the association has been the mandatory provision for peoples' participation, adoption of Environmental and Social Management Framework (ESMF), developing maintenance management capacity of the States and exposure to global good practices through training.

Quality with transparency

Under the PMGSY, a three-tier quality control system has been put in place to ensure quality in road works. This will be applicable throughout the country.

- The first tier is at the District Project Implementation Unit (PIU), led by a senior Executive Engineer, where all aspects of operational monitoring are held. Contractors are also required to maintain field level laboratories for testing at each stage. The PIU field engineers periodically conduct quality control tests at the site and record the results in a quality control register.
- The second tier involves quality monitoring at the State level, where district wise quality monitors of the State government, working independently of the PIU, cross-check the work and verify the entries in the register.
- The third tier, added under the Rural Roads Project, is of National Quality Monitors. It is mandatory for a reputed independent agency to be specifically contracted to carry out random tests on the quality of work. Retired Chief Engineers from neighbouring States are also taken on board for inspection of works alongside representatives of reputed engineering colleges and other specialized institutes.

Uniformity in governance and management

To build a strong foundation, from the inception of the program, the Government in Bihar announced many path-breaking decisions. Meanwhile, the Central Government adopted an enabling role, endorsing its strong commitment to the PMGSY.

The Central Government, provided a regular and continuous flow of funds, though this was linked to performance and expenditure. Sufficient funds were released as and when required to the state government. At no point of time was any construction work held up or slowed down because of financial restrictions thus facilitating construction to roll on smoothly. This worked as an additional incentive for engineers and contractors to meet their periodic deadlines as more funds were in the pipeline for the next schedule.

The Government of Bihar played a major role in ensuring that the program was implemented in accordance with the cluster-based criteria. The PMGSY was regarded as a rare opportunity for correcting the historical imbalances of development in the poorer regions of the State.

Other key decisions taken by the State governments that led to speeding up the decision-making processes were:

- Delegation of financial powers to the field staff to scrutinize and select bids and to announce a closure on the awards within 30 days;
- Providing stability of tenure in the department for senior managers, chief engineers, and senior administrative officers so that there was continuity in the program;
- Institutionalizing a model document that listed the guiding principle to be followed for making tenders and selection procedures. In addition to security of tenure, the roles and responsibilities of the project staff were clearly defined leading to greater efficiency and quality output.

The cornerstone of the program was the setting up of institutional and implementation structures. In each State the main implementing agency was the State Rural Road Development Agency (SRRDA). In Bihar the SRRDA worked through their respective government department- the Public Works Department (PWD) as it was the oldest department with a strong field presence and a vast network that covered the entire State.

Socio-Economic Development by Rural Roads

Rural roads are the basic infrastructure requirement and play a vital role in the socio-economic upliftment of rural community. They contribute significantly in rural development by creating opportunities to access goods and services located in nearby villages or major town/market centres. Provision of rural roads increases mobility of men and materials thus facilitating economic growth. These, in turn, assist in reducing poverty and leads to over all socio-economic development.

Several studies have already established that there exist a strong relationship between rural roads and socio-economic development. Hine (1982) reviewed several impact studies conducted in about 16 countries. Most of these case studies considered are optimistic about the relationship between road investment and agricultural development.

In India, even during the '80s, studies on socio-economic aspects of rural roads were conducted in selected nine districts under the aegis of Indian Roads Congress. The objective of these studies was to find out and quantify the possible impact of roads on socio-economic development in rural areas. CRRI (1987) carried out the compilation and analysis of the data for the nine districts, to quantify the aggregate impacts. Some of the findings are:

1. increase in agricultural production due to road facility
2. increase in fertiliser consumption
3. increase in non-agricultural activities
4. better utilisation of existing facilities like, school, health, banks and post offices.

Similarly, a socio-economic survey conducted in a remote area in India by CRRI in 1989, showed that the villages located on the main road are comparatively well developed than those away from the road. The rural transport study carried out (NCAER and IIMB, 1989) for two different periods in 1979 and 1989 revealed that after the development of rural roads, there was a change in transport modes in rural areas and also an increase in economic activities.

The economic analysis of rural roads carried out for selected rural road projects financed by World Bank in Morocco (World Bank, 1996) is one of the major studies which attempted to find out the rate of return on the investment made.

The study quantified the benefits based on savings in vehicle operating cost (VOC) compared to the original i.e. unpaved roads. The economic analysis carried out for rural access project (World Bank, 1999) in Bhutan has shown significant transport cost saving. The mule transport costs are as high as 6 times of truck transport cost. The net agricultural benefits, educational benefits and health benefits were calculated and added in the benefit stream. Recently, a similar study by CRRI (2001) has been carried out to conduct the comparative evaluation of rural roads. The major aim of the study was to compute the Internal Rate of Return (IRR) for the investment made on project roads constructed under the Agricultural Development Programme (ADP) in Rajasthan. The benefits are estimated by taking net incremental agricultural production value, net agricultural transport cost savings and non-agricultural vehicle operating cost savings. The overall average IRR for the selected 21 road projects was found to be 15.64 per cent. In addition, this study results also showed positive relationship between the road improvement interventions with socio-economic parameters.

The impacts of rural roads are summarized as given below:

- **Improvement in transportation services:-** which leads to improved access to market centres for the rural producers, better availability of farm inputs at reduced prices;
- **Diversification of agriculture:–** improved market access promotes shift in favour of cash crops and commercialization of agricultural activities.
- **Diversification of livelihood opportunities:–** better connectivity enhances employment opportunities in the non-agricultural sectors.
- **Improved services:–** improved road connectivity, interalia, enhances access to education, health, communication and financial services.
- **Increase in the outreach of the State:–** Improved rural roads facilitates better availability of public services and functionaries in rural areas.

Poverty Alleviation

Asian Development Bank (2002) also conducted a study on 'Impact of Rural Roads on Poverty Reduction – A Case Study'. The study concluded that rural roads are the important enabling conditions for livelihood development for people in rural areas. The poor and very poor primarily benefit through the indirect impact of road improvements, of better access to state services and improved provision of services to the villages, and opportunities in alternative livelihood income stream.

Better rural infrastructure has primarily two effects – promotion of economic growth and decline in the incidence of poverty. Jocelyn A Songco (Columbia University and the World Bank, 2002) in a study pointed out that rural infrastructure investments benefit the rural poor through increased incomes and improved consumption patterns. Some empirical studies illustrate a strong relationship between infrastructure and economic growth. According to World Bank sources, 1% increase in infrastructure stock is associated with a proportionate increase in GDP across all countries. A specific sectoral study by Deichman et al for Mexico shows that a 10% increase in market access leads to increase in labour productivity by 6%.

Linkages between (i) public investment on rural connectivity, agricultural growth and (ii) poverty alleviation in the Indian context - were investigated in a research report authored by Shengenn Fan, Peter Hazell and Sukhadeo Thorat (Research Paper No.110, IFPRI, 1999). Using State-level data on Government spending from 1970 to 1993, this study attempted to quantitatively measure how different types public or investment affect agricultural growth and rural poverty.

The model estimated the number of poor people who would be raised above the poverty line for each Rs.1 million (1993 constant prices) of additional investment in eight different components of public spending — roads, research and extension, education, rural development, health, irrigation, soil and water conservation and power. Accordingly, Government expenditures were ranked in terms of their effectiveness in poverty alleviation. The findings of this study are striking. Government spending on roads was found to have the largest impact on rural poverty. For each Rs.1 million increase in investment in roads, 165 poor people would be enabled to cross the poverty line. Its impact on poverty was nearly twice as large as that of the next best poverty reducer – Government investment in agricultural R&D. Investment in roads was also found to be contributing significantly to productivity growth. An additional Rs.100 billion (in 1993 prices) invested in roads would increase productivity growth by more than 3 percent.

Recommendations

1. Rural roads have been proved to be catalytic for economic development and poverty alleviation in rural areas. This objective should be pursued further with more vigor. They are also essential for providing basic access to the services like health, education, administration, etc.
2. In future, the target should be to connect all habitations with all-weather rural roads instead of fair weather roads as was done earlier.
3. For integrated development of rural connectivity, upgradation is required to be included in addition to new connectivity links, as envisaged in Bharat Nirman.
4. Rural roads development targets (based on 2001 census and to modify after next census) will require continuance of the programme even beyond 11th Plan period.
5. The structure and systems of delivery developed so far should be strengthened and continued.

The taste of success

Capacity building of local contractors

A major intervention is raising the project implementation capacity of the contractors. In the first instance, selection is through a transparent tendering process. Additionally, small and medium size contractors have benefited by a waiver of excise duty on the purchase of machinery and equipment. Access to finance, with continuous work for 3-4 years to recover costs, has helped even smaller contractors to make heavy investments to purchase machinery.

After handling larger road-building segments and raising their capacity, many contractors are now bidding for larger projects in other States of the country either by applying individually or by forming a consortium.

- The above road is built under PMGSY by contractor Sharmaji in the village chaklashahi of Samastipur district. Prior to the construction of the road, the village was very remote and had absolutely no access to the basic facilities of education, health care and livelihood. Life was hard, particularly for the women. Several families were unwilling to marry their daughters in this village. During the initial phase of the construction of the road, the contractor was facing difficulties in procuring soil for raising the height of the road to a considerable extent, as the area was prone to flooding during the monsoon season. The people of the village were so desperate for proper connectivity that they left their fields fallow for that season and offered the contractor, soil from their own fields instead. It is the result of this community participation, the village today, is enjoying its full benefits. The people now have an access to almost all the governmental facilities such as schools, health centres, banks, post office, transport etc. The village which mainly grew cash crops such as tobacco, turmeric and mustard, saw a tremendous increase in its per capita income. On the other side the waves of prosperity attracted several families to the village for matrimonial alliance leading to an increase in the dowry of that region!!!!

- Better markets - Better incomes
- Brahmapur, a small nondescript bloc in darbhanga district, is bustling with activity today. It has become the market hub for the villagers to buy and sell their farm produce. They directly collect fresh vegetables and fruits from the farms that are stacked up on the curbs of the newly built roads, next to their fields
- Up in Sagarpur, farmers Naresh Kumar and Shamsher Singh are pleased with their extra earnings this year. It is the first time the produce did not perish because of a lack of proper transportation facilities.

Family bonds

- With accessibility, distances get shortened and visits between family members become more frequent. Shanti Devi of Bhawanipur said

  "Our pace of life has suddenly changed, people are earning better and travel is less time consuming. **Even our sons, working in big cities, are visiting us for festivals as just three days leave is enough for a home visit.**" In the lush green landscape of Darbhanga, young Kalyani Devi is happy with the road. Busy working in her fields, she smilingly said that she could **slip away to the next village every second day to chat with her mother.**
- For the village of Haiderpur in Samastipur, rural roads have meant better marriage offers for their sons and daughters. "Few people were willing to give their daughter in marriage into a village where access was difficult and time consuming. All marriage ceremonies were held by the side of the main highway as getting in the village was difficult," said Dhana Sahni.

Now, the marriage procession comes down the village road enabling the old and the children to join in as it winds its way to their doorstep.

A spurt in house building

Better connectivity has also led to a spurt in building activity. "I could never think of building a concrete house because carting building material on tractors was impossible and financially out of my reach," said Anil Rai. His uncle, Ghasi Ram, 75, said, "I had never dreamt that I would see a road in my village. But now it runs right through our lands and the price of my land has jumped from Rs 50,000 a bigha to Rs 1 lakh," He smiled.

Medicine on time

The primary health centre (PHC) is bustling with activity. The road has joined the neighbouring villages and, as a result, more mothers come for their ante natal-check up. The villagers are pleased that women are able to come to the PHC for their delivery. Complicated cases can now be referred quickly to the Community Health Centre or to the District Hospital.

With better connectivity, the PHC is not facing shortages of polio vaccine any more. Children are being immunized at regular intervals due to frequent visits of the para medical staff and the health education camps at the Anganwadi have better attendance with women from other clusters joining in. Roads have also helped with better follow-up of TB patients. The doctors now insist on the patients coming to the centre each day to take their tablets in the presence of the medical staff. Cases of road or field accidents are also being attended to at the PHC itself.

Road to earning

In the clusters around Bharavballias, in Madhubani district, people lived under conditions of extreme poverty with poor lands and high unemployment. Now they take the bus to reach work. With the road connectivity the people find it easier to commute long distance. However, Daulat Ram, a cycle shop owner complained loudly that with the building of the all weather roads, the cycle tires last longer and thus he was forced to go out of business of cycle repair and now sells bicycles instead.

The Challenge

Road maintenance and management systems

The bane of most civic construction work is the follow-up maintenance work. Shortage of funds with the State government - posed a challenge for maintenance. The Rural Roads Project has built in maintenance as part of the contractor's responsibility for a period of five years after the completion of the road. Thereafter, the State government takes over. In Rajasthan, the government has already earmarked resources from the central pool and identified areas from where additional revenue will be raised to meet the demand for maintaining roads falling under the PMGSY and other programs.

Key interventions for the successful management of the rural roads program

1. Institutional development by setting up a rural roads development agency to undertake the work in a program mode at the State-level
2. Participation of people's representatives at all stages of planning and proposal formulation for greater community ownership and support
3. A three-tier quality control mechanism to achieve high quality through regular and random checks by professionals.
4. Adoption of the environmental code of practice to avoid or minimise adverse environmental impact
5. Setting up operational guidelines, norms and standards at various levels of project implementation
6. Better human resource development through capacity building, skill-enhancement and clarity of role
7. Inclusion of a five-year maintenance clause in all road building contracts from the date of completion of a particular road
8. Complete transparency in contractual bidding and awarding process.

Conclusion

In a developing country like India where 73 percentage of the population lives in rural areas and only 27 percentage in urban areas - a very structured planning procedure should be used for developmental activities and infrastructure facilities available in a rural area. Rural roads are an integral part of rural development and it stimulates overall development by providing access to economic and social infrastructure and facilities. Finally, it needs to be noted that the planning process is a dynamic process which needs temporal modification as per the requirements of the people concerned. The need is to identify the basic hindrance in the policy and use the best possible way to address it. A government does not become popular or unpopular on the basis of its policy. Worth nothing here is that solely depends on the manner in which the policy is implemented.

References

1. Acharya, S. (2004). India's growth prospects revisited. Economic and Political Weekly, 4537-4542.
2. Ahmad, E. (1961). The rural population of Bihar. Geographical Review, 51(2), 253-276.
3. Ahmad, I. (2007). Madhubani, through the ages: a regional history of Madhubani. Image Impressions.
4. Bazmi, S. H., & Shahabuddin, M. (2005). Biodiversity and wise-use of wetlands of Madhubani in Bihar. Nature, Environment and Pollution Technology, 4(4), 507-514.
5. Bell, C. (2010). Goods, Education and Health: A Combined Model for Evaluating PMGSY. University of Heidelberg, Germany.
6. Corbridge, S., Williams, G., Veron, R., & Srivastava, M. (2003). Making Social Science Matter-II: How the Rural Poor See the State in Bihar, Jharkhand and West Bengal. Economic and political weekly, 2561-2569.
7. Dalal, J., Mohapatra, P. K., & Mitra, G. C. (2010). Prioritization of rural roads: AHP in group decision. Engineering, Construction and Architectural Management, 17(2), 135-158.
8. Edgar, T. The Pearson Current Events Digest 2009. Pearson Education India.
9. Etienne, G. (1992). Employment and Wages in Rural India: The Fight against Poverty and the Economic Reforms. Indian Journal of Labour Economics,35(3).
10. Mohapatra, J. K., & Chandrasekhar, B. P. (2007). Rural Roads. 3i Network (2007), India Infrastructure Report 2007: Rural Infrastructure.
11. Mukherji, A., & Mukherji, A. (2012). Bihar: What Went Wrong? And What Changed?.
12. Rodgers, G., & Rodgers, J. (2011). Inclusive development, Migration, governance and social change in rural Bihar. Economic and Political Weekly, 46(23), 43-50.
13. Finance Department, February (2012-13), Economic Survey, Government of Bihar.
14. Ministry of Rural Development (2004), Guidelines for Pradhan Manatri Gram Sadak Yojana (PMGSY), Ministry of Rural Development, Government of India.
15. Ministry of Rural Development (2004)., Impact Assessment of Pradhan Mantri Gram Sadak Yojana – PMGSY.
16. Ministry of Rural Development (2005), PMGSY - Operational Manual. Government of India.
17. Ministry of Rural Development (2006), Rural Roads Development Plan: Vision -2025 (Draft), Government of India.

✦✦✦

Chapter Five

Urban Sanitation in Slums: A Study in Solid Waste Management Policy Implementation

Vanshree Agarwal[5]*

Abstract

As developing countries - increasingly move from the notion of 'government' to 'governance' in a technology dominated world populated by millennials - policy implementation has acquired newer nuances and challenges along with new possibilities to deliver essential services for the public good. During the implementation phase, public policy intention is translated into action, generally by peripheral units of government in which the bureaucracy at various levels, play a crucial role. Policy program implementation by the administrator often feeds back into policy formulation so that he can advise authoritatively from experience on the feasibility of different policy options. In today' environment, simple hierarchies in the system have been replaced by a policy delivery system which uses a mix of partnership between the public and private sector, market mechanism and the voluntary sector.

It is in this context that - we wish to examine the policy on urban sanitation in the country with special focus on solid waste management. The program under this namely the 'Swachh Bharat Mission' captured the popular imagination in the last five years of its inception and made many new breakthroughs in the policy delivery mechanisms. We wish to investigate the implementation of this program at the ward level of an urban local body in Delhi with respect to an urban slum to understand if the implementation process has made headway amidst the most neglected sections of the urban population. This would add to the understanding of the working, success and gaps in the implementation of a central policy as adopted under the federal structure of our country in a milieu where both public scrutiny and awareness has acquired newer dimensions owing to easy access to information through social media and other instruments.

5. *PhD Research Scholar, Department of Political Science, Jamia Millia Islamia, New Delhi

Keywords: Swachh Bharat Mission, Sustainable Development Goals, Open Defecation Free, Solid waste management, community engagement, policy implementation.

Introduction

Effective waste management across urban India is a mammoth challenge given the rapid pace of rise in population and urbanisation. It is estimated that about 65 million tons of waste is generated annually in the country out of which about 62 million tons is Municipal Solid Waste (MSW) comprising of organic waste and recyclable material like paper, plastic, wood, glass etc. About 45-50% of this MSW is biodegradable, 20-25 % is recyclable and about 30-35% is debris. Only about 75-80% of the total municipal waste gets collected and out of this only 22- 28% is processed and treated while the remaining lands up at land- fill sites.[1] It has been estimated that the Urban Local Bodies (ULBs) spend less than 5% on municipal disposal of waste indicating the scant attention given to scientific disposal of waste. If the current annual 62 million tons of MSW continues to be dumped without treatment, it will need 3.40 lakh cubic meter of landfill space every day which is not plausible owing to the other pressing demands on precious land in the wake of the country's huge population besides causing numerous other environmental and health problems. Eliminating dumping and minimizing release of hazardous chemicals by paying special attention to water and air quality, municipal and other waste management and reducing waste generation globally have been one of the UN Sustainable Development Goals (SDGs). In its commitment to fulfil this goal in India, the government turned its attention to solid waste management when the euphoria around making urban India free from open defecation began to fade away. This paper examines the gaps in the implementation of the current sanitation policy in India in the area of solid waste management with a case study of a slum in Delhi. The objective is to understand the shortcomings in the management of municipal solid waste for urban slum population.

Policy Framework

The National Urban Sanitation Policy (NUSP) of 2008 can be described as the first comprehensive policy dedicated to urban sanitation. It was launched with the objective of developing state sanitation strategies and city sanitation plans that would lead to open defecation free cities, as well as sanitary and safe disposal of all human and liquid wastes. In 2010, the Nirmal Shahar Puraskar (i.e. clean city award) was instituted to reward the cities that achieve total sanitation including open defecation free (ODF) status and 100 per cent safe waste disposal. By 2012 , 29 out of 36 states and Union Territories were preparing state sanitation plans and 158 cities had begun developing city sanitation plans. Service level benchmarking of urban services was introduced and scaled up to more than 1,756 cities. Despite such developments, many stakeholders noted that the program fell short of driving investment into municipal-level plans to enable their execution and could not succeed in achieving its objectives. Sanitation as a subject rose to national prominence in 2014 due to the political fervour to create a clean India by 2019. It was envisaged to be achieved by the setting up of sanitation and urban infrastructure related programs namely, the Swachh Bharat Mission (SBM/Clean India Mission), Atal Mission for Rejuvenation and Urban Transformation (AMRUT) and Smart Cities Mission under the Ministry of Housing and Urban Affairs.

Institutional structure

The Ministry of Housing and Urban Affairs (MoHUA) is the nodal Ministry at the central level, for the formulation of policies for development of water supply and sanitation infrastructure in the cities and towns and administers waste management in the country through the **'Swachh Bharat Mission- Urban' (SBM-U)** program.

The Ministry of Environment, Forest & Climate Change (MoEF&CC) is the monitoring authority and is responsible for issuing guidelines for environmentally sound management of hazardous and other wastes. The Central Pollution Control Board (CPCB) issues guidelines for safe handling, storage and transport of wastes.

As water supply and sanitation are a State subject, the responsibility for planning, design, implementation, operation and maintenance of water supply and sanitation systems rests with the concerned ULBs, Parastatal agencies and State Governments. The State Governments have the prime responsibility for enforcing and implementing various provisions of the Rules related to the above subjects.

Regulatory structure

The different types of wastes are regulated under the following Rules notified by the MoEF&CC:

1. Solid Waste Management (SWM) Rules, 2016.
2. Plastic Waste Management (PWM) Rules, 2016.
3. E-Waste Management (EWM) Rules, 2016.
4. Bio-Medical Waste Management Rules, 2016.
5. Hazardous Waste Management Rules, 2016.

The prescribed authorities for the enforcement of the aforementioned legislative and regulatory measures in States/Union Territories are local agencies such as:- State Environment Departments, State Pollution Control Boards, Pollution Control Committees in respect of Union Territories, State Urban Development Departments, Urban Local Bodies etc.

Administrative structure

Under the MoHUA, the SBM-U program was launched in 2014, as a flagship program of the newly elected government with the aim of making the country free from the practice of open defecation and achieving 100% scientific waste management.

As per the National Housing Federation, 'Solid Waste' comprises of plastics, food waste, bottles, paper and glass. Solid waste management is one of the two key components of SBM-U with the objective of 100% scientific processing of solid waste in all 4041 Urban Local Bodies (ULBs). The scheme includes the following areas:

1. Collection
2. Transportation
3. Processing

The Ministry supports States/UTs in achieving safe, eco-friendly disposal of waste under SBM through funding support for segregation of waste at household level in wet and dry waste category. While wet waste is processed through biological decomposition, dry waste follows the route of reuse/ recycling. The Ministry provides advisory support and monitors the progress and conducts reviews of all the States and UTs to achieve higher rate of door to door collection. It has introduced a country wide annual cleanliness survey ('the Swachh Survekshan') and the Garbage Free Star Rating System for the Cities to ensure a competition between them for the holistic management of sanitation related facilities. It has been claimed that all States have prepared Swachh City

Plans (SCPs) for all their ULBs as per guidelines of SBM-U and DPRs have been prepared by the States for SWM as per the needs of each ULB in the State. Major IEC Campaigns have also been initiated at city, state and national levels to motivate citizens to desist from indiscriminate disposal of waste and to segregate waste at source.

The SWM Rules-2016 have laid down the relevant regulatory framework. Further, all major cities have existing bye-laws which lay down penalties to be imposed for littering. The states/ULBs are said to be implementing anti-littering measures as per SWM Rules, 2016 and Municipal Acts.

SWM in DELHI

The five municipal corporations, comprising over 280 wards, generate approximately 14,000 tonnes per day (TPD) of solid waste. As per the figures provided by the MCDs, over 10,500 TPD of garbage is collected. The city has a processing capacity of 6,100 TPD through three incineration plants and two centralised composting units. Approximately 4,600 TPD is disposed in three dumping sites of Delhi at Okhla, Bhalswa and Ghazipur.

The Solid Waste Management Bye-Laws, 2018 for the National Capital Territory of Delhi (NCT) were notified on January 15, 2018. All the five local bodies—NDMC, South DMC, North DMC, East DMC and Delhi Cantonment Board (DCB) are - to enforce the bye-laws in their jurisdiction.

Initiation of waste segregation at source

Section 4 of the bye-laws emphasises the generator's responsibility to segregate at source and thus every waste generator has to segregate waste into three streams in colour coded bins: biodegradable (wet waste) in green bin, non-biodegradable (dry waste) in blue bin and domestic hazardous waste in black bin.

Door-to-door collection and transportation of segregated solid waste

Under Section 5 of the bye-laws, MCD will provide door-to-door collection and transportation of segregated solid waste, **including in slums and informal settlements** by integrating informal door-to-door collection system with the municipality. Area-wise time slots for waste collection will be set and published on the website of MCDs.

As per section 6 of the bye-laws, all the secondary storage points (*dhalaos*) are to have covered colour-coded containers for storing wet, dry and domestic hazardous waste. The MCDs will convert the existing *dhalaos* into recycling centres for further segregation of dry waste by involving the informal sector. Households should be able to directly deposit or sell their recyclable waste to authorised waste dealers at these recycling centres at pre-notified rates. Moreover, a deposition centre will be made available in each ward for collecting domestic hazardous waste.

User fees and penalty

As per section 11 of the bye-laws, user fee will be fixed for services like garbage collection, transportation and disposal from waste generators by the MCDs. The MCDs have been asked to evolve a mechanism for collection of user charges within three months of the notification of these bye-laws. Under the bye-laws, penalty shall also be imposed for non-segregation, dumping of solid waste in vacant plots and burning it in the open.

It is evident that the SWM bye-laws have provided adequate legal teeth to ensure an improvement in the status of solid waste management in the capital. But it is for the MCDs to create systems to support end-to- end segregation, collection and transportation, processing and appropriate disposal of solid waste.

Theoretical Framework

The above - started policy framework tries to accommodate all the requirements of a good policy. Yet the fact remains, as argued by Brinkerhoff and Hoff (2002), that successful policy outcomes depend not only upon designing good policies but on managing their implementation.

There are various definitions of policy implementation and the common element in them is the gap that exists between policy intent and outcomes (Maznamin & Sabatier, 1989; Smith & Larimer, 2009). Implementation studies, therefore, place emphasis on understanding the success or failure of public policy by elaborating on factors that affect it. Implementation of a particular policy is context dependent as it is affected by various political, social, economic, organisational and attitudinal factors that influence how well or how poorly a policy or program has been implemented (Meter & Horn, 1975; Stewart et al., 2008), and it also varies considerably over time, across policies, and from one state to the next (Goggin et al., 1990). This is because policy implementation is linked with the realities of a specific and dynamic environment (Fox, et al., 2006). Sinclair puts it succinctly when he argues that programs are applied unevenly across units because each local unit can react differently to the mix of constraints and incentives depending upon the management of the local context (2001). The model of implementation followed for SWM under SBM can be largely described as the 'top- down' approach to policy implementation as illustrated by scholars like Meter and Horn and Maznamin and Sabatier. This is because the policy drafted at the top is implemented across the country in accordance with the rules stipulated under SBM. It does suffer from the anomalies of this approach as it does not account for local factors and fails to address the concern of some key stakeholders.

E. Bardach's 1977 study provides an understanding of the factors which appear to be operational in the implementation gaps in the slum under my study. Bardach lists the following four factors that cause implementation delay or failure.: (1) the diversion of resources, (2) the deflection of policy goals, (3) the dilemmas of administration, and (4) the dissipation of energies. The dilemmas of administration include '*tokenism*' (attempt to appear contributing a policy element publicly but privately conceding a small token gesture) apart from other factors. The dissipation of energies includes '*tenacity*' (concerned people do not want to change) and '*not our problem*' (failure to establish clear liability, nobody wants to shoulder the responsibility) along with several other elements. These appear to be playing a dominant role in the failure of SWM program in the slum under study.

Similarly, the elaboration by Rossi et al. (2004) about the constraints associated with policy implementation also throw light on the gaps in SWM in the slum under study. As per them, a policy intervention may suffer due to poor management, political interference and a lack of personnel and facilities. Moreover, sometimes the indented policy participants may not may not be identified precisely or may be found to be non- cooperative. Other factors that can undermine the proper implementation of any policy are lack of sufficient resources (Meter & Horn, 1975; Mazmanian & Sabatier, 1989; Lipsky, 2010), impact of economic, political, and social conditions, etc. (Meter & Horn, 1975), increased demand for services; difficulties in goal achievements; and involuntary clients (Lipsky, 2010). These factors would be found operational in the mismanagement of solid waste in the case study ahead.

Indira Camp – A Case Study

This case study is based on this researcher's intensive field work in the Indira camp slum cluster, Pahari No. 2, in Taimoor Nagar near an upmarket residential colony of Delhi, New Friends colony. Housing nearly 4000 people, it derives its name from the mountain like garbage dump on which it is situated. The slum is situated besides an open nullah (big storm water drain) which is hidden from the public view through a high wall partitioning it from the main road. The scene behind the wall is a classic case of indiscriminate proliferation of solid waste and it is difficult to conceive of the squalor from the road. The nullah is filled to the brim with solid waste-filled polythene bags. The entry to the cluster is through a bridge over the nullah. Waste filled bags are strewn on the bridge as well and one has to walk over the waste to reach the cluster. The cluster is home to big black water pipes passing through the colony around which people have made their homes and shops. The main passage inside the cluster is underneath such a pipe so that all passers-by and two- wheelers have to duck and reach the other side. This researcher conducted a survey through administering questionnaires to the residents to ascertain the actual situation of solid waste management in the cluster.

Waste generation and segregation at source

Household waste, vegetable refuse, dust, plastic etc. compose the total waste generated by a household on daily basis. Faecal matter also constitutes a part of this garbage in many homes especially those having children below 5 years of age. Small children are discouraged from using the community toilet and are made to relieve themselves on a newspaper/polythene bag which is then disposed along with the household garbage the next day. It was found to our dismay that this garbage may also contain adult faeces, in case a female needs to defecate after the toilet closure timing at night, in which case she will be compelled to most likely take the same route as that of a small child.

The responses of people revealed the prevalence of two colloquial terms, "*kooda*" and "*kabaad*" for the household waste. While "kooda" refers to the household garbage, "*kabaad*" is used to denote the recyclables such as cardboard, plastic bottles etc. traded in exchange for new clothes, utensils etc. or sold to the rag- picker. Most of the respondents did not admit to segregating the waste as per the guidelines of the ULB and told that they throw the waste as a whole and rag-pickers later collect recyclables from the garbage dumps. Few respondents also admitted to selling these recyclables to the rag-pickers.

Waste collection

Despite SBM guidelines and directives to MCD - to arrange for door–to door collection of waste, there was no such facility available for any part of the cluster. All the people interviewed admitted to collecting the waste in polythene bags and throwing it in the "naala" at whichever time convenient to them. They were aware that this was not a hygienic practice yet were practising the same, in the absence of any alternate arrangement. Many said that the nullah should be covered and a big waste collection bin should be kept there to solve the problem. No community bins were kept anywhere in the cluster to facilitate any waste disposal by the residents and no one came from the municipality to collect any garbage from the cluster.

Waste transportation and processing

People were unaware of this part of the waste management cycle since all they knew was that the nullah was the main dump-yard for all household refuse. Some respondents informed that residents from nearby colonies too threw their waste in the nullah and their cluster had earned a reputation of being a neighbourhood "*koodeydaan*" (waste dump-yard). On being asked about the cleaning of the nullah, the respondents informed that it is cleaned once a year and immediately returns back to its usual state due to lack of options of waste disposal.

Drainage related problems

Open drains were criss-crossing the cluster. Drinking water pipes ran close to them, making water contamination a widely prevalent reality than a possibility. The houses had their waste water draining directly into the outside drains, some of which were covered with stone slabs where there were passages but were open in the sides of alleys. The drains were filthy and had black sewage type waste clogging them at various points. Residents told that most people clean the portion of drain in front of their house but several people did not cooperate, leading to fights and skirmishes over dirt in the colony. People complained that when choked, they are cleaned only on payment and repeated calls to the MCD sweeper. Fights among neighbours was common with respect to street sweeping and maintenance of general cleanliness around the houses. Cesspools of black water were noticed at each corner of the cluster and even near houses. People were wading through them doing their daily chores. Almost all the women we talked to, complained about the open nullah carrying waste-water. It often gets clogged and sewage water backflows into the colony drains. Then a sweeper has to be called who opens the choking point and then the problem is solved after incurring further expenses.

The residents informed that sewage backflows in drains during the rainy season and spreads dirt and disease everywhere. The description of the living conditions in the cluster during rains were horrifying to say the least!

People's feedback on cluster's cleanliness

A five point Likert scale question was administered to the respondents to understand their feedback on the sanitation situation in their cluster. It was not surprising to receive most responses to the "Not at all happy with the situation" option, given the anger of people regarding their situation which they blamed on the apathy of civic agencies. Most of them wanted to leave the cluster to settle in a better place with a hygienic environment but were constrained to live here owing to financial woes.

Key Findings

The hopeless situation created by the indiscriminate dumping of solid waste in the slum led to a deterioration in the quality of life of people and affected them on various levels. In a nutshell, the people experienced the following problems:

Physical Problems- It was difficult to traverse through the waste strewn colony on a daily basis and it was unnerving to bear the stench, filth and squalor spread everywhere while leading daily life. There was neither a place for children to play nor any community space of any sort.

Physiological Problems- People reported as falling sick often though they could not relate its cause to their unhygienic physical environment always. During rains, the incidence of disease, skin infections and accidents increased many-fold.

Psychological Problems- The researcher found the respondents to be quite aggressive in their behaviour. They were mostly non-cooperative during the interviews - viewing the whole exercise with utmost scepticism since they knew very well that no one was going to bring any change to their situation. They expressed anger and anxiety beneath which could be discerned a loss of hope due to the apathetic treatment at the hand of civic agencies and successive governments alike.

Social problems:- The dirt and squalor made the cluster an inviting den for anti-social elements who indulged in drug peddling and other nefarious activities. Residents were ashamed to invite guests to their home because of the shabby state in which they lived. They locked themselves in their houses after dark, fearing anti-social elements who openly used the colony for their activities. The colony had earned a bad reputation and people informed how they had difficulty in finding transportation back home at night because most people wanted to avoid the colony and its vicinity. A general environment of mistrust was also found among the different communities living there. People from one region stayed close to each other and away from the other community. Fights and blame-game over waste disposal and drain cleaning were common, vitiating the daily living environment.

The poor waste management clearly points to the need of the policy / program implementation to be sensitive to its context, which is the big open nullah flowing by the slum, in this case. It has no embankment or any other boundary which often led to the flooding of the colony with sewage water, falling and drowning of children and spread of filth in general. Though a waste collection dhalao (shed) was constructed outside the colony, no waste was carried to it from inside the colony. The local municipal body clearly seemed to be facing a crunch of personnel and resources, if not entirely the intention, to maintain a clean and sanitised environment in the cluster. Success in sanitation programs is also dependent on bringing a behavioural change in the residents which is perhaps the toughest to achieve. People were aware of their actions being unhygienic but lacked the motivation to cooperate even for the sake of keeping their own street clean. They relegated all responsibility on to the government and MCD to pull them out of the situation they were in. On the government 's part, it did seem a case of 'tokenism' done in the name of sanitation by building a community toilet for the purpose of fulfilling - the primary requirement of making the cluster open defecation free, which was the primary objective under SBM. No other efforts were apparent to address the other objectives of SBM, let alone improve the overall sanitation situation of the cluster. The open nullah also seemed to have provided the officials with an alibi of 'what can we do' as most nullahs are not to be covered as per laws and thus become the breeding hub of open defecation and disposal of solid waste.

Conclusion

SBM has numerous success stories around SWM from many parts of the country. Examples of cities are available where land-fills vanished owing to the successful implementation of cohesive waste management and recycling plans. What is lacking is the administrative will to introduce sanitation initiatives other than community toilets in illegal settlements and JJ clusters to improve the living quality for the residents there. With the success stories and tools for implementation already available for reference, it should not be difficult for local bodies to tackle the case of slums like Indira camp in partnership with the state government. To begin with, a special plan can be devised for areas with open nullahs/other water bodies to avoid making them as waste dumping beds. Innovative solutions are required to tackle the problem of door to door collection of solid waste even from slums where the by-lanes are very narrow, as is done for authorized colonies.

Over a period of time, a nominal waste collection charge can be levied so as to make people conscious of the service they are being provided. Experience in other such settlements has shown that people are willing to pay butit is the local politicians who wave off any such levies for the sake of populism, thus defeating the system in its infancy. Once waste collection is operationalized, civil society cooperation can be sought by local bodies to sensitize the slum residents on segregating and proper disposal of waste, backing it up with proper collection and management. This slum is home to a large number of rag-pickers who can be made to register with the municipality and made the first priority group which is integrated in all kinds of collection and waste – processing treatment contracts so that their work conditions can be enhanced and improved. In this way, they can be made as stakeholders in the sanitation of their colony as several of them work at cleaning jobs outside but are consigned to a life of filth around their own home. There is need for conducting awareness campaigns to address the toilet, drainage and water related problems of the residents which have a bearing on the overall sanitation situation of the slum. This will usher in a long term behavioral change among the local people who are not currently involved in SWM or sanitation of the cluster in general.

These functions are treated as government's sole responsibility to manage but people themselves do not cooperate in maintaining them. A gradual process of handholding through civil society initiatives can help in making the residents become stakeholders in maintaining the sanitation of their own colony.

At the level of the municipality, a robust monitoring system should be put in place along with a helpline for the citizens to register their complaints and feedback regarding the services offered. This micro-data when captured would go into making a ward effectively 'swachh' (clean) and enable the ULB to apply for the star rating system of the SBM, in real terms. Though it is easier said than done, a strong administrative will to implement the program with letter and spirit along with a sensitivity to the most disadvantaged sections of the society is what is required to make the chimera of clean and livable settlements a reality.

End Notes

1. Source: 25th Report of Standing Committee on Urban Development.
2. Sustainable Development Goal 6. United Nations.

References

1. Bardach,E., 1977 , *The implementation game* ,Chicago,University of Chicago press.
2. Brinkerhoff, D. W. and B.L., 2002, *Managing policy reform*, Bloomfiled, Kumarian Press.
3. Centre for Policy Research, 2019, "Budget Briefs: Swachh Bharat Mission-Urban (SBM-U), GOI, 2019- 20, Volume 11, Issue 8. Available at https://cprindia.org/sites/default/files/SBM-U-.pdf
4. Fox, W., S. Bayat, and Ferriera , N. (eds.), 2006, *A guide to managing public policy* ,Cape Town, Juta andCo.
5. Lipsky, M., 2010, *Street-level bureaucracy* (expanded edition), New York, Russell Sage Foundation.
6. Mazmanian, D. A. and P. A. Sabatier, 1989, *Implementation and public policy*, Lahham, University Press of America.
7. Meter, D.S.V. and C.E.V. Horn, 1975, "The Policy Implementation Process: A Conceptual Framework", *Administration and Society*, 6 (4), 445-488.
8. Ministry of Housing and Urban Affairs, 2019, "Solid Waste Management including hazardous waste, medical waste and E-waste". 25th Report of Standing Committee on Urban Development.
9. Ministry of Housing and Urban Affairs, 2014, "Guidelines for Swachh Bharat Mission", Government of India: New Delhi.
10. Rossi, P. H., M. W. Lipsey and H. E. Freeman, 2004, *Evaluation: A systematic approach*, 7th edition, Sage, Thousand Oaks.
11. Sapru, R., 2017, *Public Policy: A Contemporary Perspective*, Sage, New Delhi.
12. Sinclair, Thomas A. P., 2001, "Implementation Theory and Practice", *International Journal of Public Administration*, 24(1), pp. 77–94.
13. Smith, K. B. and C. W. Larimer, 2009, *The public policy primer*, Boulder, Westview Press.
14. Stewart, J. J., D. M. Hedge and J.P. Lester, 2008, *Public policy: An evolutionary approach* (3rd ed.), Boston, Thomsom Wordsworth.

15. SuSanA ,2008), "Planning for sustainable sanitation in cities. Factsheet Sustainable Sanitation Alliance". Retrieved February 9,2019 from http://www.susana.org/lang-en/work-ing-groups/wg06.
16. https://www.downtoearth.org.in/news/governance/delhi-gets-it-new-byelaws-on-solid-waste-management- 59559. Accessed on November 8, 2019.
17. swachhbharaturban.gov.in. Accessed on November 18, 200

✦✦✦

Chapter Six

Digital India: An Initiative to Transform the Nation

T. Sadashivam[6]

Abstract

India is going through a significant transformation in the past more than one decade in terms of economic growth, demographic change, rapid urbanization etc. However, one important transformation which not only affects us, but the whole humanity is the rapid technological advancements. In today's world,any country's growth, progress and development depend upon the adoption of Digital Technology with particular focus on governance; and without it, we cannot respond to the changing needs of the society (i.e. to deliver public services economically, efficiently and effectively). As we progressed, our focus from 'Government' to 'Governance', or as the present Modi Government says, 'Minimum Government and Maximum Governance', to accelerate the latter we need to adopt Digital Technology.

In this context, this paper attempts to examine various digital initiatives under the Digital India Programme initiated by Narendra Modi led government in 2015, and its current implementation status.

Keywords: *Digital Technology; Digital India; Sustainable Development Goals; Common Services Centres.*

Introduction

Makind a has seen a number of transformations in society, which changed the face of humanity. However, the one transformation which we are experiencing more or less throughout the world is the adoption of 'Digital Technology'. So,it is not wrong to call the present time as 'Digital Age', the impact of which is felt in almost all aspects of an individual's life, from the way individuals interact with each other, express their feelings, share ideas to managing their daily activities like health and finances etc (Kachhal, 2018).The one such field, where digital

6. Assistant Professor, Department of Public Administration, Pachhunga University College, Aizawl, Mizoram.

technology is playing an important role is, 'Governance'. There exist always a challenge for the governments around the world, how to provide various public services to the citizens in an affordable, transparent, efficient, and effective manner with limited time. The only way, this can be done is through the adoption of digital technology, which is emerging as very important integral part of the governance system. In this context, the 'Digital India Programme', which was started by the Government of India on July 2015, aims at transformation of delivery of services to the citizen or in other words, providing citizen-centric e-services. As the new mantra of the government has been moving from 'Government-Centric to Citizens-Centric', citizens will be empowered to participate in the governance system of the country not as passive participants, but as active participants.

Pre-cursor to Digital India Programme

The adoption of digital technology in governance is not new in India.During the period 1976-1996, the Government of India focused on digitisation with the help of National Informatics Centre (NIC) on establishing in-house office management systems on how to improve efficiency, preserve records and processing of data and storage, especially in number-crunching departments like:- Statistics, Finance (Treasuries), Taxation (Commercial Taxes, Income Tax, Excise) besides those departments like Public Distribution System (PDS), Rural Development etc, which deals with a large number of beneficiaries(Chandrashekhar, 2018). The main focus during this period was the automation of internal government functions rather than improving service delivery to citizens (Second Administrative Reforms Commission, 2008).

In the late 90s,some States in India started implementing e-Governance initiatives and the lead was taken by the State of Andhra Pradesh.In the first decade of the 21st century, we saw various e-Governance initiatives at the State level in the field of PDS, Land Records, Transportation etc; and similarly at the national level, it was in Income Tax, Ministry of Corporate Affairs (MCA), Excise etc. Of course, the success of e-Governance initiatives at the State level was not uniform. Nevertheless, these initiatives laid the foundation for the emergence of National e-Governance Plan (NeGP), approved by the Government of India on 18th May 2006. It was the first such kind of initiative implemented anywhere in the world with a large scale roll-out of e-Governance projects across the country. The main vision of NeGP was to "*make all government services accessible to the common man in his locality, through common service delivery outlets and ensure efficiency, transparency & reliability of such services at affordable costs to realise the basic needs of the common man*"(Second Administrative Reforms Commission, 2008). Originally, there were 27 Mission Mode Projects (MMPs) and 8 Components, but in July 2011,4 more MMPs added i.e. Public Distribution System, Health, Educationand Post to make it a total of 31 MMPs.To support these MMPs, a necessary core ICT infrastructure has been set up in the form of State Data Centres(SDCs), State Wide Area Networks (SWANs), Common Services Centres(CSCs) and State Services Delivery Gateway (SSDG) in various States/UTs in the country.

Under the Digital India programme, NeGP has been rechristened to e-Kranti, which is one of the nine pillars of the Digital India programme. The vision of e-Kranti is '*Transforming e-Governance for Transforming Governance*'. At present, Government of India through MeITY is implementing a total of 44 MMPs(13 Central MMPs- Income Tax, Passport, Posts etc; 17 State MMPs-Land Records, Health, Agriculture etc; and 14 Integrated MMPs-E-Courts, Urban Governance, India Portal etc) under the e-Kranti programme.

Digital India Programme

The Government of India approved the Digital India programme on 20th August, 2014 which was formally launched on 1st July, 2015. Digital India is an umbrella programme that covers many projects of the Central Government Ministries/Departments and States/UTs, to prepare India for a knowledge-based transformation. It restructured existing schemes, brought new ones and implemented them in a synchronized manner(MeitY, Annual Report 2016-17).

The Digital India programme has three key vision areas:

1. Digital Infrastructure as a utility to every citizen.
2. Governance and services on demand.
3. Digital empowerment of citizens.

To achieve the above-mentioned vision areas, 9 pillars have been identified, which are: i)Broadband Highways; ii)Universal Access to Mobile Connectivity; iii)Public Internet Access Programme; iv)e-Governance-Reforming Government through Technology; v)e-Kranti-Electronic Delivery of Services; vi)Information for All; vii) Electronics Manufacturing-Target Net Zero Imports; viii)IT for Jobs, and ix)Early Harvest Programmes. The main aim of Digital India programme is to transform India into a knowledge-based economy and digitally empowered society in the 21st century. For achieving the aforementioned, various initiatives have been undertaken under Digital India programme, which have shown significant progress like:-

Common Services Centres (CSCs)

For delivering various e-Governance services to the people in rural and remote areas of the country, a front-end ICT enabled service delivery access points in the form of Common Services Centres (CSCs) have been established(CSC, Annual Report 2015-16). It was initially launched in September 2006, under National e-Governance Plan, with an aim of covering six lakh villages in the ratio of one CSC per six villages, spread across rural India. The Village Level Entrepreneurs (VLEs) are private entities and running the CSCs under the guidance and control of CSC e-Governance Services India Limited, a Special Purpose Vehicle (CSC-SPV). Based on experiences and learnings from CSC scheme under NeGP, the Government of India in August, 2015, initiated 'CSC 2.0' scheme under Digital India programme, to improve access to technology and digital services for citizens. It also proposes the expansion of CSCs network to at least one CSC in every Gram Panchayat(CSC, Annual Report 2015-16).These CSCs provides major categories of services to the citizens, like Government to Citizen (G2C) services from both Central and State Governments; Financial Services; Educational Services; Health Services; Skill Development; Tours and Travels; Aadhaar Services; Utility Bill Payment and Other Business to Citizen (B2C) services.

At present (as on 31st May, 2019), the total number of CSCs functional across the States/UTs is 3,65,918, out of which 2,65,398 are at Gram Panchayat level. There has been a total increase of 2,81,968 CSCs during the period from 2014 to 2019 (83,950 to 3,65,918); while at Gram Panchayat level total increase registered 2,01,139 CSCs during the aforementioned period (64,259 to 2,65,398). So, 72.52 per cent of CSCs are existing at the Gram Panchayat level in the country. Here, only top ten States and three UTs have been discussed, which are having the highest number of CSCs. The State of Uttar Pradesh has got the highest number of CSCs (including Gram Panchayat level) with 78,350 CSCs, which is (21.41%) of the country's total CSCs. The second comes Maharashtra with 51,487 CSCs, which is (14.07%) of the country's total CSCs; followed by Bihar 31,758 CSCs (8.67%); Madhya Pradesh 29,318 CSCs (8.01%); West Bengal 18,444 CSCs(5.04%); Rajasthan 16,148 CSCs (4.41%); Chhattisgarh 14,716 CSC (4.02%); Jharkhand 14,345 CSCs (3.92%); Odisha 13,815 CSCs(3.77%) and Tamil Nadu 10,860 CSCs (2.96%). The Union Territories are: Delhi 1971 CSCs (0.53%); Puducherry 197 CSCs (0.05%) and Chandigarh 84 CSCs (0.02%)(see Table 1 at next page).

Similarly, for the CSCs (only exist at the Gram Panchayat level), the State of Uttar Pradesh got the highest number of 58,444 CSCs, which is (22.02%) of the country's total CSCs at Gram Panchayat level only. This is followed by, Maharashtra 35,341CSCs (13.31%); Bihar 26,012 CSCs (9.80%); Madhya Pradesh 20,472 CSCs (7.71%); West Bengal 14,993 CSCs (5.64%); Rajasthan 11,611 CSCs (4.37%); Jharkhand 11,468 CSCs (4.32%); Odisha 11,432 CSCs (4.30%); Chhattisgarh 10,478 CSCs (3.94%) and Tamil Nadu 5,936 CSCs (2.23%). At the Union Territories level, the UT list comprises Puducherry 107 CSCs (0.04%); Andaman & Nicobar Islands 27 CSCs (0.004%) and Dadra & Nagar Haveli 26 CSCs (0.009%).

The CSCs number of transactions from the year 2014 to 2018(as per latest data) show a four-fold increase i.e. 4.57 crore in the financial year 2014-15, increase to 10.10 crore in 2015-16; 13.72 crore in 2016-17; 17.37 crore in 2017-18 and finally, it is 17.38 crore in 2018-19. The value of CSCs transactions saw an increase from Rupees 1,558 crore during the financial year 2014-15 to Rupees 3,717 crore in 2015-16; Rupees 7,120 crore in 2016-17; Rupees 23,795 crore in 2017-18 and, Rupees 28,243 crore in 2018-19 (Mehrotra, 2019). The top 10 categories of services, in terms of value of CSCs transactions during the financial year 2018-19 are:- a)Banking-Business Correspondents(BCAs) Rupees 21,800 crore; b)Banking (Aadhaar enabled Payments System) Rupees 3090 crore; c) Electricity Bill Payment Rupees 1198 crore; d)Insurance Renewal Rupees 674 crore; e)PM FasalBima Yojana Rupees 434 crore; f) Pradhan Mantri Gramin Digital SakshartaAbhiyaan (PMGDISHA) Rupees 200 crore; g)Tours and Travels Rupees 113 crore; h)Pan Card Applications Rupees 79 crore; i)Insurance Product Sales Rupees 77 crore and; j)Indian Railway (IRCTC) Rupees 66 crore (MeitY, Annual Report 2018-19).

Table 1: States/UTs-wise Status of Rollout of Common Services Centres (CSCs)

States/UTs#	No. of Functional CSCs at Gram Panchayat Level		Total No. of Functional CSCs including Gram Panchayat Level	
	As on 31st May2014	As on 31st May2019	As on 31st May 2014	As on 31st May2019
Andhra Pradesh	3,256	6,560	5,542	9,305
Arunachal Pradesh	123	122	168	203
Assam	1,890	5,439	3,167	6,370
Bihar	4,743	26,012	6,046	31,758
Chhattisgarh	1,149	10,478	1,347	14,716
Goa	0	64	5	94
Gujarat	5,346	7,973	5,392	12,582
Haryana	36	8,579	46	12,527
Himachal Pradesh	849	3,253	2,095	3,708
Jammu & Kashmir	203	2,430	891	3,158
Jharkhand	2,859	11,468	4,217	14,345
Karnataka	287	4,646	288	8,937
Kerala	1,002	2,981	1,837	4,004
Madhya Pradesh	5,226	20,472	6,673	29,318
Maharashtra	16,997	35,341	21,116	51,487
Manipur	54	546	243	803
Meghalaya	3	491	151	599
Mizoram	43	55	98	248
Nagaland	44	40	121	279
Odisha	2,364	11,432	3,018	13,815
Punjab	563	6,825	1,566	8,829
Rajasthan	3,107	11,611	3,113	16,148
Sikkim	19	36	24	50
Tamil Nadu	480	5,936	482	10,860
Telangana	0	3,293	N/A	5,206
Tripura	113	764	146	959
Uttar Pradesh	10,048	58,444	11,258	78,350
Uttarakhand	456	4,918	989	6405
West Bengal	2,949	14,993	3,771	18,444
States Total	64,209	2,65,202	83,810	3,63,507
UTs				
Andaman & Nicobar	1	27	1	54
Chandigarh	1	11	1	84
Dadra & Nagar Haveli	0	26	0	54
Daman & Diu	01	13	0	39
Delhi	0	0	77	1,971
Lakshadweep	10	12	13	12
Puducherry	38	107	48	197
UTs Total	50	196	140	2,411
Grand Total	64,259	2,65,398	83,950	3,65,918

Note: #means - Union Territories.

Source: Shri Ravi Shankar Prasad, Minister for Electronics and Information Technology, Government of India, while giving reply to Unstarred Question No. 878, in Lok Sabha, Parliament of India on 26/06/2019. And S.S. Ahluwalia, Minister of State for Electronics and Information Technology, Government of India, while giving reply to Unstarred Question No. 1594, in Lok Sabha, Parliament of India on 19/12/2018. Retrieved http://164.100.47.194/Loksabha/Questions/Qtextsearch.aspx on 24/11/2019.

Some of the key achievements of CSCs are: To provide various banking and financial services across the country, especially in rural areas. A total of 26 banks, consist of public and private sector banks and regional rural banks have engaged CSC SPV, as a corporate business correspondent. The CSC SPV through its 12,242 VLEs or CSC operator (as on 31st May 2019) acting as business correspondent agents/customer service points (Prasad, Shankar Ravi, 2019). Also, CSC SPV started a unique initiative in the name of 'StreeSwabhiman', under which corporate houses through Corporate Social Responsibility (CSR) funds ask to take up initiatives the field of women's health, hygiene & empowerment. The VLEs at their own cost set up micro-manufacturing unit, where low cost bio-degradable sanitary pads are manufactured and supplied to women and girls in rural areas. As of 30th June, 2018 a total of 204 units have been set up in 18 States (Ahluwalia, S.S, 2018).The CSCs have been promoting entrepreneurship, especially in rural India by creating jobs for 12 lakh people, out of which 61,055 are women. Thus, it is empowering the marginalised sections of the society(Prasad, Shankar Ravi, 2018).

There are also some challenges in the functioning of CSCs, especially complaints of irregularities against some CSCs in delivery of services to the customers, related to Overcharging of services, Banking, Digi Pay. As a result, during the year from 2015-16 to 2017-18, action has been taken against 335 CSCs (Ahluwalia, S.S, 2018a).

Pradhan Mantri Gramin Digital SakshartaAbhiyaan (PMDISHA)

One of the integral components of the Digital India programme is, making people 'Digitally Literate' in the country. In this regard, Pradhan Mantri Gramin Digital SakshartaAbhiyaan(PMGDISHA) scheme, approved by the Government of India in February 2017 aims to empower the 6 crore rural persons digitally literate. So, one digitally illiterate person from every eligible rural households initially by 31st March, 2019, however, now extended to 31st March, 2020. This scheme is one of the largest digital literacy programmes, covers 40 per cent of rural households across States/UTs in the country, and; importantly aims to bridge the digital divide specifically targeting marginalised sections of the society, like Scheduled Castes and Tribes, Women, Minorities, Below Poverty Line (BPL) and differently-abled persons. The selected beneficiaries under this scheme need to get themselves enrolled in nearby Common Services Centres/Training Centres. There is no fee for attending training, and the target group would be in the age-group of 14 to 60 years. The course duration will be of 20 hours (minimum 10 days and maximum 30 days); and the broad content of digital literacy training will cover topics like introduction to digital devices; operating digital devices; introduction to the internet; communications using the internet and application of internet (includes citizen-centric services and use of digital financial tools for undertaking cashless transactions). Every candidate after the completion of training has togive online examination at a centre of the certifying agency(PMGDISHA, 2019).Here, one thing to remember is that, for the success of Digital India programme 'capacity building' is critical, which is the main objective of PMGDISHA.

Table 2: States/UTs wise Status of Pradhan Mantri Gramin Digital Saksharta Abhiyaan (PMGDISHA) Scheme

States/UTs#	Targets (No. of Candidates)	Achievement Status (No. of Candidates) *		
		Registered	Trained	Certified
Andaman & Nicobar Islands	18,000	167	116	0
Andhra Pradesh	20,28,000	4,55,029	4,30,501	1,95,782
Arunachal Pradesh	77,000	1,666	1,621	317
Assam	19,29,000	6,78,511	6,60,467	1,15,305
Bihar	66,30,000	11,66,927	11,34,536	6,43,406
Chandigarh	2,000	0	0	0
Chhattisgarh	14,12,000	9,44,369	9,09,522	5,20,404
Dadra & Nagar Haveli	13,000	1	1	0
Daman & Diu	4,000	330	317	33
Delhi	30,000	0	0	0
Goa	40,000	11	11	0
Gujarat	24,97,000	9,56,276	9,36,897	5,61,363
Haryana	11,91,000	8,91,874	8,65,176	5,18,048
Himachal Pradesh	4,44,000	1,04,918	1,02,130	43,761
Jammu & Kashmir	6,58,000	2,12,996	2,12,134	1,22,649
Jharkhand	18,03,000	11,18,984	11,06,199	5,98,247
Karnataka	27,05,000	3,71,215	3,57,601	1,96,317
Kerala	12,57,000	16,715	16,320	6,203
Lakshadweep	1,000	6	6	0
Madhya Pradesh	37,84,000	10,72,029	10,37,768	5,56,597
Maharashtra	44,33,000	8,11,223	7,85,396	4,27,559
Manipur	1,37,000	7,395	7,339	2,236
Meghalaya	1,71,000	20,930	19,229	329
Mizoram	38,000	4,768	4,760	2,325
Nagaland	1,01,000	2,023	1,962	1,050
Odisha	25,17,000	10,54,859	10,33,450	5,71,662
Puducherry	28,000	8,831	8,653	3,791
Punjab	12,47,000	5,38,290	5,11,727	3,19,563
Rajasthan	37,12,000	9,47,416	9,17,311	4,83,318
Sikkim	33,000	40	40	3
Tamil Nadu	26,79,000	4,53,885	4,45,105	2,54,002
Telangana	20,28,000	3,16,217	3,11,795	1,75,467
Tripura	1,95,000	53,483	50,633	25,475
Uttarakhand	5,06,000	2,20,435	2,13,296	1,27,659

Uttar Pradesh	1,11,71,000	36,38,480	35,18,498	19,10,513
West Bengal	44,81,000	4,24,075	4,18,329	2,14,100
Total	6,00,00,000	1,64,94,374	1,60,18,846	85,97,484

Note: #It means Union Territories.

**The data as on 7/12/2018.*

Source: Shri S.S. Ahluwalia, Minister of State for Electronics and Information Technology, Government of India, while giving reply to Unstarred Question No.251 in Lok Sabha, Parliament of India on 12/12/2018. Retrieved http://164.100.47.194/Loksabha/Questions/Qtextsearch.aspx on 24/11/2019.

As per Table 2(as on 7th December 2018); more than 1.64 crore candidates have been registered, out of which, training has been imparted to more than 1.60 crore candidates, and more than 85.97 lakh candidates have been duly certified under the PMGDISHA Scheme. So, the percentage of certified candidates in comparison with the total targets has been only 14.32 per cent. Here,only those States/UTs are discussed, which achieved more than the national average i.e. 14.32 per cent. The State of Haryana stands first, against a target of 11,91,000 candidates, so far 5,18,048 candidates have been duly certified with achievement status of 43.49 per cent. Similarly, in Chhattisgarh, out of 14,12,000 candidates, 5,20,404 candidates certified (36.85 per cent); Jharkhand, out of 18,03,000 candidates, 5,98,247 candidates certified (33.18 per cent); Punjab, out of 12,47,000 candidates, 3,19,563 candidates certified (25.62 per cent); Uttarakhand, out of 5,06,000 candidates, 1,27,659 certified (25.22 per cent); Odisha, out of 25,17,000 candidates, 5,71,662 candidates certified (22.7 per cent); Gujarat, out of 24,97,000 candidates, 5,61,363 candidates certified (22.48 per cent); Jammu & Kashmir, out of 6,58,000 candidates, 1,22,649 candidates certified (18.63 per cent); Uttar Pradesh, out of 1,11,71,000 candidates, 19,10,513 candidates certified (17.10 per cent); and finally, in Madhya Pradesh, out of 37,84,000 candidates, 5,56,597 candidates certified (14.70 per cent), just marginally ahead of the national average.

Also, it can be observed in Table 2, achievement status of (duly certified candidates) for some big States in India, which is less than 10 per cent, like West Bengal 4.77 per cent; Karnataka 7.25 per cent; Telangana 8.65 per cent; Tamil Nadu 9.48 per cent; Maharashtra 9.64 per cent; Andhra Pradesh 9.65 per cent; Bihar 9.70 per cent; Assam 5.97 per cent respectively. There are still some States/UTs, where no candidates have been certified since the inception of PMGDISHA, they are Andaman & Nicobar Islands, Chandigarh, Dadra &

Nagar Haveli, Delhi, Goa, Lakshadweep. According to the government, main reason for the slow progress of PMGDISHA has been lack of awareness about digital literacy programme and its benefits; and low internet connection in rural and remote areas of the country.

Unified Mobile Application for New-age Governance (UMANG)

According to Ericsson Mobility Report (June, 2019), there are 1.2 billion mobile phone subscriptions in the country, 560 million internet subscribers (which is 40% of the Indian population) and going to increase between 750 to 800 million by 2023. Similarly, the number of Smartphone users are 354 million, which is going to increase between 650 million and 700 million by 2023(Ericsson Mobility Report,2019).In this situation, mobile can be used as an effective service delivery channel by all the stakeholders (including government) by creating mobile apps, portals or websites. The use of mobile channel for providing services in e-Governance is also referred as 'Mobile Government or M-Government'. The Mobile Government is not only cost-effective and flexible, but importantly, it is in close proximity to its users and action-oriented, meaning that one uses the mobile phone to 'do something' (United Nations E-Government Survey- 2014).

To promote Mobile Governance in India, Ministry of Electronics and Information Technology (MeitY) and National e-Governance Division (NeGD), Government of India, developed - one application to avail various citizen-centric services in a single platform called Unified Mobile Application for New-age Governance (UMANG). It provided citizens Pan India e-Governance services offered by Central, State, Local Governments; and some utility services from private organizations. The UMANG service can be accessed through multiple types of devices, such as feature phones, smartphones, desktops and tablets; through multiple online and offline channels (Mobile Application, Web, Interactive Voice Response (IVR) and Short Message Service(SMS) (UMANG, 2019). The UMANG App users can access various services through 12 Indian(Hindi, Assamese, Bengali, Gujarati, Kannada, Marathi, Malayalam, Punjabi, Telugu, Tamil, Odia and Urdu) and English languages, with a dedicated customer support service. As on 14th December, 2019, this App providing citizens, access to 490 services of 104 government organizations of 21 States and Central governments. The UMANG aims to increase the current services to 600 services by March 2020, further 900 services by March, 2022 and 1200 services by March, 2024.

Table 3: Major Services available Department-wise across the country on UMANG App

Departments	Services
Pension	1. Jeevan Praman 2. Employee Provident Fund 3. National Pension System 4. Pensioners Welfare Services
Education	1. Central Board of Secondary Education (CBSE) 2. e-Pathshala (NCERT) 3. All India Council for Technical Education (AICTE) 4. National Scholarship Portal (NSP) 5. National Digital Library
Health	1. Hospital Booking 2. e-Raktkosh 3. Pharma SahiDaam from NPPA 4. Employees State Insurance Corporation
Agriculture	1. Crop Insurance 2. Soil Health Card 3. AgMarknet 4. Weather Forecast 5. Agro Advisory
Utilities	1. Electricity 2. Gas 3. Direct to Home (DTH) 4. Telephone/Mobile
Other Services	1. Passport 2. Permanent Account Number (PAN) 3. Income Tax 4. Grievance/ Complaints

Source: negd.gov.in/umang, accessed on 14th December, 2019.

Table 4: States/Union Territories wise Segregation of Users of UMANG App#

States	No. of Users	States	No. of Users
Andhra Pradesh	1,72,921	Punjab	96,113
Arunachal Pradesh	1,471	Rajasthan	1,85,681
Assam	38,398	Sikkim	1,599
Bihar	1,74,304	Tamil Nadu	2,63,615
Chhattisgarh	52,844	Telangana	1,62,764
Goa	8,676	Tripura	5,400
Gujarat	2,78,995	Uttarakhand	67,228
Haryana	1,51,562	Uttar Pradesh	4,55,862
Himachal Pradesh	43,925	West Bengal	1,66,853
Jammu & Kashmir	13,697	**Total of States**	36,09,464*
Jharkhand	65,980		
Karnataka	2,87,964	**Union Territories (UTs)**	
Kerala	79,365	Andaman & Nicobar Islands	1,347
Madhya Pradesh	1,56,903	Chandigarh	16,884
Maharashtra	5,57,685	Dadra & Nagar Haveli	3,166
Manipur	3,803	Daman & Diu	1,626
Meghalaya	1,515	Delhi	1,97,031
Mizoram	551	Lakshadweep	84
Nagaland	1,099	Puducherry	5,938
Odisha	1,12,691	**Total of UTs**	2,26,076*
		Grand Total (States+ Union Territories)	38,35,540*

Note: *The data provided is for the registered users who have given their demographic details.

#The data as on 14th July, 2018.

Source: Shri S.S. Ahluwalia, Minister of State for Electronics and Information Technology, Government of India, while giving reply to Unstarred Question No.2362 in Lok Sabha, Parliament of India on 1/08/2018. Retrieved http://164.100.47.194/Loksabha/Questions/Qtextsearch.aspx on 24/11/2019.

The State of Maharashtra got the highest number of registered users on UMANG with (5,57,685) users; followed by Uttar Pradesh (4,55,862); Karnataka (2,87,964); Gujarat (2,78,995); Tamil Nadu (2,63,615); Rajasthan (1,85,681); Bihar (1,74,304); Andhra Pradesh (1,72,921); West Bengal (1,66,853) and Telangana (1,62,764) etc. So, total of (36,09,464) registered users on UMANG App from all the States. Among the UTs, Delhi has the highest number of registered users with (1,97,031); followed by Chandigarh (16,884); and Puducherry (5,938), etc (see Table 4). The total number of registered users on UMANG (as on 14th July 2018), is 68,25,170 out of which 38,35,540 registered users have been given their demographic details; while 29,89,630 registered users have not given their demographic data. During the 6th edition of the World Government Summit held at Dubai, UAE, 2016, UMANG has won the 'Best m-Government Service Award', under accessible government category. Similarly, during National e-Governance Awards 2018-19 in February 2019, won the Special Jury Choice Award in the category of 'Excellence in providing Citizen-Centric Delivery'(MeitY,Annual Report 2018-19).

As mentioned, there are few services which are available on UMANG App; so, there is a need to add many more services from various Central/States/Union Territories governments departments and other agencies. Similarly there is a need to make people aware of this App through publicity and campaigns both (offline and online) methods, about its use and benefits.

Progress of India's e-Governance

E-Government Development Index (E-GDI)

Since the year 2001, the United Nations has been publishing the United Nations e-Government Survey, the latest being in the year 2018. It is the only global report, which measures each member country's progress in e-Government development.It examines, how digital technologies are impacting public sector and changing people's everyday lives. It tracks the progress of e-Government development via the E-Government Development Index (E-GDI). The E-GDI, is a composite indicator comprise of three factors, which are equally weighted. Firstly, Telecommunications Infrastructure Index (TII); secondly, Human Capital Index (HCI) and thirdly, Online Service Index (OSI)(United Nations E-Government Survey- 2018).

Table 5: E-Government Development Index (E-GDI)

Year	Rank	E-Government Development Index (EGDI)	Online Service Index (OSI)[1]	Telecommunication Infrastructure Index (TII)[2]	Human Capital Index (HCI)[3]
2014					
India	118	0.3834	0.5433	0.1372	0.4698
World Average		0.4712	0.3919	0.3650	0.6566
2016					
India	107	0.4637	0.7464	0.1430	0.5019
World Average		0.4922	0.4623	0.3711	0.6433
2018					
India	96	0.5669	0.9514	0.2009	0.5484
World Average		0.5491	0.5691	0.4155	0.4155
2019					

Note: [1]It means the scope and quality of online services quantified as OSI. 2It consists of five components: a) estimated internet users per 100 inhabitants; b) number of main fixed telephone lines per 100 inhabitants; c) number of mobile subscribers per 100 inhabitants; d) number of wireless broadband subscriptions per 100 inhabitants; and e) number of fixed broadband subscriptions per 100 inhabitants. 3It consists of four components: a) adult literacy rate; b) the combined primary, secondary and tertiary gross enrolment ratio; c) expected years of schooling; and d) average years of schooling.

Source: United Nations E-Government Survey- 2014, pp.201, 204; 2016, pp.149, 153; and 2018, pp.223, 233. United Nations, New York.

Table 5 above shows that India has climbed up by 22 ranks on its E-GDI from (2014 to 2018). In 2014, it ranked 118th, jumped to 107th rank in 2016, and 96th rank in 2018. India's E-GDI score also improved from (0.3834) in 2014 to (0.4637) in 2016, and (0.5669) in 2018. Interestingly, comparison with the world average E-GDI score from (2014 to 2018), only in the year 2018, India's E-GDI score was higher. Also, India has moved from 'Low E-GDI' level group of countries in 2014 to 'High E-GDI' level group of countries in 2018. The performance score of India on 'Online Service Index' (OSI) in comparison with other two (Telecommunication Infrastructure Index and Human Capital Index) is much better, even the world average OSI score is much lower. The OSI score in 2014 for India was (0.5433), which increased to (0.7464) and (0.9514) in 2016 and 2018 respectively. Out of the three composite indicators given in (Table 5), where India still needs to improve is in the, Telecommunication Infrastructure Index (TII), which even in comparison with the world average score is much lower.

E-Participation Index (E-PI)

The United Nations has included, hence, since the year 2010; another index was named as 'E-Participation Index (E-PI). This index is very important because the focus of governments around the world have shifted to participatory forms of governance; where citizens become more important in participating in governance (decision making), more so; in the digital age with the use of ICTs. The United Nations e-Government Survey defined E-PI, 'as the process of engaging citizens through ICTs in policy, decision-making and service design and delivery so as to make it participatory, inclusive and deliberative' (Malhotra, Charru, 2018). E-Participation Index (E-PI) based on: a) E-Information: availability of Online Information; b) E-Consultation: online public consultations c) E-Decision-Making: directly involving citizens in decision processes (United Nations E-Government Survey- 2018).

Table 6: E-Participation Index (E-PI) and its Utilisation by Stages

Year	Rank	E-Partici-pation Index (E-PI)	Total %	Stage 1 (E-Infor-mation%)	Stage 2 (E-Consul-tation%)	Stage 3 (E-Decision-Making %)
2014						
India	40	0.6275	56.9%	92.5%	36.6%	0%
World Average		0.3947	36.4%	55.7%	24.6%	7.3%
2016						
India	27	0.7627	76.7%	79.4%	94.7%	14.3%
World Average		0.4625	47.1%	56.4%	43.1%	12.9%
2018						
India	15	0.9551	95.6%	100%	95.65%	90.9%
World Average		N/A	N/A	N/A	N/A	N/A

Note: N/A means data not available.

Source: United Nations E-Government Survey- 2014, pp. 238, 242; 2016, pp.172, 175; and 2018, pp.246, 250. United Nations, New York.

India has jumped 25 ranks on its E-PI during the year (2014 to 2018). In the year 2014, it was ranked 40th with an E-PI score of (0.6275), while in 2016 it jumps to 27th rank and E-PI score (0.7627) and finally, in 2018, it got 15th rank with E-PI score (0.9551). In comparing India's scores in E-GDI, with E-PI, the latter index shows a better position. In 2014, India scores 92.5 per cent in stage one, 36.6 per cent in stage two, and zero per cent in stage three, with an overall score of 56.9 per cent (see Table 6). The world average scores in stage one, two and three are 55.7 per cent, 24.6 per cent and 7.3 per cent respectively with an overall score of 36.4 per cent. In the year 2016, the scores for India was

79.4 per cent (decrease of 13.1 per cent) in comparison with 2014 in stage one. In stage two, it was an (increase of 58.1 per cent) with 94.7 per cent; whereas in stage three, it opens its account from zero per cent in 2014 to 14.3 per cent in 2016. An Overall score was 76.7 per cent an (increase of 19.8 per cent) in comparison with 2014. Finally, in the year 2018, the stage one score is 100 per cent (increase of 20.6 per cent) in comparison with 2016; similarly, in stage two; it is 95.65 per cent (increase of 0.95 per cent) and, stage three - saw the largest (increase of 76.6 per cent) with 90.9 per cent. The overall score is 95.6 per cent an (increase of 18.9 per cent) in comparison with 2016. In both years (2014 and 2016); except for stage three in 2014, India's scores in all three stages are higher than the world average scores. Still, some improvements need to be done in stage 2 (E-Consultation) and stage 3 (E-Decision-Making) of the E-PI, to achieve 100 per cent.

The overall improvement in India's performance in both E-GDI and E-PI, (from 2014 to 2018) can be attributed to a number of initiatives taken by various stakeholders (more importantly governments). However, one such important initiative, impossible to be forgotten is - the Digital India programme.

Digital India and Sustainable Development Goals (SDGs)

The members of the United Nations adopted Sustainable Development Goals (SDGs) in the United Nations Summit, held in September, 2015. These are 17 SDGs and 169 Targets, which needs to be adopted by all member states by 2030. The adoption of ICTs will go a long way in helping to achievie SDGs, especially in terms of providing the quality basic services like health, education and other utility services to the people, more efficiently and effectively. Besides, bringing more transparency and accountability on the part of the government and other concerned stakeholders. It increases two-way communication and participation between government and the citizens, and try to design and deliver public services regardless of time and location, even to remote and hinterland areas. It is beneficial to both government and citizens, for the former, it is more cost effective than the traditional public service delivery channels. Similarly, for the latter, it provides more benefits in terms of access, cost, time saving and convenience.

The main vision of both, Digital India and Sustainable Development Goals (SDGs) have been the overall well-being and empowerment of the people. The National Institution for Transforming India (NITI) Aayog, under the Government of India, has identified 62 priority indicators, guided by the

National Indicator Framework, developed by the Ministry of Statistics and Programme Implementation (MOSPI), Government of India. These 62 priority indicators, identified aligned with the 17 SDGs and their 169 targets.Based on the progress of these indicators, the SDG India Index score was computed for India as a whole and separately for each States and UTs(SDG India Index: Baseline Report 2018).

In this context, some of the Digital India initiatives try to achieve directly or indirectly, some of the goals of SDGs, discussed in the following paragraphs:-

The (SDG No.1) talk about '*No Poverty-End poverty in all its forms everywhere*'. One of the national level indicators (out of five)identified for (measure India's performance) SDG India Index for (SDG No.1) is, 'persons provided employment as a percentage of persons who demanded employment under MGNREGA.' The (SDG No.2) aims to achieve '*Zero Hunger-End hunger, achieve food security and improved nutrition and promote sustainable agriculture*'. Out of four national level indicators,the one identified was, - 'ratio of rural households covered under public distribution system to rural households where the monthly income of highest earning member is less than Rupees 5,000.' The (SDG No.4) purpose is to achieve '*Quality Education-Ensure inclusive and equitable quality education and promote lifelong learning opportunities for all*'. In general, for achieving this goal, the Government of India is promoting the use of digital technology in the education sector through digital boards; smart classrooms; and direct to home channels. Also, some digital initiatives like Shala Kosh; Shagun; ShaalaSaarthi; Massive Open Online Courses (MOOCs), are helping in providing affordable and quality education for all women and men.

The (SDG No.7) focus on '*Affordable and Clean Energy-Ensure access to affordable, reliable, sustainable and modern energy for all*'. For achieving this goal, out of three national level indicators,the one which has been identified is, 'percentage of household's using clean cooking fuel'. The (SDG No.8) state that '*Decent Work and Economic Growth-Promote sustained, inclusive and sustainable economic growth, full and productive employment and decent work for all*.' One of the national level indicators, out of four identified were 'percentage of households with a bank account'. Out of all the SDGs, which discussed above, the (SDG No.9) is directly linked with the Digital India initiatives. This goal aims to achieve '*Industry, Innovation and Infrastructure-Build resilient infrastructure, promote inclusive and sustainable industrialization and foster innovation*'. Out of the four national indicators, the three identified were:- firstly, 'number of mobile connections per 100 persons in rural and urban areas (Mobile Tele Density)'; Secondly, 'number of internet subscribers per 100 population'; and thirdly, 'percentage of Gram Panchayats covered under Bharat Net'(SDG India Index: Baseline Report 2018).

Below are discussed some of the Digital India initiatives, which are aforementioned aligned with achieving SDGs:-

Jan Dhan-Aadhaar-Mobile (JAM) Trinity

Jan Dhan-Aadhaar-Mobile (JAM) trinity is one of the important initiative of the Government of India, to directly transfer subsidies to the eligible beneficiaries by eliminating intermediaries and leakages. It has done by linking Jan Dhan account, Aadhaar card and Mobile number of the beneficiaries. The JAM solves three challenges that confront the service delivery. Firstly, the challenge of identification; secondly, the challenge of payment; and thirdly, the challenge of last-mile of getting money from banks into the beneficiaries hands (JAM Trinity, 2018). It also minimises the steps involved in fund flow and thus, reduces delay in payment. According to our Prime Minister Shri Narendra Modi, JAM is about 'Just Achieving Maximum' i.e. Maximum value for every rupee spent; Maximum empowerment for our poor; and Maximum technology penetration among the masses(PM India Website).It helps the government in implementing Direct Benefit Transfer (DBT) on a large scale and provide more fiscal space for it.

Pradhan Mantri Jan Dhan Yojana (PMJDY)

The Government of India on 28th August 2014, started one of its flagship programmes called, Pradhan Mantri Jan Dhan Yojana (PMJDY), which is one of the biggest financial inclusion programmes implemented anywhere in the world; particularly for the weaker sections and lower-income groups in the society. The PMJDY provides a platform for universal access to banking facilities with at least one basic banking account for every household, financial literacy, and access to credit, pension and insurance facility (PMJDY, PM India Website). As on 20th November 2019, more than 37 crore bank accounts have been opened under this programme, and so far deposits worth Rupees 1,07,172.54 crore recorded (PMJDY, Government of India). These accounts have been used through DBT for transferring money under various government schemes.

Direct Benefit Transfer (DBT)

These benefits related to pensions, Mahatma Gandhi National Rural Employment Guarantee Scheme (MGNREGS), scholarship, subsidies etc, are directly transferred to the intended beneficiary through Direct Benefit Transfer (DBT). As on 29th November, 2019, 436 schemes implemented by 56 Ministries/Departments use DBT. The total number of eligible beneficiaries under both (cash and in-kind schemes) is 138.3 crore. The total DBT transfer cumulative both (cash and in-kind schemes) is Rupees 8,75,816.5 crore (see Table 7). The number of DBT schemes started with (28) during 2013-14, which increased to (34) in 2014-15; (59) in 2015-16; (142) in 2016-17; and drastically increase to (436) in 2017-18; (437) in 2018-19; and till 29th November, 2019 it is (440) schemes. Similarly, the number of beneficiaries who are eligible for various benefits from the government through DBT is increasing every year. During 2013-14 it was (10.8 crore) beneficiaries, gradually increases in 2014-15 with (22.8 crore); 2015-16 (31.2 crore); 2016-17 (35.7 crore); and near about four-fold increase in 2017-18 with (124 crore); 2018-19 (129.2 crore); and 2019-20 (138.3 crore). The total funds transferred (cash and in-kind schemes) through DBT is increasing every year, in 2013-14 it was (Rupees 7,367.7 crore) increased in 2014-15 to (Rupees 38,926.2 crore); 2015-16 (Rupees 61,942.4 crore); 2016-17 (Rupees 74,689.4 crore); 2017-18 (Rupees 1,90,870.9 crore); 2018-19 (Rupees 3,29,796.3 crore); and 2019-20 (Rupees 1,72,223.6).

Table 7: Overall Direct Benefit Transfer (DBT) Progress Report

	2013-14	2014-15	2015-16	2016-17	2017-18	2018-19	2019-20 (As on 29/11/2019)
No. of DBT Schemes	28	34	59	142	437	440	436
Eligible Beneficiaries (in crore)	10.8	22.8	31.2	35.7	124	129.2	138.3
Funds Transferred in Cash Schemes (in crore)	7,367.7	38,926.2	61,942.4	74,689.4	1,70,292.2	2,14,092	1,00,731.5
Funds Transferred In-Kind Schemes (in crore)	N/A	N/A	N/A	N/A	20,578.7	1,15,704.3	71,492.1
Total Funds Transferred (Cash+In-Kind Schemes) (in crore)	7,367.7	38,926.2	61,942.4	74,689.4	1,90,870.9	3,29,796.3	1,72,223.6
Total DBT Cumulative (in crore) (As on 29/11/2019)	8, 75,816.5						

Note: N/A it means data is not available.

Source: Direct Benefit Transfer, Government of India. Retrieved on dbtbharat.gov.in, 29/11/2019.

The data from (Table 8) shows, with the use of information technology, duplicate or fake beneficiaries can be eliminated, which saves a lot of money. The official data shows that savings from DBT from its inception,i.e. 2013 till March, 2018 were, Rupees 90,012.71 crore; while for the period April 2018 to March, 2019, it was Rupees 51,664.85 crore. Similarly, the cumulative saving from DBT from its inception until March 2019 was, Rupees 1,41,677.56 crore.

Table 8: Estimated Benefits/Gains from Direct Benefit Transfer (DBT)

Ministry/ Department	Scheme	Estimated Savings/Benefits (in Rs. crore)			Remarks
		Cumulative upto March 2018	April 2018 to March 2019	Cumulative upto March 2019	
Department of Fertilizers	Fertilizer	0	10,000	10,000	Reduction of 120.88 lakh metric tonnes of fertilizer sale to retailers
Department of Rural Development	MGNREGS[1]	16,073	4717.45	20,790.45	Deletion of duplicate, fake/ non-existent, ineligible beneficiaries resulted into 10 per cent savings on wages(According to Field Studies).
	NSAP[2]	438.60	77.41	516.01	Deletion of 4.77 lakh duplicate, fake/non-existent, ineligible beneficiaries (including some due to migration, death etc)
Ministry of Women & Child Development	Others	0	1523.75	1523.75	Reduction of 98.8 lakh duplicate, fake/non-existent beneficiaries
Ministry of Petroleum & Natural Gas	PAHAL[3]	42,275	17,324	59,599	4.23 crore duplicate, fake/ non-existent, inactive LPG connections eliminated. In addition, there are 1.86 crore non-subsidized LPG consumers, including 1.03 crore 'Give It Up' consumers.
Department of Food & Public Distribution	PDS[4]	29,708	17,925	47,633	Deletion of 2.98 crore duplicate and fake/ non-existent ration cards (including some due to migration, death etc).

Ministry of Minority Affairs	Scholarship Scheme	159.15	0	159.15	Deletion of 5.26 lakh duplicate, fake/non-existent beneficiaries
Department of Social Justice & Empowerment	Scholarship Scheme	238.27	97.24	335.51	Deletion of 1.91 lakh duplicate, fake/non-existent beneficiaries
Others	Others	1,120.69	0	1,120.69	
Total		90,012.71	51,664.85	1,41,677.56	

Note: *[1]MGNREGS (Mahatma Gandhi National Rural Employment Guarantee Scheme); 2NSAP (National Social Assistance Programme); 3PAHAL (PratyakshHanstantaritLabh); 4PDS (Public Distribution Scheme).*

Source: *Direct Benefit Transfer, Government of India. Retrieved on dbtbharat.gov.in/estimated gain, 29/11/2019.*

Below are discussed some of the schemes, which fall under various categories of anti-poverty, employment and support schemes for which government transfers directly to the beneficiaries:

Pratyaksh Hanstantarit Labh Yojana (PAHAL)

The Direct Benefit Transfer of LPG (DBTL) scheme Pratyaksh Hanstantarit Labh (PAHAL) Yojana was launched on 1st June 2013, but because of some difficulties faced by the consumer, it has been re-launched on 15th November, 2014. Being one of the largest direct cash transfer schemes in the world, it entered the Guinness Book of World Records. Under this yojana, beneficiaries are directly getting their Liquified Petroleum Gas (LPG) subsidies into their bank accounts. Under this scheme, more than 30 crore beneficiaries are receiving direct cash and in-kind subsidies. For subsidy on LPG cylinders, 4.23 crore duplicate, fake/non-existent or inactive connections have been eliminated.The cumulative savings upto March, 2019 under PAHAL Yojana was the highest amongst all the schemes with Rupees 59,599 crore. During the period from April 2018 to March 2019, it was Rupees 17,324 crore; while the cumulative savings till March 2018 was Rupees 42,275(see Table 8).

Public Distribution System (PDS)

Under this system, both union and state governments try to tackle food scarcity through the distribution of food grains especially to the poor (Below Poverty Line families and households under Antyodaya Anna Yojana-Poorest of the Poor) through the fair price shops at affordable prices. There are 58.41 crore beneficiaries receiving direct in-kind subsidies, which is the largest among all the schemes run by the government. Because of DBT, there were deletion of 2.98 crore duplicate, fake/non-existent ration-cards (including some due to migration, death etc). The cumulative savings till March, 2019 was Rupees 47,633 crore; while between April, 2018 to March, 2019 it was Rupees 17,925 crore. Similarly, since its inception until March, 2018, the cumulative savings were Rupees 29,708 crore (see Table 8).

Mahatma Gandhi National Rural Employment Guarantee Scheme (MGNREGS)

The Mahatma Gandhi National Rural Employment Guarantee Scheme (MGNREGS) aims to provide at least 100 days of wage employment in rural areas for one adult member from a family willing to do unskilled manual work in a financial year. At present, more than 12 crore beneficiaries are receiving direct cash subsidies under DBT. It is estimated (through field studies) that there has been a 10 per cent savings on wages on account of the deletion of duplicate, fake/non-existent, ineligible beneficiaries. The cumulative savings upto March 2019 for MGNREGS is Rupees 20,790.45 crore; while from April, 2018 to March, 2019 it was Rupees 4717.45 crore (see Table 8).

Apart from aforementioned schemes, the government also managed to delete 5.26 lakh beneficiaries under scholarship scheme given by Ministry of Minority Affairs; 4.77 lakh such beneficiaries under the National Social Assistance Programme; 1.91 lakh beneficiaries under scholarship scheme of Department of Social Justice and Empowerment; and 98.3 lakh reduction under the scheme operated by Ministry of Women and Child Development resulting in a lot of savings for the government. Thus, the aforementioned interventions from the government side through the use of ICTs (Digital India) are likely to yield better results over time, in terms of achieving some of the SDGs by 2030.

Conclusions

The paradigm of governance has been changed, as discussed previously from government-centric to citizen-centric; and this happens because of increase in citizen awareness about their rights and entitlements, also the expectation from the government to deliver various services to them. So, the only inevitable option for the government is to adopt Information and Communication Technologies (ICTs), in order to bring about reforms in governance systems, structures and processes, which was also emphasised by the Second Administrative Reforms Commission in its 11th report on 'Promoting e-Governance: The Smart Way

Forward'. As a result, e-Governance becomes an integral part of governance, and this was necessitated with the emergence of the Fourth Industrial Revolution, also known as 'Digital Revolution'. The adoption of e-Governance in India (both at Central and State Governments) is not new, there existed National e-Governance Plan (NeGP), which was one of the largest programmes in the world. However, there were some limitations to this programme, as a result, a new programme called Digital India came into existence, which is trying to cover many projects under one umbrella programme in order to achieve the goal of knowledge-based economy and digitally empowered society in the 21st century. The various initiatives under Digital India programme are at different stages of implementation,like Common Services Centres (CSCs), Unified Mobile Application for New-age Governance (UMANG), Pradhan Mantri Gramin Digital Saksharta Abhiyaan (PMGDISHA) etc.

There has been a close relationship between Digital India initiatives and Sustainable Development Goals (SDGs) and through the former, the Government can achieve the goals of the latter by 2030. Already, not only citizens are benefitting from easy access to various government services, but the government is also saving a lot of money,especially with the use of Direct Benefit Transfer (DBT). Still, the big challenge for India in the way of achieving the goals of the Digital India programme is,lack of infrastructure, which can be seen from the ranking of India in United Nations E-Government Development Index(E-GDI). Similarly,due to digital disruptions taking place frequently, government should keep abreastnot only with technology, but the changing needs and aspirations of the citizens. No doubt, in the 21st century, the Digital India programme can help to improve governance through transformation in the public service delivery system in our country.

References

1. Ahluwalia, S.S, 2018, Minister of State for Electronics and Information Technology, Government of India, while giving reply to Unstarred Question No.183, in Lok Sabha, Parliament of India on 18/07/2018.
2. Ahluwalia, S.S, 2018a, Minister of State for Electronics and Information Technology, Government of India, while giving reply to Unstarred Question No.1594, in Lok Sabha, Parliament of India on 19/12/2018.
3. Chandrashekhar, R, 2018, "Towards a Digital Future", *Yojana*, Vol.62, December, p.13.
4. CSC, Annual Report 2015-16, Common Services Centres, CSC e-Governance Services India Limited, Ministry of Communication & Information Technology, Government of India, New Delhi, pp.8-9.

5. Ericsson Mobility Report, 2019, June, p.viii. Retrieved from https://www.ericsson.com/en/mobility-report/reports/june-2019 on 20th December 2019.
6. JAM Trinity, 2018, Indian Brand Equity Foundation (IBEF), August. Retrieved from-ibef.org/research/india-study/jam-trinity on 28th November 2019.
7. Kachhal, Deepika, 2018, "Reshaping development", *Yojana*, Vol.62, December, p.5.
8. Malhotra, Charru, 2018, 'Theme paper on Role of Digital Technologies in Governance', Indian Institute of Public Administration, New Delhi, p.6.
9. Mehrotra, Karishma, 2019, 'Online Payment of Bills: Four-Fold surge in rural and semi-urban India', *Indian Express Newspaper*, 17th June, Monday, New Delhi.
10. MeitY, Annual Report 2016-17, Ministry of Electronics and Information Technology, Government of India, pp.17-18.
11. MeitY, Annual Report 2018-19, Ministry of Electronics and Information Technology, Government of India, pp.40, 60.
12. Prasad, Shankar Ravi, 2019, Minister for Electronics and Information Technology, Government of India, while giving reply to Unstarred Question No. 652, in Lok Sabha, Parliament of India on 26/06/2019.
13. Prasad, Shankar Ravi, 2018, 'Towards An Inclusive and Empowered Nation', *Yojana*, Vol.62, December, p.10.
14. PM India Website, Leveraging the power of JAM: Jan Dhan, Aadhar and Mobile. Retrieved from-pmindia.gov.in/en/government_tr_rec/leveraging-the-power-of-jan-dhan-aadhar-and-mobile on 28th November 2019.
15. PMJDY, PM India Website. Retrieved from pmindia.gov.in/en/major_initiatives/Pradhan-mantri-jan-dhan-yojana/ on 28th November 2019.
16. PMJDY, Government of India. Retrieved from pmjdy.gov.in/account, on 28th November 2019.
17. PMGDISHA, 2019. Pradhan Mantri Gramin Digital SakshartaAbhiyaan, Government of India. Retrieved from pmgdisha.in on 9th December 2019.
18. Second Administrative Reforms Commission, 2008, "11th Report on Promoting e-Governance-The SMART Way Forward', Department of Administrative Reforms and Public Grievances, Government of India, December, New Delhi, p.106.
19. SDG India Index: Baseline Report 2018, NITI Aayog, Government of India, New Delhi, pp.5, 6, 17, 29, 59, 89, 101,113.
20. United Nations E-Government Survey- 2014, Department of Economic and Social Affairs, United Nations, New York, p.100.
21. United Nations E-Government Survey- 2018, Department of Economic and Social Affairs, United Nations, New York, pp.iii, xx, 112.
22. UMANG, 2019, Unified Mobile Application for New-age Governance, Government of India. Retrieved from web.umang.gov.in/web/#/ on 14th December 2019.

+++

Chapter Seven

Choice Based Credit System in Universities and Colleges: An Analysis

Neeru Snehi[7]

Abstract

One of the major academic reforms initiated by UGC for improving the quality of higher education is the introduction of the Choice Based Credit System in recent times. Twelfth plan period (2012-2017) and the initiatives outlined under Rashtriya Uchchattar Shiksha Abhiyan (RUSA) plan 2013 include transition to semester based academic calendar, introduction of choice based credit system and examination and assessment reforms. University Grants Commission (UGC) has framed guidelines for adoption of Choice Based Credit System (CBCS) programme for all undergraduate and postgraduate level degree, diploma and certificate programmes under the credit system awarded by Central,' State and Deemed to be Universities. The CBCS aims to introduce 'cafeteria' type approach in which the students can take courses of their choice, learn at their own pace, undergo additional courses and acquire more than the required credits, and adopt an interdisciplinary approach to learning. In return, it is expected that this will bring flexibility in curriculum development, enhance quality of education programmes, increased student choice and student mobility in higher education. Introduction of these reforms would also contribute in bringing Indian higher education institutions at par with global practices in academic standards and evaluation strategies in the present structure of undergraduate and postgraduate education.

Keywords: *CBCS, Higher Education, Universities and Colleges*

Introduction

One of the major academic reforms initiated by UGC for improving the quality of higher education is the introduction of Choice Based Credit System in recent

7. Associate Professor, Department of Higher and Professional Education, National Institute of Educational Planning and Administration, New Delhi

times. The Twelfth plan period (2012-2017) and the initiatives outlined under Rashtriya Uchchattar Shiksha Abhiyan (RUSA) plan 2013 include transition to semester based academic calendar, introduction of choice based credit system and examination and assessment reforms. The focus of these reforms is not only on raising standards but also bringing Indian higher education institutions at par with global practices in academic standards and evaluation strategies in the present structure of undergraduate and postgraduate education. Further, this will drive higher education institutions to become globally competitive and contribute more in national development. Consequently, the University Grants Commission (UGC) has framed guidelines for adoption of Choice Based Credit System (CBCS) programme for all undergraduate and postgraduate level degrees, diploma and certificate programmes under the credit system awarded by Central, State and Deemed to be Universities. Introduction of CBCS has been made mandatory in all undergraduate and postgraduate programmes since 2015-16. However, the transition to the system is continuing. In this context, the article focuses on the conceptualization of CBCS, its implementation and challenges in Indian higher education institutions.

Developing of Choice Based Credit System

Academic reforms for development and improvement in the quality of teaching learning experience have been continuous. The credit system came into existence, in US with the practice of developing and offering of elective courses for increasing flexibility and to enhance student choice. These aspects got facilitated with the introduction of semesterisation and modularization as proactive strategies in the end of 19th century and early 20th century. Thus, the classical curricula whose major purpose was to train elites for nearly 200 years, entered a second stage in the middle of the 19th century and became industrial-professional oriented and emphasized on useful knowledge and employment; while from 1960, a consumer era brought a third change and introduction of more electives, more courses for arts, non-majors in various fields, part time, extension, evening and community services etc. (Westmeyer, 1985). Resultantly, most of the general education programmes, distribution of core and electives resembled a cafeteria line where one can enter at any point, choose food as per their whim (Miller, 1990).

In the second half of the twentieth century, credit system/framework gained acceptance and became part of the higher education system in many countries.

The credit system introduced in UK is known as Credit Accumulation and Transfer Scheme (CATS). In Europe, European Credit Transfer System (ECTS) was introduced in 1989, which has been successfully tested and used across Europe. In recent times, ECTS has developed into an accumulation and transfer of credits system at institutional, regional, national and European level for the students. The implementation of credit system reflects that though most UK universities/ institutions use a common approach to credit; there is no top- down initiative aimed at making credit systems in US Higher Education converge. In Europe, on the other hand, a top down initiative stemming from the Bologna Process ministerial decision has definitely accelerated the implementation of the European Credit Transfer and Accumulation System (ECTS). Other countries such as Australia, has introduced the 'National Qualifications Framework' in Australian universities but there is no unified credit system across all institutions, the Pan-Canadian Protocol on the Transferability of University Credits in Canada, Japan, China etc. have implemented credit system across their universities. Subsequently, the developing countries also started the adoption of credit system and in many Asian countries this led to diversification of programs as well as institutions.

CBCS in Indian Higher Education

Higher education sector is growing at break-neck speed in recent years. In the year 2018-19, there are 993 Universities, 39931 Colleges and 10725 Stand Alone Institutions; Total enrolment in higher education has been estimated to be 37.4 million while the number of teachers has grown to 1416299. The GER at present is 26.3 percent (AISHE Report, 2018-19). This widened access for higher education has also enhanced the need for academic reforms in order to improve the quality. In this context, one of the reforms initiated by UGC is introduction of CBCS in the year 2015.

The UGC articulated the need for developing a flexible higher education system for the students. It observed that, "Majority of Indian higher education institutions have been following the system which obscures the flexibility for the students to study the subjects /courses of their choice and their mobility to different institutions. There is need to allow the flexibility in education systems, so that students depending upon their interests can choose inter-disciplinary, intra disciplinary and skill based courses." This can only be possible when choice based credit system (CBCS), an internationally acknowledged system is adopted. The choice based credit system not only offers opportunities and avenues of learning beyond the core subjects for holistic development of an individual (UGC, 2015, p.2). Resultantly, introduction of CBCS was made mandatory in all the public universities from the next academic session i.e. 2016-17. At present, the transition to CBCS by different universities is continuing and is at different stages of implementation.

Looking back, it is observed that introduction of CBCS had its seeding period. In the post independence period, establishment of higher education institutions received attention from the policy makers. Although, the existing universities were following the traditional pattern of an annual examination involving internal and external examinations, examination reforms were initiated in the 1960s and 1970s. The education systems being adopted by these newly set up institutions revealed exposure to new concepts, as they were being mentored by different reputed universities of United States of America and Europe. The reforms included semester system, continuous internal assessment and end of term examinations was implemented in all the professional institutions and professional faculties/departments of most of the conventional universities. Thus the professional institutions established during the period namely Indian Institutes of Technology and Indian Institutes of Management, Jawaharlal Nehru University etc. adopted semester system for developing their programmes while the majority of conventional universities namely, Delhi, Bombay, Calcutta, Madras, Andhra, Mysore, Pune etc. followed the annual system of examinations. Nevertheless, some universities adopted semester system for professional and engineering courses, while continuing in annual mode for the liberal arts programmes. Manonmaniam Sundaranar University was the first in Tamil Nadu to introduce this CBCS pattern in university departments from 1996. Madras University also followed. Autonomous colleges in Tamil Nadu, with one or two exceptions, had also adopted this Choice-Based Credit System around this time. In the next 10 years, almost all universities in Tamil Nadu have followed the CBCS. But there is no uniform pattern followed amongst these institutions. Universities in, Karnataka such as Kuvempu University, Bangalore University also introduced credit system. The credit system has been implemented for degree courses affiliated to Bangalore University since 2004-05.

To improve the quality of Indian higher education and provide relevant knowledge, skills and competencies in tandem with the requirements of industry and society reforms and innovations are essential. Therefore, the persistence of academic structures and practices adopted during their inception in the post independent period warranted change. The concerns regarding disconnect between the higher education system and the societal needs were raised by The Radhakrishnan Commission report (1948) and The Kothari Commission Report (1966) that had recommended for developing a dynamic and robust system responsive to the changing environment of the country. Consequently, the New Education Policy, 1986 (revised in 1992) taking into consideration the ongoing structural reforms, globalization and ICT expansion paved the way for introducing change in higher education across the country. Several changes were suggested including 'redesigning of courses' along with 'increasing flexibility in combination of courses' and 'transformation of teaching methods'. Several reforms were initiated; however their implementation nationwide was not uniform. The Ambani- Birla Report (2000) made recommendations for improving education. In case of higher education, the Report advocated for easier student mobility from one institution to the other based on a system of transfer of proportional credits along with other recommendations. In 2006, The Report of National Knowledge Commission (NKC) which was set up in 2005, reiterated the need for allowing students to move from one institution to the other, and opportunity for opting for skill based courses.

The NKC also argued in favour of providing students with choices in courses, and shift to course credit system as being used in various universities abroad. The premise was introduction of greater diversity and flexibility in the course structure for students which implied improving quality by enhancing competition between institutions and making them more accountable. In addition, NKC Report, 2009 again suggested for use of semester format for teaching, providing choice to students and offering of skill based courses to make higher education relevant and graduates employable. The Yashpal Committee Report (2009) also supported the ideas floated by NKC and recommended for 'autonomy of learner' and said that they should be allowed to choose courses for study from different universities and then be awarded degree based on the credits they earned (Yashpal, 2009).

Meanwhile, few universities in the last few decades adopted semester system using a system of credits though largely the general universities continued with teaching in annual mode (Rajivlochan and Rajivlochan, 2018). However, those universities which introduced the semester system did it in selected courses and programmes based on the experiences of the other universities. For instance, DU had semester system (no credits) in postgraduate science courses and professional /engineering courses in late 1970s onwards. Mysore University adopted it in engineering courses in 1967. In University of Mumbai, the semester pattern was followed in B. Sc. IT and B.E. courses. Pondicherry University also started with introduction of CBCS in PG programmes in 1992-93. The emphasis on semester system by NKC, Yashpal Commission and UGC led the idea flowed into the Eleventh FYP with an aim to improve the quality of higher education. The Eleventh Five Year Plan (2007-2012) advocated the need for all Indian academic institutions to introduce examination reforms based upon the credit based semester system, evolve a system of grading that is in consonance with international practices so that grant of equivalence could be facilitated to adopt appropriate credit transfer mechanisms etc. In 2008, UGC asked universities to take necessary steps to introduce semester system at undergraduate level vide its Circular No. D.O.No. F.1-2/2008 (XI Plan) dated 31 Jan 2008. It also put forward its action plan for academic and administrative reforms for all the universities and specifically urged all the central universities again in March, 2009 to initiate these reforms.

Thus, the introduction of structural reform in academic degree programs in all universities and colleges in India started in 2009. The central universities and state universities in many states in India embraced the semester system at undergraduate and postgraduate level. Under this, UGC introduced the CBCS system, which is a student centric system and the traditional annual system to be replaced with the semester system. The key areas include Semesterisation of curricula; standardization of examinations; reformation of syllabi in the form of modules, and switching over from the numerical marking system to the grading system. This move by the UGC was aimed at bringing higher education in India in conformity with the best academic practices and standards being followed globally. Nevertheless, in some states, state universities and state governments were resistant to introducing it and in many universities it was implemented only for selected courses and not all. This situation of partial implementation is still continuing in many universities even after more than a decade.

Structure of Choice Based Credit System

The introduction of academic reforms received a greater push under the Ministry of Human Resource Development's 2013 Rashtriya Uchchatar Shiksha Abhiyan

(RUSA). The RUSA initiatives build on plans first circulated in 2009 under the UGC's Action Plan for Academic and Administrative Reforms. These academic reforms were designed to promote more responsive, diverse and flexible learning opportunities through adoption of semester system, choice based credit system, flexible curriculum framework, assessment and examination reforms.

Universities and colleges in India have traditionally followed the annual academic calendar with evaluation (usually in marks) based on end-of year examinations. Although, many professional and technical institutions and few universities such as IITs, IIMs, BITS Pilani, Jawaharlal Nehru University etc. had adopted semester system at their inception.

The major characteristic of CBCS is its allowance for more flexible learning framework with greater course choices, the ability to transfer credits between institutions, improved quality standards, and greater flexibility for mature students to complete programs over an extended period of time. It is also expected that in this way, the curriculum offered to students would be regularly updated and more relevant to current needs. Further, under CBCS credits will be awarded based on the successful completion of a course of study in terms of classroom contact hours and type of content. One credit is equivalent to 15 clock hours of teaching or in other words a semester credit is measured as one lecture (one hour) per week over the course of the semester, a minimum of two hours of tutorials a week, or one practical session per week. A course may be developed to combine all three - lecture, tutorial and practical. The specific credit make-up of a course will vary from subject to subject and from institution to institution based on curriculum design and desired learning outcomes. In addition marks-based assessment of coursework is weighted at 25 marks per credit, or 100 marks for a four-credit course. In general credits allocated to different programmes range between:

- Undergraduate degree program (three year): 120-150 credits.
- Undergraduate technical program (four year): 150-240 credits.
- Master's program: 100-120 credits.
- Technical master's program: 150-180 credits.
- Research degrees (M.Phil, M.Tech, LLM): 50-60 credits, with 25-credit thesis.
- Doctoral degree (coursework): 25 credits.

The structure of programmes (UGC, 2015) as constructed includes:

- Core Course (compulsory)
- Elective Course (courses which can be chosen from a pool of courses)-
  - Discipline Specific Elective,
  - Dissertation/Project and –
  - Generic Elective (GE) Course)
- Ability Enhancement Courses (AEC) (two types –
  - Ability Enhancement Compulsory Courses (AECC) -Environmental Science, English Communication/MIL Communication; and -
  - Skill Enhancement Courses (SEC)) - These courses may be chosen from a pool of courses designed to provide value-based and/or skill-based knowledge.

The structure also provides options for coursework and self study projects if desired and allowed by the department or institution. It is evident that this structure provides opportunity to students to diversify their study experience and develop a broader knowledge base outside their core discipline. Thus, the paradigm shifts towards student-centric higher education.

Introduction of CBCS also called for the introduction of a new assessment and grading system so as to improve student choice and academic mobility in Indian higher education institutions. It was expected that the semester-based assessment system would lead to better assessment of students through a combination of continuous internal and external (end term) evaluation. For this purpose, UGC recommended the relative weightage to continuous internal evaluation may range from 25-40 percent. Internal evaluations would include essays, tutorial presentations, lab work, and term papers. End-of-semester evaluation would seek to assess the skills and knowledge of students, moving away from examinations that require students to memorize and reproduce information. Further to bring uniformity in evaluation system, UGC formulated guidelines for uniform grading system and computation of the Cumulative Grade Point Average (CGPA) based on students' performance in examination (UGC, 2015). UGC recommended that the cut-off marks for grade B shall not be less than 50% and for grade B+, it should not be less than 55% under the absolute grading system. Based on the 10 point scale, letter grades, grade points and their performance description prescribed are given below in the Table 1:-

Table 1: Grade and Grade Points

Letter Grade	Grade Point	Performance description
O	10	Outstanding
A+	9	Excellent
A	8	Very Good
B+	7	Good
B	6	Above Average
C	5	Average
P	4	Pass
F	0	Fail
Ab	0	Absent

Source: UGC Guidelines 2015

Implementation of CBCS: Current status

The current status of implementation of CBCS system in the public. HEIs of the country reflects wide variations. Based on the extent of implementation of Semester/CBCS, the degree awarding institutions may be categorized into groups as given below:

Group A: The institutions who have adopted CBCS in all programmes of studies include- IITs, IIMs, NITs, IIITs, IISERs and many Central Universities (e.g. Jammu, Himachal Pradesh, Rajasthan, Karnataka, JNU, MANUU)

Group B: The institutions/universities that have adopted CBCS partially in some programmes of studies but not all programmes of studies. Large number of universities has introduced semester and credit system for Post-Graduate courses in the University Departments, are in the process of introduction of CBCS in Under Graduate courses in the affiliated colleges in the last 2-3 years, or in the session 2018-19 and some have introduced in 2019-20 session. In addition these universities continue to have some educational programmes in annual mode e.g. at the undergraduate level B.El. Ed, B.Ed. course at University of Delhi

Group C: The third group constitutes universities and their affiliated colleges which have not introduced semester and/or credit in undergraduate programs in humanities, sciences and commerce while undergraduate professional programs are offered in semesters and credit. For example UG programmes in colleges affiliated to Pune University, Maharashtra, UG programmes are in annual mode in affiliated colleges of state universities in Bihar and few other states.

Group D: Few states such as Kashmir, Himachal Pradesh and Madhya Pradesh introduced semester and credit system but have been facing representations by the teachers, students and unions for rolling back the CBCS system at the undergraduate level in affiliated colleges and their programmes. Despite the representations, CBCS is continuing in institutions/colleges of Kashmir. Major reasons cited by the faculty are problems in implementation of CBCS system mainly due to lack of infrastructure, shortage of faculty, conflict prone region and weather conditions. In addition, it was pointed out that the higher education system is not yet adequately prepared to manage such system, resulting in problems related to holding of examinations and prolonging of course durations and for students. Resultantly, only non professional UG and PG and a few professional courses like M.Ed are running under CBCS, while rest are continuing as usual. The colleges in the state are facing problems particularly in case of inadequate infrastructure and subject experts for teaching in various disciplines. The large enrollments in colleges make it difficult to do justice with the CBCS learning outcomes. Inadequate physical and administrative infrastructure creates hurdle in conducting of exams and declaration of results in time thereby increasing the duration of a degree.

Some examples related to introduction of CBCS in different universities include:-

In North Eastern States, NEHU implemented CBCS in 2008 in Master's Degree Programmes in Arts, Sciences and Commerce at postgraduate level while introduced it by UG from 2016-17. In Maharashtra, The University of Mumbai is planning to introduce CBCS in its UG and PG programmes in a phased manner, while it introduced credit and grading system in undergraduate and postgraduate programmes of engineering in the year 2012-13. Pune University introduced CBCS in engineering and PG courses, while UG is under semester system. On the other hand, Calcutta University has introduced CBCS for UG

2018-19 and PG (2017-18) courses from the academic session in university departments and affiliated colleges, Maulana Azad National Urdu University in 2016-17 at all levels.

In the states like Madhya Pradesh, Bihar and Haryana; the decision to implement took long i.e. by 2018. Most of the universities in these states are following annual mode at UG and PG level, though engineering/ professional institutions have semester system for example Barkatullah University, Patna University. Both the universities planned to introduce it in the forthcoming session i.e 2019-20. Patna Girls College (an autonomous college) which is affiliated to Patna University has introduced CBCS from 2019-20 session while other colleges are offering UG courses in annual mode. One of the significant reasons for introduction of CBCS by the university and college is getting better grade of accreditation too as CBCS is the prerequisite for NAAC accreditation presently. In Karnataka, Banglore University introduced semester system in 2004-05. Similarly in Goa, semester system was adopted since 2011-12 for post graduate courses and in UG from 2016-17. In case of University of Rajasthan, B.A, B.Sc., B.Com. programs are in annual mode while BBA and/B.Voc are in semester mode. For PG programmes, the courses are in annual mode as well as in semester mode with grading. The university pulled out of the introduction of CBCS in 2015-16 at the last moment citing lack of teachers and infrastructure (Oct 2017, TOI, Jaipur).

It is evident from these examples that the implementation of CBCS in various universities across the country is at varying stages. There are institutions who implemented the system more than twenty years back and on the other end are institutions that are in the process of implementation of the semester system and/or have recently implemented from the session 2019-20. Although, as per UGC plans i.e. implementation of CBCS from the academic year 2015-16, by 2019 the higher education programmes in the institutions of the country will shift towards learner centered education, increased interdisciplinarity and flexibility thereby having direct influence on enhancing quality of higher education .

CBCS: Continuing Challenges

The review of implementation of CBCS system in Indian universities reveals that in terms of implementation there are large variations among the universities. Nevertheless, the CBCS has started taking roots in the colleges and universities and credit transfer to ease student mobility is also shaping up as institutions are developing policy of equivalence and transfer. However, institutionalization of CBCS in the universities and colleges is raising issues and mechanisms are being developed to address them. Following paragraphs attempt to highlight these challenges being faced by the administrators and academics of the higher education institutions. These issues and concerns have emerged during the discussions and interview of administrators, faculty as well as students from different universities and colleges.

Implementation of CBCS

Many universities introduced the semester and credit system at the post graduate level in the early years of the 21st Century. Adoption of these reforms at the university level requires them to become part of the University Act and Ordinances. Role of State Governments is significant as in many States there is State Common Acts for State Universities. Thus, administrative processes and procedures for developing and passing Ordinances take long time. Some state governments have been able to implement the system such as Kerala and other south Indian states, state of Gujarat while in most states its implementation is partial. Some courses in the university are continuing in annual, semester and others in CBCS mode. There are States which are facing representations for rolling back to annual mode e.g. Himachal Pradesh, Punjab, Madhya Pradesh and Kashmir. Major reasons cited for these concerns include inadequate infrastructure-physical and administrative, teacher shortage. Institutional inertia and unpreparedness in terms of inadequately equipped libraries, laboratories, classrooms etc. are major factors resisting the change. Forcing universities to adopt CBCS, a structural change in the institution got associated with the issue of autonomy-institutional as well as academic autonomy. However, the concerns continue.

Credit allocation of educational programmes/courses:

Although UGC provided the template for credit allocation of undergraduate and post graduate programmes, the data from the sampled institutions revealed variations in credit allocation of the same programme offered by different universities. For successful completion of undergraduate (general/pass course/ honors) three year programme the credits range from 120 credits to 148 credits. While most of the Central and some State universities followed the UGC guideline others still need to transit. Allocations of credits to undergraduate professional courses also show varying trends for the similar duration courses. The credits required for successful completion of PG programmes also reveal large variations. For example a Masters in Computer Applications course is of 144 Credits in MANUU, 136-138 in DU, 120 credits in Goa University, 150 in Pune University. These variations have major implications for equivalence and course recognition and credit transfer for students.

Curriculum

The model curriculum to be taught under CBCS was developed by UGC and universities were expected to develop their curriculum with maximum contextual/locally relevant modifications of 20-30 percent. In addition to the concern for local relevance of the curriculum, the increasing student diversity in the class-room is also becoming a challenge for the teacher. Unfortunately, the continuing concerns relate to the division of the syllabus. The syllabi of core, foundation courses, generic and elective subjects need continuity and flow from one semester to the other. The apprehensions related to quality of curriculum are very high. The observation that the study load for the students is said to be higher in CBCS mode than annual mode. This is due to the increase in the number of papers though content is limited. This has also impacted the extra and co curricular activities of the students

The Cafeteria Approach-Choice of subjects

Though, the choice to students is the inherent mechanism in CBCS, yet in actual sense the implementation of choice is limited. Majority of the students and teachers from different institutions reported that the elective papers offered are limited and are directly related to the availability of staff and infrastructural resources. For instance, in Universities and colleges seats are fixed for each course, so accommodation of all students who want to study a particular subject is not feasible. This restriction is also placed with a view to balance the work load of the faculty. In order to offer, choice to students, the CBCS has found better acceptance in postgraduate subjects than at undergraduate level. In colleges, major problems are being faced. Many universities are offering open electives in a particular semester e.g. Kerala university, Bangalore University, NEHU etc. The instances about lack of genuine implementation of CBCS in private affiliated colleges emerged many a times. The mechanism for monitoring of choice to the student, the essence of the system is essentially needed.

Assessment challenges

Assessment of student performance reflects that the extent of defined learning outcomes/objectives achieved. The core concern emerges due to non existence of well-articulated and clear-cut assessment policy at the university level. In case the assessment policy is there, it is skeletal in framework, for instance, Total Marks for each course = 100% , Continuous assessment (C1) = 15% marks , Continuous assessment (C2) = 15% marks and Semester End Examination (C3) = 70%, the C1 and C2 are carried out after completion of 50% course and 100% course respectively and then the final end of semester exams. These assessments may be based on test, assignment, seminar, case study, field work, project work etc. In fact no university has fully internal assessment based practice of giving results. The reason underlying the assessment practices as prevalent in Indian universities education system reveals that it is charged with distrust. Assessment feedback is also not given timely and properly. The more open teachers are about assessment procedures, what is required and how grades are awarded, the more comfortable students are likely to be. In many universities and colleges teachers have started showing the graded end of semester sheets too.

Teacher related challenges

In addition to the major shortage of teachers in universities and colleges, the Indian university education system does not have any provision to have a dedicated agency to help university teachers how to design the curriculum/ content of any course/ programme, improve assessment practices by devising suitable assessment strategies and methodologies. Opportunities for continuous professional development for teaching, learning and assessment are in dire need. In addition, at present the perception is that higher education teachers are more concerned with testing and examinations and need to be oriented towards use of formative assessment as a tool to facilitate and enhance learning.

Conclusion

Introduction of CBCS in the public universities by UGC started in the year 2009. CBCS, a student-centric reform package replaces traditional academic annual structure with a semester system. The intended goals of introduction are to enhance learning opportunities to meet student's aspirations, improve educational quality and excellence, flexibility for working students to complete the programme, standardization and comparability of educational programmes across the country. The earlier discussion reveals that the shift towards CBCS from annual system and change in assessment methodology from traditional Indian marks system to credits and grading system are gaining acceptance but there is need for more awareness about the processes and mechanisms. It is also evident from the earlier discussion that implementation of CBCS in the universities all over the country is progressing slowly and they are at varying stages. Largely the universities have adopted the system only partially i.e. some programmes at both UG and PG level are continuing in annual mode too. In view of the continuing challenges for implementation, strategies and mechanisms for dealing with resource crunch, faculty shortage and administrative facilitation need to be developed and strengthened at institutional level to achieve the intended goals of the CBCS academic reform.

References

1. Ambani, M., & Birla, K., 2000, Report on a policy frame work for reforms in education. Special subject group on policy framework for private investment in education, health and rural development, Prime Minister's Council on Trade and Industry, pp. 840-845. New Delhi: Government of India.
2. ECTS Guide 2019, Available at https://europass.cedefop.europa.eu/sites/default/files/ects-users-guide_en.pdf
3. Government of India, 2013, *Rashtriya Uchchtar Shiksha Abhiyan*. Available at https://mhrd.gov.in/sites/upload_files/mhrd/files/RUSA_final090913.pdf
4. Government of India 1992: *Programme of Action, NPE 1986*, New Delhi: GOI.
5. Pitroda, Sam, 2009, "*National Knowledge Commission : Report to Nation, 2006-2009*". Advisory Report, Government of India. New Delhi: Ministry of Human Resource Development (Department of Higher Education) Government of India.
6. Planning Commission, 2008, "*Eleventh Five Year Plan 2007-2012*" New Delhi, Oxford University Press.
7. Planning Commission, 2013, "Twelfth *Five Year Plan 2012-2017*", New Delhi, Sage Publications.
8. Radhakrishnan, S, 1948, "*The Report of University Education Commission*", New Delhi: Government of India.
9. Rajivlochan.M and Rajivlochan. Meeta, 2018, Choice-based Credit System(CBCS) and Semester System in Indian Higher Education, in Varghese N V, Pachouri Anupam and Mandal Sayantan(Eds): *India Higher Education Report 2017: Teaching, Learning and Quality in Higher Education*, New Delhi, Sage Publications.
10. UGC, 2008, From Chairman on Examination Reforms. D.O. No. F1-2/2008 (XI Plan), dated Jan 31,2008: Annexure-II, Action Plan for Academic and Administrative Reforms.

11. UGC, 2009, Guidelines on Adoption of Choice Based Credit System. University Grants Commission, Bhadurshah Zafar Marg New Delhi.110002. Available at https://www.ugc.ac.in/pdfnews/8023719_Guidelines-for-CBCS.pdf
12. UGC 2015, Instructional template for facilitating implementation of choice based credit system (CBCS). Retrieved 11 June 2019, from https://www.ugc.ac.in/pdfnews/4426331_Instructional-Template.pdf
13. UGC, Report on Evaluation Reforms,
14. Available at https://www.ugc.ac.in/pdfnews/4258605_Report-of-the-Committee-on-Evaluation-Reforms.pdf
15. Yashpal, 2009, "*Report of the Committee to advise on 'The renovation and rejuvenation of higher education*". Advise, Government of India, Ministry of Human Resource Development (Department of Higher Education). New Delhi. GOI.

✦✦✦

Chapter Eight

Right to Inclusive and Quality Education of Muslim Children: A Quagmire of Identity, Security and Exclusion

Nuzhat Parveen Khan[8] *& Muzaffar Hussain Mir*[9]

Abstract

The Constitution of India proclaims that there should be free and compulsory "education for all" which includes within its ambit the ideals of universal access, universal enrolment, and universal retention. However, these terms obscure the term "all" which, in principle should encompass all the deprived sections of the society who suffer from distinctive kinds of socio-economic deprivation. The minorities in India especially Muslims suffer from this distinctive kind of deprivation due to a combination of economic, political, religious, socio-cultural and gender factors. Despite the fact that Muslims are a heterogeneous minority, they carry the historical burden of the homogeneous other. The otherwing gives way to stigmatization and demonization of community that combine with class and gender inequalities leading to deprivation and exclusion of the community. Education occupies the pivotal role in the process of empowerment of minorities especially Muslims in contemporary India. Educational backwardness is the main cause of real or perceived "alienation" of the Muslim community and inclusive education at the same time is seen as the panacea given its role as an instrument of socialization, empowerment, social mobilization, and national integration. But the form of education should be such that is diversified and reinforces the Muslim identity and at the same time does not become another factor for the exclusion of Muslims. However, Muslims are at the double disadvantage with low levels of education combined with low quality of education. This paper analyses the whole concourse of Muslim identity, security and equity, which affect the participation of Muslim children in elementary education in India.

Keywords: *Education, Identity, Security, Exclusion, Deprivation, Participation.*

8. Professor, Faculty of Law Jamia Millia Islamia New Delhi
9. Senior Research Fellow (UGC), Faculty of Law, Jamia Millia Islamia, New Delhi

Introduction

The United Nation Declaration on The Rights of Persons Belonging to National, Ethnic, Religious, and Linguistic Minorities, 1992(UNO, 1992) enjoins upon the state that they ought to promote and protect the rights of religious and linguistic minorities so as to contribute to political and social stability of the countries they live in. The ultimate goal of the U.N. Declaration is to make it clear to the state parties that the meeting of the aspirations and attributing dignity to the persons belonging to the minority community leads to the fulfillment of the goal of equality and participatory development. Equality and participatory development in turn lead to the lowering of tensions between various communities and groups within the country. In order to achieve political and social stability in a country especially a developing country, it becomes necessary to give due attention the socio-economic development and rights of minorities. The acid test of just and impartial state having minority population depends on the fact of how much faith and confidence the minorities have on the government of the country in which they are living (Drèze& Sen, 2016:352).

With the unfolding of the various contours of economic development, pressures emerge and intensify from various corners of society when there is unequal development and various minority groups get left behind in this story of economic development. When these groups get left behind, they become the breeding ground for the alienation and discontent in society. Ideally, the development process should lead to the overall and equal development of all groups of society which in turn lead to social and political stability and mutual respect. When development moves in the reverse gear, it may lead to flux and mutual distrust (Sen, 2000:3).

Equality (Sen, 2006:12) of the citizens and the assurance, protection and preservation of the rights (Parr, Lawson-Remer & Randolph, 2015) of the minorities in the matters of language, culture and religion are the watchwords of the Indian Constitution. That is why, the founding fathers of the Indian constitution have tried to emulate the ideal of 'unity in diversity' in these watchwords in light of the multi-cultural, multi-religious and multi-linguistic character of our country (Chelameswar & Naidu, 2018).

Since independence, India has made various commendable efforts to reduce poverty and to improve various other human development indicators like education, health services, etc. But it appears from the official statistics

(Census, 2001; GOI Report, 2006; GOI Report, 2007; Census, 2011) that all the religious communities are not reaping the benefits of India's development story. Muslims, being the largest religious minority, comprising about 14.2% lags behind in almost all the human development indicators like education, per-capita income, health indicators etc. (Census, 2001).This lagging behind of the Muslim community in key development indices combined with the historical burden of the "*other*"[1] leads to the demonization and the stigmatization of the community as a whole. This process of the demonization and stigmatization paves the way for alienation and ghettoisation of the community leading further to the shrinking of common public spaces.

Contesting Educational Dilemma of Muslims: Insights from Legal Frameworks and Official Data

The Constitution of India proclaims that the state shall provide free and compulsory education to all children between the ages of six to fourteen years.[2]This particular progressive provision was introduced after the judgment in the *Mohini Jain* case[3] and its subsequent reconsideration in the *Unnikrishnan* case.[4] Besides these provisions there are provisions in the Constitution of India which call for the protection and promotion of the education and culture of the religious and linguistic minorities under Articles 29[5] and 30.[6] The Supreme Court in *T.M.A. Pai foundation v. State of Karnataka*[7] has tried to define "religious minority" and held that the religious minorities are to be defined with respect to their population at the state level and minorities have right to establish educational institutions of "their own choice" which includes institutions offering professional courses. The *T.M,A. Pai foundation* case[8] was further elucidated in the case of the *Islamic Academy of Education and another v. State of Karnataka and others*[9]where it was laid down that the minority community has the precedence or better footing than non-minorities in establishing educational institutions and has the constitutional protection granted by Articles 29 and 30 but still there are minority schools or institutes which are unrecognized and operating illegally. Although Articles 29 and 30 call for the autonomy of the minority educational institutions but it does not dispense with the requirement of acting fairly and in a transparent manner.[10]

In order to give effect to this Constitutional Mandate, the Parliament of India enacted the Right of Children to Free and Compulsory Education Act in 2009. This Act provides that every child of the ages six to fourteen shall have a right to free and compulsory education in the neighbourhood school till the completion of elementary education. No child shall be charged any fees or other expenses till the completion of elementary education.[11] The constitutional validity of the Act was challenged in the case of the *Society for unaided Private Schools of Rajasthan v. Union of India* [12] where the three-judge bench of Supreme Court upheld the constitutional validity of 2009 Act with the rider that the Act is not applicable to the unaided minority institutions as they are protected under Article 30(1) of the Constitution.

In order to know how much has percolated in reality on the ground, it is better to analyse the official data under four parameters:

A. Literacy Rates
B. Proportion of Population Completing Specified Level of Education
C. Mean Years of Schooling:
D. Enrollment Rates

Literacy Rates

In 2001, the Muslim literacy rate was 59.1% which was lower than the national average of 64.8 by 5.7% (Census, 2001). Surprisingly, the Muslims fared better than the Scheduled Castes and Tribes whose rates were abysmally low at 54.7% and 47.1% respectively. Literacy rate among the Muslims was lower than the other minorities: Christians (80.3%); Sikhs (69.4%); Buddhists (72.7%); Jains (94.1%). As far as the Hindu-Muslim Gap (HMG) is concerned, the Hindu literacy rate was at 65.1%, which was above the national average, as compared to 59.1% among the Muslims leading to the gap of 6%.

The next visible feature of the literacy rate was the division within the community due to the dismal participation of women in education among the Muslims. The literacy rate among the Muslim females was 50.1% as compared to the 67.6% among the Muslim males leading to the Male-Female gap (MFG) of 17.5%. If the MFG is analysed among other minorities, there is no such higher gap between the males and females: Christain-males-84.4%, females-76.2% (Gap=8.2%) and Sikh Males-75.2% Females- 63.1% (Gap=12.1%)

Proportion of population completing specified level of education

To measure the proportion of the population completing a specified level of education, graduation level education was taken as the measuring indices. As per the Census (2001) data, percentage of Muslims having education of graduation level is mere 3.6% as compared to the national average of 6.72%. The religious community having highest graduates among its members are the Jains (21.47%). The proportion of people having educational qualification of graduate level among the Hindus (7.01%) is higher than the national average.

Mean Years of Schooling

The Mean years of schooling means the average number of years a person attends school during a specified period of age. In India it is taken for the age group of seven to sixteen years. The national average Mean years of schooling is four years while as for the Muslims this is approximately three years four months which is abysmally below the national average(GOI Report, 2006).

Enrollment Rates

The enrollment rates have increased among all the social and religious communities at the elementary level (up to primary level) highest being among the scheduled castes and the scheduled tribes (95%) followed by the Muslims (65%) as the national average of 55.57%. There is a bit of erratic pattern in the enrollment (or attendance) of Muslims and the enrollment at the primary level does not translate in the higher proportion of Muslims at higher echelons of education. This is evident from the statistics of enrollment at the Primary Level (65.31%) which is the highest in India, but this goes on decreasing at the Middle level (15.14%) and secondary (10.96%) dipping to the all time low at Senior Secondary level where the enrollment is 4.53%. The enrollment of the Muslims at the Diploma and Graduation level, which is seen as the qualification which helps the individual to participate in the job market, is 0.41% and 3.6% respectively(GOI Report, 2007). In this statistical rhetoric it can be seen that the Muslim community has one of the highest rates of dropouts. There is a pattern in this dropout rate of the Muslims and the causes which affect this enrollment have to be probed and this paper is a step in that endeavor.

Education of Muslims and the Underlying Hyperbole: A Quagmire of Identity, Security and Exclusion

Muslim Identity, Security and the Access to Public Facilities

Nation-building process in a nation-state having heterogeneous population - goes through the process of defining the core and the periphery. When that core has been defined and affirmed, all other groups at the border of the core become the marginalized, minority and the periphery of that core. The defining process of that core can be based on ethnicity, religion or other cultural aspects in case of heterogeneous societies like India. It has been the two-stage process, one that the nation is established by defining the majoritarian core of the nation and secondly the emergence of the minorities which are the means of constituting the majority in a nation (Pandey, 1999). Like the race or the tribal labels, ethnicity has been a marker of those groups who are at the borders of the nation or state. In case of homogeneous states, these borders are created by the ideology of the mainstream and the periphery of the social order (Williams, 1989).

Partition and independence of India has been the pincer-moment in the process of the definition of a nationalist core whereby the loyalty of this core towards the nation is taken as beyond any acid test. The loyalty towards the nation has to be proved by those who do not belong to this core – marginalized, minorities and groups at the periphery. In India, after the Partition and independence, this nationalist core comprised of the Hindus and the group at the periphery were the Muslims who have stayed behind in India after the creation of Pakistan. Partition led to the ideological division of Hindus into, "*Hindu Nationalists*" and "*Secular Hindus*", whereas the Muslims were grouped into "*Nationalist Muslims*" and "*Muslims*". The term *"Hindu Nationalists"* do not signify the Hindus who are nationalists, but the term carries the baggage of a nationalism which is defined by Hindu culture, Hindu traditions and Hindu community at large.The general perception was that the loyalty of the Hindus was beforehand established in light of the thinking that "*Hindus have no other country to go besides India*" whereas Muslims who fought for the creation of Pakistan but stayed back in India can any time move to Pakistan if they like. This perception gave birth to the rhetoric that the Muslims who remained in India were a kind of 'collaborators' of Pakistan and if they want to live in India, they will have to show they loyalty to this nation (Khaliquzzaman, 1961:411).

Pubic Spaces for Muslims: Shrinking

Even after six decades of Partition and independence that perception has not waned out of the public horizon and still Muslims have to parade their patriotism in India. This perception is evident from the communal riots, social boycott and ghettoisation of Muslims (Kirmani, 2009). These processes have led to the '*double burdening*' of the Indian Muslims who on the one hand have been hounded as anti-national and on the other hand been victims of appeasement politics. These two processes have pushed the Indian Muslims to the edge where on the one hand they have to prove their loyalty on a daily-basis that they are patriots and not terrorists collaborating with the 'enemy', and on the other hand, "appeasement politics" has not led to any socio-economic development of Muslims in India but rather to their neglect and abandonment. In this whole phenomenon, identity of Muslims has been the main factor that leads to the shrinking of the public spaces for Muslims.

The historical burden of the homogenous *other*, despite being a heterogeneous community, has led to the stigmatization and demonization of the Indian Muslims. The stigmatization and demonization combined with the class and gender inequalities led to the marginalization and exclusion of the Muslim community. The identity markers –*topi, burkha or purdah, beard* - of Muslims although showing their distinctive culture has a daunting impact in public spaces like schools, market, bus stops and trains. These identity markers have been the site of their public ridicule and stereotyping as the terrorists or anti-nationals. Muslim men wearing *topi* or *beard* are often picked and detained by the enforcement agencies on the suspicion that they are involved in anti-national activities. Muslim women often complain of their harassment in public spaces like trains, buses, police stations etc and there have been cases where in case of communal riots they have been sexually assaulted(Nussbaum, 2004).

General lack of security combined with the halfhearted attitude of the law enforcement agencies like police has led to the shifting of Muslims to the "*ghettos*"[13] (Census, 2001). And whenever there are communal riots or other religious skirmishes, Muslims being in minority fear for their safety and security and leading to further flux and rush of Muslims to ghettos. Ghettos in India are generally characterized by lack of basic amenities, water, electricity, banking facilities, health services, schools, etc, and overcrowding. The locality of *Jamia Nagar* illustrates the complete picture of the ghettoisation process. This locality being in the heart of the national capital lacks in all the facilities reminding one of the ancient times when there used to be no trace of government on the ground. This whole area comprises of illegal colonies like Zakir Nagar, Gafoor Nagar, Batla House, Joga Bhai Extension, Noor Nagar, Haji Colony and Johri farm. This whole area has hardly five schools, three M.C.D. primary schools and two Government senior secondary schools for a population of approximately 1.2 lakhs as per the official records, (Census, 2001; Census, 2011). However, unofficial reports peg it near about four lakhs(Borker, 2011).Thus, there is lack of access and availability of schools in this area which leads the children to resort to unrecognized minority schools.

There are cases which have been elaborately documented by Hem Borker(2011) in her study where many Muslim children have been denied admission in the public and private educational institutes due to their identity as Muslims on the general perception that they (Muslim children) will vitiate the environment of these schools. It is generally the perception that Muslims don't like education but Borker (2011) has surveyed that majority of Muslim parents want their children to take the mainstream education. When these children are denied admission to public facilities, (Borker, 2016) it gives rise to a number of Muslim denominational schools which mostly are unrecognized. Muslim children are left with the "*only option*" (GOI Report, 2006; GOI Report, 2007) that is to resort to these unrecognized schools. This was not the intent of the Constitution of India in every way therefore these developments violating this pious document.

Muslim Identity, Education and Exclusion: Why 'they' are? Where 'they' are?

Education of the community, although not a magic potion, is the *'fertile functioning'* which leads to the fertilization of other capabilities which a community needs in its path to development and stability. Education can be a plinth leading to the achievement of the goals like economic empowerment, human security, social mobilization, political empowerment and gender justice for which a community aspires(Nussbaum, 2011:42). When the community is failing in this main arena, the other areas are likely to get affected and that is the problem of the minorities especially Muslims in India. In the words of Jonathan Wolff and Avner De-Shalit (2007:121), the lower level of education can be called as a 'corrosive disadvantage' Corrosive disadvantage, the other side of the fertility functioning, affects other aspects of life for instance if there is lower level of education among the community that community is likely to see lower economic development, low political participation and marginalization in general.

Education of the community is seen as the main armour in its fight against economic penury and for social mobilization but the Muslim community is failing in this area. The question remains what holds Muslims back from educating its children and making them the generators of empowerment of the community? As per the author, there are various factors that hold back its members from education leading to their marginalization in general and these factors can be divided into: *Supply-side factors* and *Demand-side factors*. Here the author will be focusing only on the *supply side factors*. The supply side factors are those which the government could have done for the betterment of the Muslim community but has shown utter disregard for these areas.

Firstly, the main impediment in the educational development has been poor access to schools or non-availability of schools near the Muslim concentration areas (Basant, 2012). Although the Right of Children to Free and Compulsory Education Act, 2009 puts an obligation on the local authorities in the state to set up schools in their jurisdiction but there has been a lackadaisical attitude of the authorities when it comes to the development of the Muslim areas. The example of the Jamia Nagar area - illustrates the attitude of the government with respect to Muslim concentration areas. In the whole area there are only five schools, three up to primary level and two up to senior secondary level leading to the higher teacher-student ratio in these schools (Bhalotra &Zamora, 2010). The higher teacher-student ratio leads many children to resort to private schools if they can afford to or else drop-out. There is also absence of specific schools meant for women in these areas leading to lower education among the Muslim girls. These girls either resort to madrasas, unrecognized schools in the locality or simply drop-out(Gupta, 2015:43).

Secondly, even if Muslim children succeed in crossing the first hurdle of access to schools, next problem begins with in the four walls of the school i.e., the '*communalization of the school spaces.* This process is evident from the "*saffronisation*" of the school texts and the attitude of the teaching as well as the non-teaching staff towards the Muslim children. Many Muslim parents perceive this as a threat to their culture and religion and therefore try to keep their children out of these schools. The other problem has been the attitude of the teachers towards the Muslim children and their identity markers. There has been many cases where teachers start to pinpoint in the whole class and calling them words like "*miyan*" and many staff members targeting the children whenever there is a terrorist act in the country, pointing towards them and saying *"yehtou in k logon ne kiyaho ga"* (this might have been done by *their* people). These types of shenanigans lead to these children being ostracized and alienated from the mainstream students and the result is dropping out of these children from these schools or resort to unrecognized schools.

Thirdly, the demonization of the Urdu language and the *sanskritization* of the school curriculum led to a dismal condition of the Urdu-medium schools. Urdu is not the language of Muslims as it is generally perceived but is the product of the composite culture of Hindustan. The identification of the Urdu language with Indian Muslims has led to the utter neglect and abandonment\ of this language and this has been made possible after the Constitution under Article 351 proclaimed that Hindi shall draw heavily from Sanskrit.

Fourthly, the government has been heavily relying on the plank of modernization of the *Madrasas* when the percentage of Muslim children studying there is only 3% (Approx) rather than the mainstreaming of the Muslim children studying in these *madrasas*(GOI Report, 2006). Even though constitution gives rights to Muslims to establish educational institutions for the development of the community these institutions get entangled in official quandary due to which these institutions remain unrecognized during their life-courses(Basant & Shariff, 2010).

Last but not the least, there has not been any effort on the part of the government to increase the political participation and representation of Muslims. They have been the victims of political appeasement and vote-bank politics by which they have been exploited by the political parties for their own ends. Political participation and representation could have helped the community by placing their interests in the power corridors of the Indian political structure. Muslims have seen their exclusion from these political structures by non-*inclusion of their names in the voter lists* and declaration of the constituencies where Muslims are in a majority as the *"reserved category constituency"*.

Conclusion

All these problems are not only the problems of the Muslims but are the problems faced by the poor (as majority of Muslims being poor) or underdogs of Indian society and all the minorities in general and Muslims in particular. That is why these issues need to be addressed and pondered over. There has been demonization, alienation and marginalization of the Muslim community in India after the Partition and independence. To ameliorate the condition of the Muslims and to give them dignity and equality they deserve as citizens of this country, the supply side factors need to be dealt with urgently otherwise; they will contribute to their further marginalization and alienation.

Further the changes need to emerge from 'within' the community, which is possible only by emergence of the *'organic intellectuals'* in the Gramscian sense(Hoare & Smith, 2014:3) who are the 'thinking' and 'organizing' element of the concerned social class. They will be less characterized by the professional qualifications but more by the manner in which they direct the 'ideas' and 'aspirations' of the class to which they 'organically' belong. The organic class has that connection with the marginalized sections of society as they are part of the same society and can easily understand the problems of that segment of the society.

References

1. Basant, Rakesh, and A. Shariff, 2010, "The State of Muslims in India: An Overview" in Rakesh Basant and A. Shariff, (eds.), *Handbook of Muslims in India: Empirical and Policy Perspectives,* New Delhi, OUP.
2. Basant, Rakesh, 2012 "Education and Employment among Muslims in India: An Analysis of Patterns and Trends". Ahmedabad, Indian Institute of Management, W.P. No. 2012-09-03, September 2012
3. Bhalotra, S. and B Zamora, 2010, "Social Divisions in Education in India", in Basant R and Shariff, A (eds.) *Handbook of Muslims in India: Empirical and Policy Perspectives,* New Delhi, OUP.
4. Borker, Hem, 2011, "Contesting Dilemmas: Muslim Identity and Education: The Case Study of Jamia Nagar New Delhi". *National CRY Research Fellowship-CRY-Child Rights and You,* 2011 *Retrieved from*: http://www.cry.org/resources/pdf/NCRRF
5. Borker, Hem, 2016, "Shutting the door on the Muslim child". *The Hindu,* April 5, 2016 *Retrieved from:*http://m.thehindu.com/opinion/op-ed/shutting-the-Door-on-the-Muslim Child/Article3281463.ece
6. Chalemeswar, Justice Jasti, and Justice Dama Seshadri Naidu, 2018, *M.P. Jain's Indian Constitutional Law*, New Delhi, lexisNexis.
7. Drèze, Jean, and Amartya Sen, 2016, *India: Development and Participation* 14th Impression, New Delhi, OUP.
8. Fukuda Parr, Sakiko, Terra Lawson-Remer, Susan Randolph, 2015 *Fulfilling Social and Economic Rights* New York, OUP.
9. Government of India (GOI) Census Report, 2001 *Retrieved from:http://*censusindia.gov.in/2011-common/censusdataonline.html
10. Government of India (GOI) Report: Report of the National Commission for Religious and Linguistic Minorities (Justice Ranganath Mishra Commission Report) (Ministry of Minority Affairs, 2007)
11. Government Of India (GOI) Report: Social, Economic and Educational Status of the Muslim Community of India (Ministry of Minority Affairs, 2006) *Retrieved from* : http://

minorityaffairs.gov.in/sachar

12. Government of India (GOI), Census Report 2011 Census Data –Population by Religious Community, *Retrieved from:* http://www.censusindia.gov.in/2011census/C-01.html
13. Gupta, Latika, 2015, *Education, Poverty and Gender: Schooling Muslim Girls in India,* New Delhi, Routledge.
14. Hoare, Quintin, and Geoffrey Nowell Smith (eds.& trans.), 2014, *Selections from the Prison Notebooks of Antonio Gramsci*, New Delhi, Orient Black Swan.
15. Khaliquzzaman, Choudhary, 1961, *Pathways to Pakistan*, London, Longman.
16. Kirmani, Nida, 2009, "Constructing 'The Other': Narrating Religious Boundaries in Zakir Nagar". *Contemporary South Asia*, Vol. 16, 2009, pp. 397-412
17. Nussbaum, Martha C., 2004, "Body of the Nation: Why Women were Mutilated in Gujarat". *Boston Review*, April 2004 Retrieved *from*: http://bostonreview.net/archives/BR29.3/nussbaum.html
18. Nussbaum, Martha, 2011, *Creating Capabilities: The Human Development Approach*,New Delhi, Permanent Black.
19. Pandey, Gyanendra, 1999 "Can Muslims Be Indians?". *Comparative Study in Society and History, Vol. 41, 1999, pp.* 608-629 *Retrieved from:* http:// www.jstor.org/stable/179423
20. Sen, Amartya, 2000 *Development as Freedom*, New York Alfred A. Knopf, Inc.
21. Sen, Amartya, 2006, *Inequality Re-examined*, New York, Reprint. OUP.
22. United Nations Organisation (UNO), United Nations Declaration on the Rights of Persons belonging to National, Ethnic, Religious, and Linguistic Minorities, 1992. A/RES/47/135,*Retrievedfrom*:http://www.un.org/Documents/Ga/Res/47/A47r135.htm
23. Williams, Brakette F., 1989, "A Class Act: Anthropology and the Race to Nation across The Ethnic Terrain". *Annual Review of Anthropology,* Vol. 18, 1989, p. 439.
24. Wolff, Jonathan, And Avner De-Shalit, 2007, Disadvantage, New York, OUP.

Endnotes

1. Indian Muslims are generally perceived to be not belonging to the India and having affection for the Pakistan on the basis of religious commonality. Further, they are taken to be one not to be trusted as *they* have already betrayed India by partitioning the country. The cultural distinctiveness and the myth of the Muslim history as one of oppression in India have been the contributing factors in this process of *othering.*
2. Constitution of India, Article 21-A (*Inserted* by Constitutional (Eighty Sixth Amendment) Act, 2002)
3. Mohini Jain v State of Karnataka AIR 1992 SC 1858.
4. Unnikrishnan, J P v State of Andhra Pradesh (1993) 1 SCC 645
5. Constitution of India, Art 29 cl.1.: *"(1) any section of the citizens residing in the territory of India or any part thereof having a distinct language, script or culture of its own shall the right to conserve the same*
6. Constitution of India, Art 30 cl. 1.: *"(1) all minorities, whether based on religion or language, shall have the right to establish and administer educational institutions of their choice."*
7. (2002) 8 SCC 481

8. (2002) 8 SCC 481
9. Writ Petition (Civil) 350 of 1993 (Decided on August 14, 2003)
10. Mrs. Ivy C. Da. Conceicao v State of Goa AIR 2017 SC 1834
11. The Right of Children to Free and Compulsory Education Act, 2009, s. 3
12. Society for unaided Private Schools of Rajasthan v. Union of India,(2012) 6 SCC 1.
13. It is generally an urban phenomenon where a part of the city is inhabited by the members of a particular group, race or religion who live in very poor condition like lack of basic amenities-water, health centers, schools etc. As per the Census Report 2001 majority of Indian Muslims (16.9%) reside in urban areas.

+++

Chapter Nine

Gender and Development- A Study of Maternal & Child Health Care Policies in Odisha

Padmalaya Mahapatra[10]

Abstract

Gender discourse within the field of development has come a long way from building a case of 'inclusive' growth which prevents the marginalization of women to questioning of the predominant notions of development itself. The body of feminist critique continues to traverse new terrains and posit new challenges. The neo-liberal vision of society with a strong undercurrent of economic determinism often celebrates the atomistic, unconnected, self-maximizing individual- a conception which largely inhibits the space of both culture and development. Women's limited access to and control of material resources and limited decision-making power within the household can produce high fertility rates, under-investment in aspects of family welfare such as child nutrition and education, and sub-optimal allocations of human capital in the economy. Maternal morbidity and mortality along with infant mortality rate is universally considered as human development indicators in a country and determines the health status of the people. In spite of very good plans and programmes, the reduction in MMR & IMR is much below the target set in Odisha. The present study is based on both primary &secondary sources of data. The paper attempts to analyse the impact of maternal health care policies on women's health status in Odisha. It mainly focuses on maternal mortality relating to socio-economic characteristics of the deceased, status of ante natal care, major causes that lead to maternal death, major steps taken through various policies & programmes initiated by Government of India / the Government of Odisha & their achievements.

Keywords: *Gender, material and child health, policies, Odisha*

10. Associate Professor, P.G Department of Public Administration, Utkal University, Vanivihar, Bhubaneswar.

Gender & Development

The Gender Related Development Index (GDI) is an index designed to measure gender equality. GDI together with the Gender Empowerment Measure (GEM) were introduced in 1995 in the Human Development Report written by the United Nations Development Programme. The GDI measures differences between male and female achievements in three basic dimensions of human development: health, education and command over economic resources. GDI is the ratio of female HDI to male HDI. To calculate it, the HDI is first calculated separately for females and for males. India ranks 130 in Gender Inequality Index: UN. According to the United Nations' Human Development Report, India is ranked 130 out of 155 countries on the Gender Inequality Index (GII). The gender index takes into account reproductive health, empowerment, and economic activity.

Maternal Health – Concept, definition, and components

Maternal health refers to the health of women during pregnancy, childbirth and the postpartum period. While motherhood is often a positive and fulfilling experience, for too many women - it is associated with suffering, ill-health and even death. Maternal health care is a concept that encompasses family planning, preconception, prenatal, and postnatal care. Goals of pre-conception-care can include providing education, health promotion, screening and interventions for women of reproductive age to reduce risk factors that might affect future pregnancies. Prenatal care is the comprehensive care that women receive and provide for themselves throughout their pregnancy. Women who begin prenatal care early in their pregnancies have better birth outcomes than women who receive little or no care during their pregnancies. Post-natal care issues include recovery from childbirth, concerns about newborn care, nutrition, breast-feeding, and family planning.

Women constitute nearly half (49.5 %) of the State's total population as per census 2011. As such their socio-economic development is a sine qua non for sustainable growth of the economy. Generally, women experience considerable disadvantage and discrimination in the society owing to gender differentiation. The gender bias propels disparities in terms of literacy, access to public health services and social development indicators. The female literacy of Odisha as per 2011 Census was 64% which was at par with the national average. But gender gap in literacy as per 2011 Census was the highest in Nuapada district and lowest in Khordha district.

Infant Mortality in Odisha has made a quantum leap with a 56 points decline by reducing IMR from 96 (SRS 2000) to 40 in 2015-16 (NFHS-4) which is the highest point decline in the country far ahead of the national average decline of 27 points and better than major States like Gujarat (28 points), Rajasthan (38 points), Chhattisgarh (25 points), Jharkhand (26 points), MP (36 points), UP (19 points). This translates into 51,000 more children being saved annually compared to the year, 2000. IMR in rural Odisha was 43 as compared to 21 in urban areas in 2015-16. At the national level, IMR stood at 41 and varied from 46 in rural areas to 29 in urban areas in 2015-16.

Infant Mortality Rate Point decrease: Odisha-56, India--27

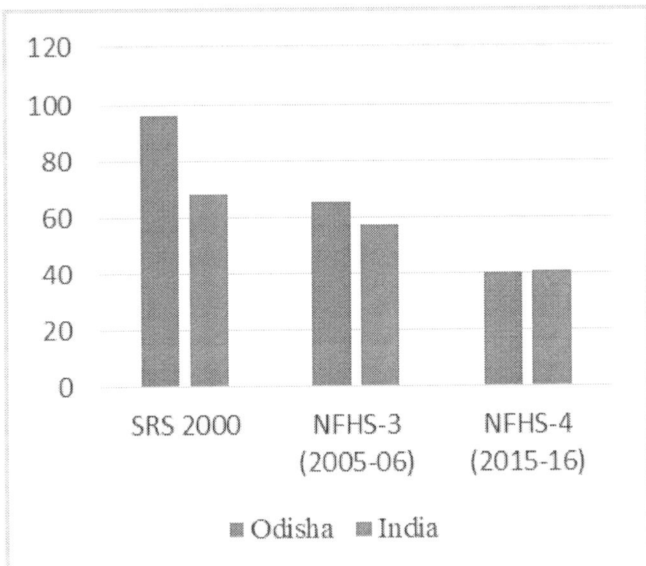

Source: National Family Health Survey

Gender inequality, human rights and its effects on maternal health

Despite the country's growing economy and an ambitious rural health initiative, over 100,000 women die from pregnancy-related causes each year, more than anywhere else in the world. Many more suffer debilitating complications that they endure in silence due to impunity and lack of accountability in the health system. The medical causes of maternal mortality are well known and largely preventable, yet government policies have failed to have an impact.

Promotion of maternal and child health has been one of the most important objectives of the Family Welfare Programme in India. The current Reproductive and Child Health Programme (RCH) was launched in October 1997.In order to improve maternal health at the community level a cadre of community level skilled birth attendants who will attend to pregnant women in the community is being considered.

Review of Literature

Miller (1989), Murthi, Anne and Dreze (1995), Gupta and Bhat (1997), George (1998), Bhat and Zavier(2003), Mishra., Roy and Rutherford (2004), Dyson and Moore (1983), Krishnaji (1987), Siddhanta, Nandy and Agnihotri (2003), Pandey (2003), Hill and Upchurch (1995) and Acharaya & Kumar (2004) explained the extent of gender differences in infant and child mortality in terms of gender differences in health status ,disease incidence, preventive and curative treatment and social status.

In many parts of the world, women receive less attention and health care than men do and particularly girls often receive very less support than boys. As a result of this gender bias, the mortality rates of females often exceed those of males in these countries. This is an important issue because gender discrimination that contributes to poorer health status for girls than for boys is likely to be the main pathway for high female child mortality rates. Such discrimination occurs when a girl receives less attention than would be bestowed upon a son. She is less warmly clad, she is probably not so well fed as a boy would be and when ill, her parents are not likely to make the same strenuous efforts to ensure her recovery.

Sugathan, Mishra and Retherford (2001), Kishor and Parasuraman (1998), Stephenson and Tusi (2002), Bourne & Walker (1991), McNay, Arokiasamy and Cassen (2003), Dyson and Moore (1983) and Rustagi(2004) evaluated the status of women in India with different indicators such as of (i) women‘s work, (ii) education, (iii) health, (iv) survival, (v) safety and (vi) participation in public/private decision-making.

Sudha, Rajan, (1999) George (2002), Rutherford and Roy (2003), Bose (2007), Visaria (2007) examined the causes for eliminating the girl child. It indicates that they are rooted in rituals and perceptions that go back centuries: the fear of having to pay for a girl‘s dowry, the belief that for true salvation, a son should perform the last rites, the conviction that lineage and inheritance run through the male line and that a son will look after his parents in their old age, whereas the daughters will belong to another family. Tied up to all this is - the old perception of seeing only men as the bread earners.

Whatever our stance is on feminist economics, however; we need to be aware of these issues when analysing the effect of gender related issues on development at the macro level. Indeed, some of the newer fields in economics, such as behavioural economics, - take some of these challenges more seriously. Another example of rising awareness of the need to consider changing social norms and culture is a recent book on economic growth by David Weil (2005), which gives considerable emphasis on culture and values.

During the 50 years from 1950 to 2000, mortality in all age groups greatly improved. The infant mortality rate (IMR) was 90% lower in 2000 than in 1950, making infants the age group that saw the greatest changes over time. Men experienced a decline of at least one-third across all age groups. Women's death rates at ages zero to 80 fell by at least 50%, while improvements above age 80 constituted at least 30% of the decline over the 50-year period. These sex specific differences in mortality declines were also reflected in life expectancy. Women's life expectancy increase was almost linear over time. Men, on the other hand, initially experienced a slower life expectancy increase. From the late 1970s onward, male mortality declined faster in relative terms than female mortality (Luy, 2004).

While at the beginning of the period, infant mortality contributed significantly to East-West differences, old age became much more important over time. Until the mid-1970s, the lower IMR and more rapid improvements in this rate in the GDR were responsible for part of the initial advantage of GDR in male life expectancy (Nolte et al. 2000a). The first few years after reunification, the IMR fell in both the East and the West, and the rates converged in 1997 (Nolte et al. 2000-2001).

In a cross-sectional study, under-5 mortality was found to be strongly associated with maternal and infant health programmes. It was also strongly associated with the proportion of births attended by trained persons. To raise the public health spending remains the main challenge in developing countries for improving the quality of maternal and child healthcare. (McGuire JW, 2006).

A study was conducted to describe the association between under-5 mortality andsocio-economic, political, and healthcare factors between rich and poor children. In this study,higher incomes were associated with lower under-5 mortality rates. (Houweling et al, 2005).

Global under-5 mortality has dropped from 11.9 million in 1990 to 7.7 million deaths in 2010.33%. Of these deaths mostly occurred in South Asia and 49.6% in sub-Saharan Africa. Less than 1% deaths occurred in developed countries. This reveals compared to 1990 to 2000, there is accelerated decline in child mortality from 2000 to2010. (Rajaratnam et al, 2010).

In a study from India, under-5 mortality rate declined at a mean rate of 3.7% per year between2001 and 2012. According to this study, 222 districts were lagging behind in the process of achieving Millennium Development Goals. Female mortality rate was higher by 25% in 303 districts. (Ramet al, 2013).

Objective

The main objective of the study is to ascertain the level and pattern of maternal mortality among the selected rural groups in Odisha. More specifically very study tries to-

- Determine the level of maternal mortality among the selected population groups in Rural Odisha.
- Identify the Risk Factors of Maternal mortality, know their operational mechanisms and find out their related risks
- Recommend appropriate intervention modes to prevent and control risk factors in order to reduce maternal & infant mortality.

Research Question

To what extent maternal and child health care policies influence to improve the health status of women in Odisha?

Method of Study

This study is based on both Primary & Secondary data. Data was collected from an empirical study in 2 Gram Panchayats of Cuttack district of Odisha. This study also involves personal interviews and discussions with several Women Leaders, Social Welfare Boards, and prominent members of NGOs etc.

A Brief this light

- Field investigations, empirical surveys, direct interviews with villagers specially women, young mothers, traditional dais, Anganwadi workers, the Auxiliary nurse midwives, doctors and Self Help groups, Panchayat sarpanchas and members.
- Extensive scanning of published material on the subject.
- Scanning of a few previous and current Five Year Plan Provisions to reduce IMR& MMR. Special attention was given to the Midterm reviews not only of the Planning Commission but also of Reports of some Ministries viz: Ministry of Health and Family Welfare, Ministry of Women and Child Development of the Centre and the States; National Rural Health Mission, selected local feedback from Panchayat Raj reviews and a few members of the Panchayats of the concerned States.

In any case, the problem of IMR & MMR is part of the Indian, "Social Complexity". To bring it down in full extent, we need to take vigorous direct and indirect systemic reform steps. It is high time, we took not one but several, "first steps". Some of them have been recommended here as we have to walk a thousand miles to bring down IMR/ MMR in India.

Reduction of maternal and child deaths is one of the major challenges of the health system in Odisha. With several efforts from the State under the RMNCH+A campaign, it has been observed from the SRS reports, that there has been a decline in the State Maternal Mortality Ratio (MMR) and Infant Mortality Rate (IMR) over the years.

(Odisha State strategy for accelerated reduction of Maternal and Infant Mortality -Odisha 2020)

The maternal mortality has been defined by WHO as death of a woman while pregnant or within 42 days of termination of pregnancy, irrespective of the cause of death (and) is intended for countries that wish to identify deaths occurring in pregnancy, child birth upto 6 weeks after the end of pregnancy but where the cause of death cannot be identified precisely. (WHO cited in Royston, Mauldin, 1994).

For women and adolescent girls of reproductive age, the biological functions of pregnancy and childbirth intersect with gender inequalities and poverty to expose women to maternal health risks. A lack of autonomy to make decisions about one's own health care, low levels of education circumscribing the ability to make informed health care decisions, limited control over financial resources, restricted mobility to access health care services and power differentials between health care providers and recipients are all factors which may preclude women from receiving the quality of care essential for ensuring healthy pregnancies and deliveries.

No doubt, the maternal mortality ratio had been declined by 37 per cent between 2000 – 2015, there were an estimated 303,000 maternal deaths worldwide in 2015 due to complications in pregnancy and childbirth. Almost all (99 per cent) occurred in developing regions, with the highest level (546 per 100,000 live births) in sub-Saharan Africa, followed by South Asia (182 per 100,000 live births).

Maternal & New Born Health

S.No	Component	Rate
1	Proportion of women aged 15-49 who received post natal care within 2 days after giving birth (%)	62
2	Antenatal care coverage for at least four visits (%)	51
3	Proportion of births attended by skilled health personnel (%)	81
4	Caesarean section (%)	17
5	Proportion of women 20-24 years old who gave birth before age of 18	22
6	Number of women age 15-49 years with a live birth delivered in a health facility	79
7	Births who had their postnatal check-up within the first two days after birth (%)	24

(Source: Other NS 2016)

Infant mortality is an indicator of the health status not only of infants, but also of the whole population and of their poverty ridden social and economic status in the country. They face excessive vulnerability, as underprivileged, to a hostile environment and suffer malnutrition and serious health problems; all this leads to high rates of infant mortality and morbidity. Infant mortality i.e. deaths under one year of age in a year per 1000 live births, is an important indicator of child health and development.

(Source: The Socio-economic determinants behind Infant Mortality & Maternal Mortality, sponsored by the Planning Commission of India, 2006)

Child Health

Sl No.	Component	% Rate
1	Children under age 5 whose births are registered (%)	72
2	Women aged 20-24 years who were first married on in union by age (%)	27
3	Children aged 5-17 years engaged in Child Labour (%)	12
4	Children aged 1 to 14 years who experienced any violent discipline (psychological aggression and/or physical punishment) in the past month (%)	Not Available
5	Justification of Wife beating (female) (%)	47
6	Justification of Wife beating (male) (%)	42
7	Women aged 15-49 who have undergone female genital mutilation (%)	Not Available

(Source: UNICEF/WHO 2017)

In 2015, the world began working towards a new global development agenda, seeking to achieve, by 2030, new targets set out in the Sustainable Development Goals (SDGs). The proposed SDG target for child mortality aims to end, by 2030, preventable deaths of newborn and children under 5 years of age, with all countries aiming to reduce neonatal mortality to at least as low as 12 deaths per 1,000 live births and under-5 mortality to at least as low as 25 deaths per 1,000 live births.

Child Survival

SL. No	COMPONENT	RATE
1	Under-five mortality rate (U5MR), deaths per 1000 births	39
2	Number of Under-five deaths	989,167
3	Infant Mortality Rate (IMR), deaths per 1000 live births	32
4	Neonatal Mortality rate (NMR), deaths per 1000 live births	24
5	Under-five mortality rate (U5MR), deaths per 1000 live births (male)	39
6	Under-five mortality rate (U5MR), deaths per 1000 live births (female)	40

(Source: IGME 2018)

The world made remarkable progress in child survival in the past few decades, and millions of children have better survival chances than in 1990–95. 1 in 26 children died before reaching age five in 2018, compared to 1 in 11 in 1990. Moreover, progress in reducing child mortality has been accelerated in the 2000–2018 period compared to the 1990s, with the annual rate of reduction in the global under-five mortality rate increasing from 2.0 per cent in 1990–2000 to 3.8 per cent in 2000–2018. Despite the global progress in reducing child mortality over the past few decades, an estimated 5.3 million children under age five died in 2018–roughly half of those deaths occurred in Sub-Saharan Africa.

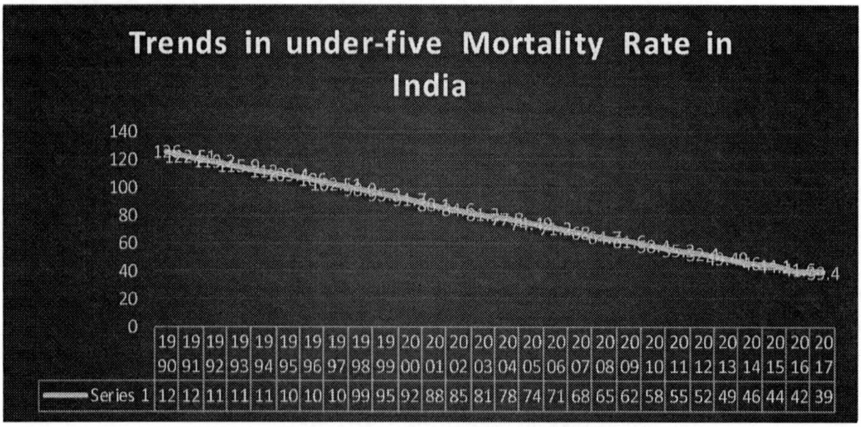

(Source: World Bank Report on Child Mortality)

Existing Interventions for Reducing IMR & MMR In The State

State is continuing its consistent efforts for reducing MMR and IMR through different strategies at community as well as facility level. The major interventions which are implemented currently are as follows:

Village Health and Nutrition Day (VHND)

These days are organized once in a month in every AWC on a fixed day basis (Tuesdays and Fridays) with joint effort of ANM, AWW and ASHA. The VHND provides quality ANC & PNC services for expecting and lactating mothers, counseling on family planning needs, Adolescent Health Day for adolescents, monitoring growth of child development where services like general health checkups (Weight for age, BMI, Anaemia detection etc), provision of essential drugs and micronutrients like IFA, albendazole, calcium are along with counseling and referral of identified high risk cases to appropriate institutions. Line listing and follow up of anaemia cases is also done in this platform.

Comprehensive Abortion Care (CAC)

To provide safe and accessible abortion care services, doctors and paramedics are trained in different methods of MTP up-to CHC DP level.

Review of Maternal Deaths

To reduce the incidence of maternal deaths, each and every cause of maternal death is analyzed and corrective action is taken accordingly at appropriate level.

These reviews are undertaken at various levels so that steps can be taken for avoiding similar deaths in future.

Screening of Syphilis and HIV in Pregnant Women

For early management of syphilis and HIV among pregnant women, all pregnant women are mobilized for a screening test which is presently available up to delivery points. ANMs and ASHAs are mobilizing pregnant women for screening at the facility level and initiation of treatment, if found positive.

ANM Mentoring

This activity aims at improving knowledge & building defined skill sets of HW (F) for providing quality services in VHNDs and Sub centre.

MAMATA Yojana

This scheme was launched in the year 2011 &is operational in the state to provide monetary support to the pregnant & lactating women of 19 years of age which enables them to seek improved nutrition and promote health seeking behavior. The beneficiary will receive a total incentive of Rs. 5000/- in four installments, subject to the fulfillment of specific conditions. Payment is made by e-transfer from the CDPO to the beneficiary account.

Janani Suraksha Yojana (JSY)

JSY is a safe motherhood intervention scheme implemented with the objective of reducing maternal and neonatal mortality by promoting institutional delivery among all pregnant women with provision of cash incentive of Rs. 1400/- and Rs.1000/- for rural and urban area & Rs-500/- for home delivery cases belonging to BPL category respectively. The payment is made to the beneficiaries through Direct Bank Transfer (DBT) method only.

Janani Sishu Surakshya Karykram (JSSK)

JSSK assures cashless services to pregnant women, post-natal women up-to 6 weeks after delivery and sick infants up to one year in government health institutions in both rural and urban areas.

New born Care Corners (NBCC)

A special corner is established in the labor room of all delivery points with a set of equipment for immediate care of the newborn and Healthcare providers conducting deliveries have been trained in Nabjat Sishu Suraksha Karyakram (NSSK) for essential newborn care and resuscitation.

Kangaroo Mother Care (KMC) units

KMC units have been established in all health facilities with SNCUs for ensuring warmth and early initiation of breastfeeding in low birth weight, preterm hypothermia & other sick newborns.

Findings

It is estimated that about 15 percent of all pregnancies can develop complications of which five percent can be life threatening. These complications cannot be predicted but if detected and timely care is provided then maternal deaths and disability can be averted. Further, there are no evidences that antenatal care alone will have considerable impact on reduction of maternal deaths. However, antenatal care is a crucial aspect of birth preparedness and complication readiness where pregnant women can be screened, danger signs can be detected, treated or referred and to ensure that the pregnant woman and her spouse or family members are educated and counselled.

(Source: Odisha State Strategy for Accelerated reduction of Maternal and Infant Mortality, 2020)

The Maternal & Infant Mortality rate has been decreased significantly in India due to the innovative schemes adopted by the Govt. of India through the implementation of family welfare programmes. To improve the accessibility and affordability of quality health care especially for those residing in rural areas particularly the poor and vulnerable women and children, the government has launched National Rural Health Mission in 2005.

(Source: Maternal Mortality in Orissa: An Epidemiological Study, by MY HEART)

Under the study, attempt was made to collect qualitative information pertaining to maternal mortality, infant mortality and challenges faced by the pregnant women, service providers, ASHAs, ANMs, Anganwadi Workers, & other medical staff or government staff etc. Members in the focus group discussions in all the Sub-centre villages were House wives who actively participated in the process of discussion. In all cases SHGs leaders as well as AWW/ ANM moderated the focus group discussion. The findings from each focus group discussion on the present theme have been enumerated below:

Year	Pregnant	Registered	Child Birth	%	Reason				
					Miscarriage	%	Child Death	%	
2017-18	49	48	46	94%	2	4%	1	2%	
2018-19	65	65	62	95%	1	2%	2	3%	

DATA: In the year 2017-18, 49 women were pregnant, 48 were covered under MAMATA Yojana (Govt. Policy) but 1 could not come under the policy due to under age (below 18). There were only 46 child births & rest 3 were child deaths 2 child deaths were due to miscarriage & 1 child death was due to disease.

In the year 2018-19, 65 women were pregnant, all were covered under MAMATA Yojana, but there were only 62 child births & rest 3 were child deaths. 1 was miscarriage & 2 were child deaths due to deficiency of vitamins.

Date on Pregnant Beneficiaries in State of Odisha

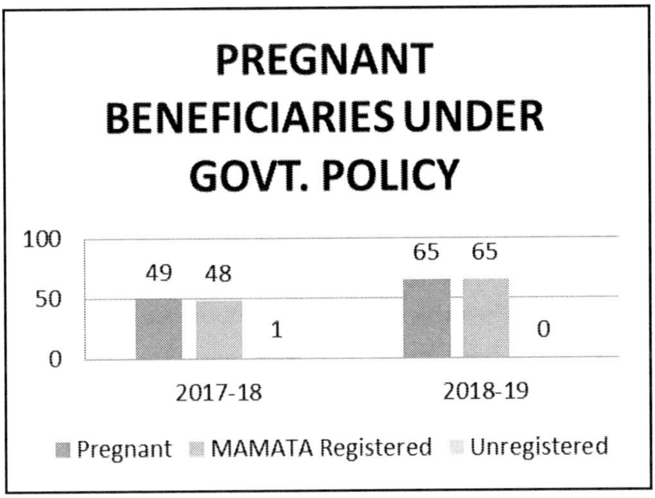

Interventions

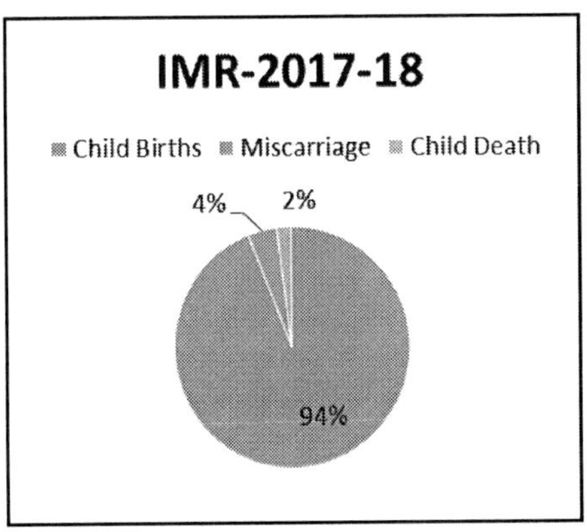

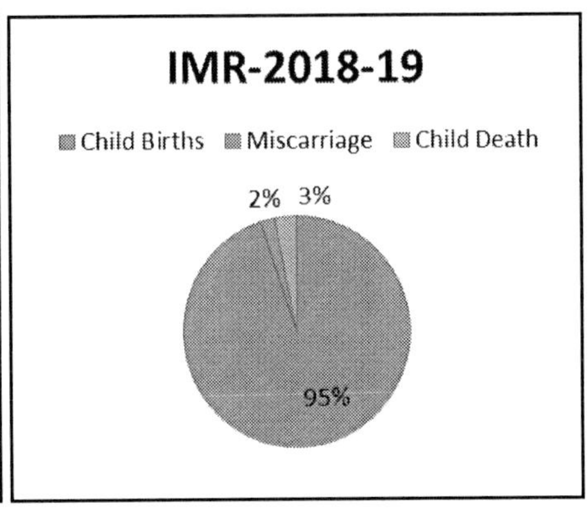

Ante-natal Status of Women

Ante natal care generally implies that either a doctor, ANM or any other trained health personnel provides pregnancy related health care so as to avoid complication during pregnancy and child birth. Proper and effective counseling is also an integral part of ANC such as preventive care, diet during pregnancy, delivery and postnatal care. According to guidelines envisaged in Reproductive and Child Health Programmes, ANC should include at least 3 health check-ups, measurement of weight, height and blood pressure, administration of 2 TT, consumption of IFA tablets and preventive measures for malaria.

Survival Status of Neo Natal

About 58% of newborns were reported to be alive in the post delivery period whereas only 29% of newborn babies could not survive. Many of the health institutions are not properly equipped to provide neo-natal care. On the other hand, there was lack of health education programme on the aspect of effective neo-natal care and a role of service providers towards community.

Concluding Observations

The present empirical study has reflected the gap between policy formulation and policy implementation. The author concludes the paper with an optimistic view point suggesting measures to remove the loopholes in Maternal and Child Health Care Policies in Odisha.

Suggestions: Panacea to availing Challenges

- There should be increased awareness programmes on maternal health and safe motherhood.
- Treatment at right time during pregnancy and sufficient nutritional food intake by PWs should be the major responsibility of elderly members in every family including the husband.
- Services and systems in sub divisional medical centers should improve to ensure quality maternal healthcare.

References

1. Bhatia Jagdish C. and John Cleland, 1995, "Determinants of Maternal Care in a Region of South India". *Health Transition Review*, Vol. 5, No. 2, October 1995, pp. 127-142.
2. Compendium of Research Projects in RCH (Min. of Health Family Welfare, Govt. of India).

3. Five year plans - Three volumes (2002-2007) Vol. I, Vol. II and Vol. III. http:// dx.doi.org/10.1016/S0140-6736(10)61888-0.
4. International Institute for Population Sciences (IIPS) and Macro International, 2008. National Family Health Survey (NFHS-3), India, 2005e06: Orissa. IIPS, Mumbai.
5. International Institute for Population Sciences (IIPS), 2010. District Level Household and Facility Survey (DLHS-3) 2007e08, Orissa, India. IIPS, Mumbai.
6. Journal of Women's Health (An analysis of the Determinants of Maternal Mortality in Sub-Saharan Africa) Oct. 2004.
7. Mapping India's Children - UNICEF in action 2004-2005.
8. Midterm appraisal of the Tenth Five Year Plan.
9. Ministry of Health and Family Welfare Govt. of India - Annual Report 2005-2006.
10. Ministry of Health and Family Welfare Govt. of India - Annual Report 2005-2006.
11. National Rural Health Mission - Mission Document Min. of Health & Family Welfare - Govt. of India.
12. National Rural Health Mission (2005-2012) Mission Document, Govt. of India.
13. Odisha Economic Survey, 2017-18, Planning and Convergence Department, Govt. of Odisha.
14. Rao, Mohan, Krishna D.R., A.K. Shiva Kumar, Mirai Chatterjee, Sundararaman, T., 2011. Human resources for health in India. Lancet, Vol. 377, Issue 9765, February 2011, pp. 587-598.

+++

Chapter Ten

Performance of Janani Suraksha Yojana in Empowered Action Group States and Assam

Prajakta Pradip Shukla[11]

Abstract

Janani Suraksha Yojana (JSY), a maternity assistance scheme, remained instrumental in increasing institutional deliveries, however it failed to reduce maternal mortality substantially and there remain wide unintended consequences of the scheme. The paper identifies the states and districts amongst the EAG+A states where JSY performed poorly and after fifteen years of the implementation of this scheme, these pockets still wait for the magic to happen.

***Keywords:** JSY, Maternal health, institutional delivery, EAG+A states*

Introduction

The Maternal Mortality Ratio(MMR) of India is 130,whereas that for poor performing states varies from 237 for Assam to 165 for Bihar and Jharkhand. In 2005, Janani Suraksha Yojana (JSY) was launched as a flagship programme under National Rural Health Mission(NRHM) to reduce maternal mortality by promoting institutional deliveries with conditional cash transfers to women.JSY is one of the largest cash transfer schemes in the world (Ng, et al. 2014)(Carvalho and Rockicki 2018)(Lim, et al. 2010) which intends to reduce mortality amongst the under served population of the country. There has been three-fold increase in institutional deliveries between 2005-2016(WHO 2018),owing to the launch of JSY scheme. With this background, the paper explores how JSY is performing in health wise poorly performing states now categorized as Empowered Action Group states along with Assam(EAG+A)in maternal health through indicators such as ante-natal care, post-partum care, institutional births, prevalence of anaemia etc. and what are roadblocks in the effective implementation of the scheme.

11. PhD, Research Scholar, Department of Political Science, Jamia Millia Islamia, New Delhi

Janani Suraksha Yojana (JSY) is a safe motherhood intervention scheme under the National Rural Health Mission (NRHM) being implemented with an objective of reducing maternal and neo-natal mortality by promoting institutional delivery among the poor pregnant women. The Yojana, launched in April, 2005 is implemented in all states and UTs with special focus on low performing states. JSY is a 100 % centrally sponsored scheme and it integrates cash assistance with delivery and post-delivery care. The success of the scheme would be determined by the increase in institutional delivery among the poor families. The scheme has identified ASHA, the accredited social health activist as an effective link between the Government and the poor pregnant women in low performing states, namely: the 8 EAG states and Assam and J&K and the remaining North East States. In this paper it is intended to i) describe the health scenario of women in EAG+ A states along with the trend in institutional deliveries coupled with JSY beneficiaries ii)the unintended consequence of JSY on woman's health iii) identify the states and districts performing poorly in the uptake of JSY. The data from NFHS-IV, NITI Aayog and other sources is used to analyse the health scenario.

Empowered Action Group States and Assam (EAG+A)

The former BIMARU states i.e. the most underdeveloped states of India viz. Bihar, Madhya Pradesh, Rajasthan and Uttar Pradesh along with their off shoot states formed in the year 2000-Jharkhand, Chhattisgarh and Uttarakhand consists of EAG states. The EAG states along with Assam (henceforth referred to as EAG+A states) consists of 48% of the total population of India and are hotspots for high fertility and mortality(AHS Bulletin 2010-11).Assam is included along with EAG states as it has the highest maternal mortality ratio (237) in India and has one of the highest out of pocket spending (Rs 3,821) per delivery in public health facility(NFHS-IV 2015-16 Assam).The development in BIMARU states has been sluggish since 1960's and continues to remain unchanged in 2018. Out of these EAG states, Uttar Pradesh, Madhya Pradesh, Jharkhand and Bihar lacked in all the major indicators such as literacy, health, governance etc and were placed at the bottom of Public affairs index created by the Public Affairs Centre, Bangalore. (Mathew, et al. 2018).

Based on National Family Health Survey-IV (NFHS-IV) the JSY related health indicators were identified and analysed to understand the performance of JSY in these states. The seven prime indicators are i)Ante-Natal Care(ANC)

ii) Post-Natal Care-PNC iii) prevalence of anaemia iv)percentage of institutional births v) monetary benefits received under JSY vi) OOPS per delivery and vii) maternal mortality ratio. The research paper identifies the states where the scheme has failed to deliver the basic healthcare services and requires close scrutiny into the failures.

Health Scenario of EAG+A states

NFHS-IV data for EAG+A states based on the seven indicators related to JSY scheme was gathered and compared to understand the performance of the scheme. All the seven indicators indicate the maternal health scenario of women. For instance low institutional deliveries indicate unsafe deliveries and serious threat to life in case of obstetric complication, low ante-natal care indicates that prevalence of anaemia or any such critical condition would not be detected beforehand whereas high out of pocket spending indicate the scheme is falling short on the promises that it made to provide 'free institutional delivery'.

Indicators Depicting Performance of Janani Suraksha Yojana in EAG+A States

Table 1: Compiled by Author; Source NFHS: IV (2015-16)

	Assam	Bihar	Jhar-khand	Madhya Pradesh	Chattis-garh	Uttar Pradesh	Uttara-khand	Odisha	Rajas-than
MMR	237	165	165	173	173	201	201	180	199
4 ANC	46.4	14.4	30.3	35.7	59.1	26.4	30.9	61.9	38.5
PNC	54	42.3	44.4	54.9	63.6	54	54.8	73.2	63.7
JSY	66.1	53.9	41.6	61.1	66.2	48.7	49.4	72.6	56.1
OOPS	3,821	1,784	1,476	1,481	1,480	1,956	2,618	4226	3,052
Institutional-Births	70.6	63.8	61.9	80.8	70.2	67.8	68.6	85.3	84
Anaemic women of all age	46	60.3	65.2	52.5	47	52.4	45.2	51	46.8
Women literacy	71.8	49.6	59	59.4	66.3	61	76.5	67.4	56.5
10 or more years	26.2	22.8	28.7	23.2	26.5	32.9	44.6	26.7	25.1

Assam has highest mortality ratio whereas Bihar and Jharkhand have lowest maternal mortality ratio amongst EAG+A states. However, this ratio is much higher than national MMR of 130.The literacy rate amongst women is worst in Bihar with half of the women being illiterate followed by Rajasthan, on the contrast in Uttarakhand and Assam nearly 3/4th women are literate. Save as otherwise Uttarakhand, nearly 70% of all women in all the EAG+A states failed to pursue 10 or more years of schooling, thus highlighting the poor track record of these states. Women are dropping out at a faster rate from schools than men and in the past decade there has been neither effective intervention to reduce female dropouts nor sufficient efforts have been taken to re-enrol the females in educational institutions. The Kerala model and Sri Lankan examples provide sufficient evidence to prove that the educational status of a woman is positively co-related to woman and infant health.

Except Uttarakhand where the instances of early marriage were limited to nearly 14%,all other EAG+A states have unexpectedly high ratio of early marriage. Bihar(42%), Jharkhand(38%) and Rajasthan(35%) top the list of high instances of early marriages, whereas Assam (30%) follows the league despite of 70% female literacy in the state. Inadequate knowledge of sexual and reproductive health, inaccessibility to counselling services and social pressure to consummate marriage early leaves female with limited choices. There is sufficient evidence proving that educated women tend to be well aware of their own health, nutrition, hygiene as well as their child's health at the same time.

Do Higher Institutional Deliveries Result in Low Maternal Mortality?

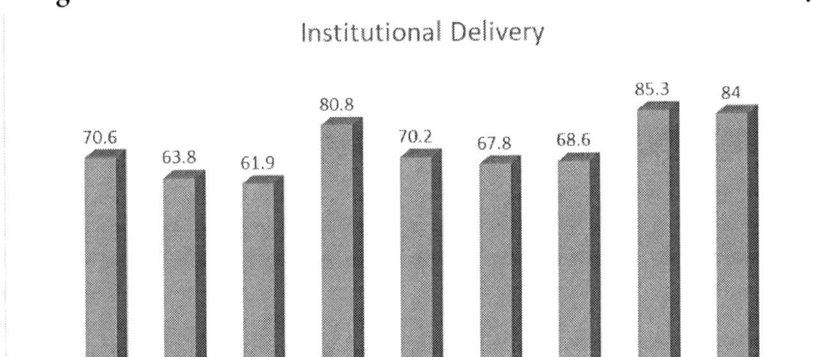

Figure 1: Trend of Institutional Deliveries in EAG+A states; Source: NFHS IV.

Previous surveys such as - District Level Household Survey(2007-08), National Family Health Survey-III (2005-06), NFHS-IV(2015-16) and

Coverage Evaluation Survey(2009) conducted by UNICEF have time and again focused on the substantial gains in institutional deliveries (upto 72%) and more post introduction of JSY, however nearly 2/5th of women from Bihar and Jharkhand are still unable to opt for institutional deliveries followed by nearly 1/3rd of Uttar Pradesh and Uttarakhand women who face similar fate.

Odisha, Rajasthan and MP witnessed the highest number of childbirths in institutions, yet these states have one of the highest MMR in India and fares average among the EAG+A states. This is in line with previous research conducted by Marie Ng et al(2014)(Randive, Diwan and De Costa, India's conditional cash transfer programme (the JSY) to promote institutional birth : Is there an association between institutional birth proportion and maternal mortality? 2013)which claims that higher institutional deliveries may not necessarily result into reduced mortality as the quality of healthcare, availability of trained obstetricians, surgeons, anaesthetists and nurses affect the overall maternal survival rate.

The undernourished -anaemic women bear greater risk of complications than others. Thus, if a woman fails to receive timely ante-natal care, the complications may be never detected till the eleventh hour endangering the life of a woman and her unborn child and enhancing the chances of obstetric complications(Sageer, et al. 2019)(WHO 2011)(Campbell and Graham 2006).

Did the Scheme Reach the Last Mile?

The bottom-most districts in every EAG+A states barring Uttarakhand reflected that in each state, one out two children were born outside the health institutions. Jharkhand Latehar, Pakur, Simdega, Sahebgunj and Paschimi Singh bum districts recorded nearly less than 50% institutional deliveries(NFHS: IV Jharkhand 2015-16) whereas in Bihar the bottom place of least deliveries rested with Madhubani, Darbhanga, Purbi Champaran, Kishanganj and Sitamarhi respectively(NFHS: IV Bihar 2015-16).Uttar Pradesh, the largest populated state in India on an average had 68% institutional deliveries with lowest institutional deliveries in Shrawasti, Siddharth Nagar, Bahraich and Balrampur. In contrast, in Uttarakhand the lowest rate of institutional deliveries was found in two districts i.e. Bagheshwar and Chamoli,yet both the districts had 56% and 53% institutional deliveries respectively(NFHS: IV Uttarakhand 2015-16). Dakshin Bastar (58%), Dantewada (58%) and Kabir Dham (45%) had least institutional deliveries in Chattisgarh(NFHS: IV Chattisgarh 2015-

16). Rajasthan outperformed all other states in the group with only Jaisalmer having least institutional deliveries at 50% in the state with Baran and Jhunjhunu recording 97% institutional births(NFHS IV: Rajasthan 2015-16). In Odisha none of the districts recorded institutional births below 50%(NFHS: IV 2015-16) whereas Barwani, Alirajpur and Singrauli in Madhya Pradesh recorded lowest deliveries amongst 51 districts of Madhya Pradesh(NFHS: IV Madhya Pradesh 2015-16).

On the other end of the spectrum there has been mixed opinion on the utilization of the scheme by the poorest of the poor. The general argument has been- since the overall rate of institutional deliveries increased it also resulted in raised institutional deliveries for SC,ST and other vulnerable women(UNFPA 2009).On the contrary research proves that owing to socio-economic barriers most vulnerable women still deliver outside the institution (Dongre and Kapur 2013)(Lingam and Yelamanchili 2011)(Sidney, et al. 2012).

Lacunae in the Scheme

The scheme used bottom up approach and without understanding the accessibility, affordability, acceptance and setting minimum quality level according to the district and the people, the scheme was launched with the presumption that for the sake of money, women will come to health care centres. The low institutional deliveries in certain pockets of every state challenges the assumption. Second the complications in claiming monetary benefits doubled with poor quality of care, neglect, undignified and rude behaviour of service providers and most importantly shortage of drugs, necessary health goods and services coupled with lack of transport missed the crucial opportunity of improving overall maternal health and healthcare seeking behaviour of women especially vulnerable women.

The poor rely more on public healthcare facilities as it is affordable and highly subsidized, however the absence of specialists, doctors, diagnostic services force the poor to forego the treatment or opt for catastrophically expensive private healthcare(Shahrawat and Rao 2012)(Garg and Karan 2009)(A. Singh 2019).The research conducted by Deshpande, 2011; Sidney, Diwan, El-Khatib, & De Costa, 2012; Dongre & Kapur, 2013; Randive, 2016 found that the poor and marginalized women for whom the JSY scheme intended were still unable to seek healthcare services owing to high OOPS and inaccessibility as the major factor.

Infrastructure facilities in EAG+A states

A Community Health Centre(CHC) acts as a referral unit to four Primary Health Centres (PHC) and consists of specialists such as Anaesthetists, Surgeons, Paediatricians, Gyanecologists etc serving the 80,000-120,000 population(MoHFW 2015).Ideally a CHC is expected to have atleast four specialists, yet the sanctioned positions in all the EAG states are lower than the required positions.

Missing Doctors in Community Health Centres(CHCs)

Table 2: Trend of vacant positions of health specialists against the sanctioned positions in EAG+A states. Source: Rural

Total Specialists at CHC's			
State	**Sanctioned**	**Vacant**	**% of Vacant positions**
Assam	NA	NA	NA
Bihar	NA	NA	NA
Jharkhand	131	3	2.29%
Madhya Pradesh	897	634	70.68%
Chattisgarh	628	550	87.58%
Uttar Pradesh	2099	1615	76.94%
Uttarakhand	197	148	75.13%
Odisha	908	552	60.79%
Rajasthan	1566	1040	66.41%

Health Statistics (2014-15) MoHFW

Chattisgarh, Uttar Pradesh and Uttarakhand record the highest number of vacant positions for specialists in CHC; nearly 3 out of 4 specialist seats are vacant. For other EAG states the vacancy of specialists is as high as 60-70%.This is bound to overburden the existing specialists, increases waiting hours forcing patients to seek treatment elsewhere. Jharkhand reported the lowest vacant seats at 2%,however looking closely into the picture, the sanctioned posts(131) for Jharkhand is much lower than the required CHC specialists (i.e. 752); nearly 600 positions were never sanctioned (MoHFW, Rural Health Statistics 2014-15).

Missing Doctors in Primary Health Centres (PHCs)

Table 3: Vacant positions of Doctors at CHCs; Bihar and Jharkhand has surplus doctors at PHC level. Source: Rural Health

Doctors at PHC's			
State Name	**Sanctioned**	**Vacant**	**% of Vacant positions**
Assam	NA	NA	NA
Bihar#	2078	Surplus	13.76%
Jharkhand#	327	Surplus	21.32%
Madhya Pradesh	1658	659	39.75%
Chattisgarh	752	384	51.06%
Uttar Pradesh	4509	2300	51.01%
Uttarakhand	325	165	50.77%
Odisha	1312	304	23.17%
Rajasthan	2807	395	14.07%

Statistics (2014-15) MoHFW

PHC is the first referral unit at the periphery serving population of 20,000-30,000(MoHFW 2015).Again,the trend of vacant positions at PHCs is repeated in the states of Chattisgarh, Uttar-Pradesh and Uttarakhand where half of the total sanctioned posts are lying vacant. On the other side of the spectrum, it is seen that Bihar and Jharkhand have surplus doctors at PHC, yet it has neither resulted into favourable health conditions of the people nor it has improved the healthcare seeking behaviour of the people.

Discussion

As aptly argued by Kanchan Mathur(Mathur 2008), reproductive and child health programmes(whose extension is JSY) are curative as they fail to address the root-cause of early marriage and pregnancies in adolescence.In the EAG+A states, substantial number of females are still getting married at an early age, thus risking their health and their lives into early pregnancies, morbidities and in some instance mortality.

Marriage at Early Age and Low Body Mass Index amongst Women

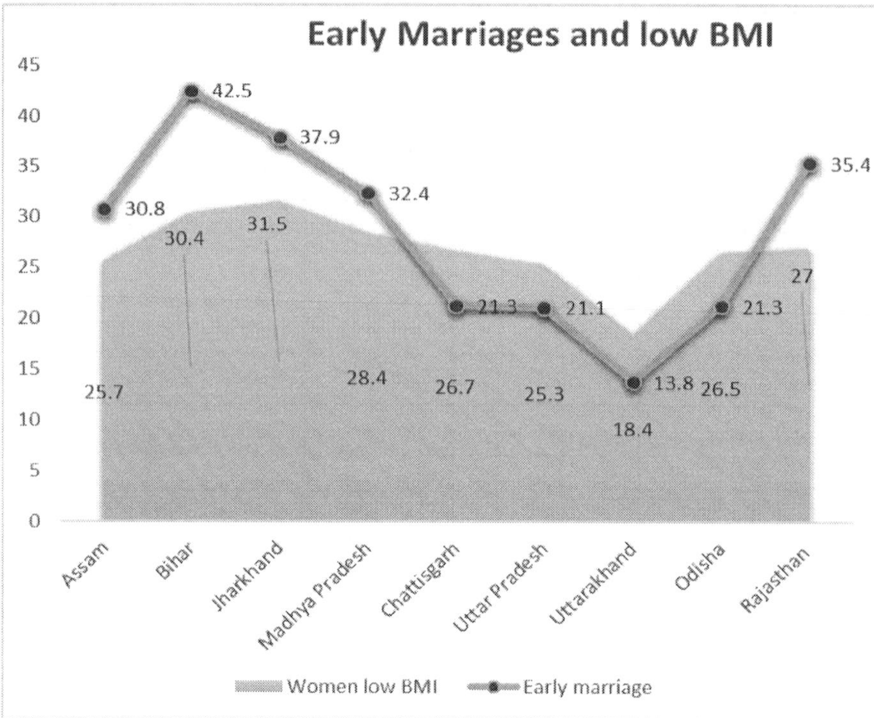

Figure 2: Trend of undernutrition compared to early marriage, Bihar, Jharkhand and Rajasthan reveals high instances of both the indicators-early marriage and low BMI; Source NFHS IV (2015-16)

As reflected in NFHS-IV data Bihar(42.5%),Jharkhand (37.9%) and Rajasthan(35.4%) has highest instances of early marriages. These states have also shown highest instances of women being undernourished, having body mass index lower than normal i.e. below 18.5. Early marriage along with low BMI coupled with pregnancy is nothing short of a critical situation for a woman, who is most likely to be also anaemic. In such situations where most of the damage is already done, the meagre amount of Rs 1400/1000 hardly could be useful in saving lives leave alone improvement in their health.

The JSY scheme therefore introduced compulsory four ante-natal care visits of a woman, delivery in health institution followed by post-natal care within 48hours either by a doctor, nurse, ANM, midwife or any other health personnel. Yet again, Bihar and Uttar Pradesh display disappointing numbers of recipients who received atleast 4 ANC and PNC within 48 hours of delivery. Jharkhand follows the trail of Bihar and UP in terms of low institutional deliveries and low post-natal care.

Maternal Health and JSY Components

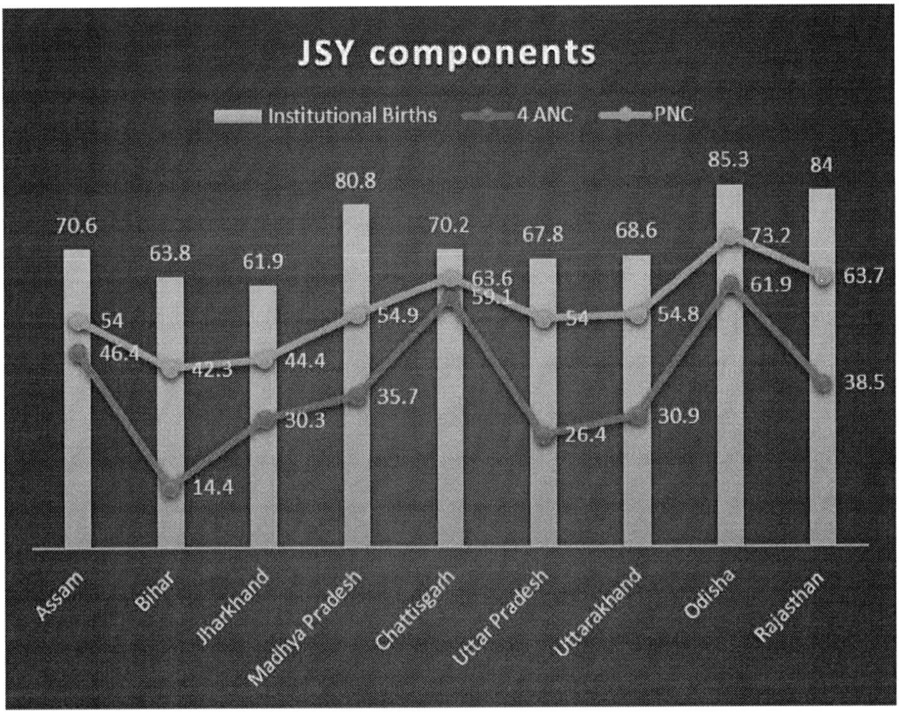

Figure 3: Trend of Institutional Births, Ante-natal care and Post-partum care; Source NFHS IV (2015-16)

In consistency with other indicators Bihar, Jharkhand and Uttar Pradesh have one of the lowest rates of institutional births as well as ANC and PNC. Earlier research sufficiently highlights the financial and opportunity cost that woman incur in availing these facilities, and when women reach these facilities they are asked for informal payments, the quality of treatment being sub-standard and the long waiting hours further worsen the situation(Kumar and Singh 2016).

Out of Pocket Spending

Various government figures have stated that post introduction of JSY institutional deliveries have increased three to four times in comparison to earlier rate of institutional deliveries. The same is true in the context of out of pocket spendings (OOPS) that women incur in health facilities. In Odisha women incurred three times the JSY benefit amount as OOPS followed by Assam and Rajasthan where women on an average spent more than twice the JSY amount. The scheme is publicized as a "free scheme" with comprehensive package of services, yet women were forced to pay for medicines, transportation, informal payments etc. Goli et al.(Goli, et al. 2016) found this maternity related expenditure ten times higher than the entitlement amount. Singh etal.(Singh, Kumar and Verma 2016) estimates these expenses to be as high as nine times(i.e. Rs 14,777 and above) if women were to seek maternity care in private hospitals when compared to OOPS in public facilities. Singh et.al further argues that the heavy maternity expenditure coupled with any additional burden has potential to push nearly 46.6% of BPL women further deep into the vicious circle of poverty.

Growing burden of sterilization on Women

Table 3: Trend revealing sharp decline of male sterilization in comparison to female sterilization, Source: NFHS IV (2015-16)

	Female Sterilization		**Male Sterilization**	
States	**2005-06**	**2015-16**	**2005-06**	**2015-16**
Assam	13	9.5	0.2	0.1
Bihar	23.8	20.7	0.6	0
Jharkhand	23.4	31.1	0.4	0.2
Madhya Pradesh	44.3	42.2	1.3	0.5
Chattisgarh	40.7	46.2	1.8	0.7
Uttar Pradesh	17.3	17.3	0.2	0.1
Uttarakhand	32.2	27.4	1.8	0.7
Odisha	33.1	28.2	1	0.2
Rajasthan	34.2	40.7	0.8	0.2

The sterilization of males in all the states have declined drastically. In Odisha the decline in male sterilization was five times, whereas in Rajasthan and Chattisgarh it reduced to nearly three times and in Bihar none of the males were sterilized. In rest of the states the decline in male sterilization was a whopping 50%. In comparison to female sterilization (tubectomy), male sterilizations are less complicated, bear low risk and 3-4 times cheaper (Smith, Taylor and Smith 1985).It is the fear of side effects such as low sex-drive, method failure and stigma associated with vasectomies along with low awareness and misleading information amongst men and women that push the burden of sterilization on women(Rajagopal, et al. 2000)(Scott, Alam and Raman 2011).The figures highlight the declining trend indicating that no intervention took place in promoting male sterilization whereas tubectomies (female sterilization) increased in three states viz. Rajasthan, Chattisgarh and Jharkhand. Post- independence, vasectomy was one of the popular modes of family planning until the excesses committed during national emergency (1975-1977) resulted in the political doom of the ruling party(Brown, 1984)(Green, 2018)(Gupte, 2017). Thus, the burden of family planning was pushed on the shoulders of women in the form of tubectomies and abortions. The irony is the JSY scheme too seeks institutional deliveries as an opportunity to pressurize women into sterilization or as pushed by the scheme post-partum intra-uterine contraceptive device(PPIUCD).

Steep rise in C-section deliveries

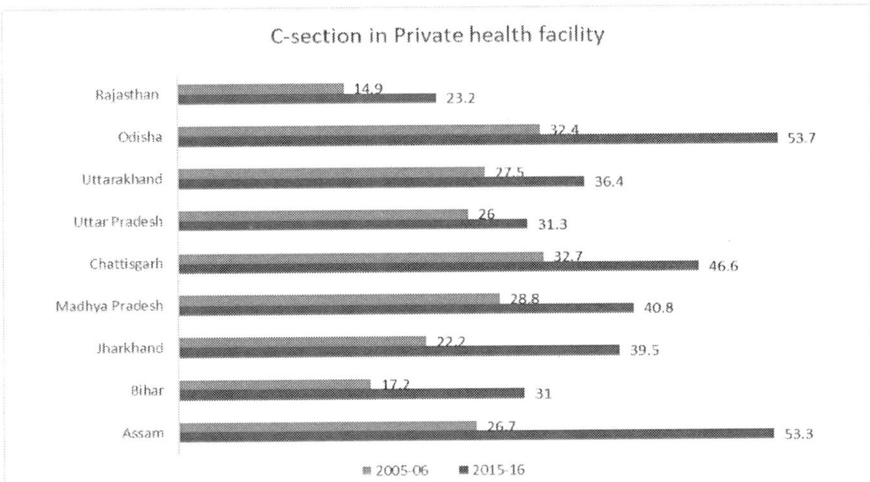

Figure 4: Rise in Caesarean deliveries in private health facility. Source: NFHS: IV (2015-16)

The figure depicts the trend of caesarean deliveries in private facilities which have increased two-fold in Assam and Jharkhand, whereas the other states witnessed the steep rise in C-section deliveries. As compared to normal delivery-section deliveries are complicated and also source of higher financial incomes for the health staff especially in private facilities. Peel et al. (2018) are of the view that commercial interests contribute indirectly to high caesarean rates. Perceptions amongst providers and consumers of caesarean section as the 'safe' option have re-defined caesareans as the new 'normal', even for low-risk deliveries. The continuous study in this sector by WHO since 1985 limits the ideal rate of CS deliveries between 10-15% as unnecessary caesareans are bound to pose risks of severe health complications to woman and infant in short term as well as in long term. [WHO statement on caesarean section rates 2015].

JSY policy covers the cost of C-section deliveries and also provides honorarium for the surgeon if called from outside the institution. However, the usual norm has been to refer the woman with complications to the higher-level facility or to the private health facility. There is no concrete data on trend of referrals from public health facility to private or so on. However, it is often perceived that private health providers intentionally choose to operate women, for higher financial gains. It is also true, that there is no methodology to determine whether the said delivery required C-section or not, yet the alarming rise in surgical deliveries points out that all is 'not well'. Singh et al.(2018) comments that referral to a private institution is also a source of commission for government doctors and in some states there seems a bias towards surgical procedures as caesarean deliveries are covered under Rashtriya Swasthya Bima Yojana (RSBY-a public-funded national health insurance scheme) indicating monetary benefit for the private healthcare provider (Nandi et al 2016; Selvaraj and Karan 2012).

Fund Allocations for JSY scheme

Assam(32% i.e. from104 crores to 71 crores),Jharkhand(9% i.e. from 94 crores to 76 crores), Odisha(9% decline from 102 crores to 92 crores) witnessed consistent reduction in JSY fund allocations in previous three years between 2015-16 to 2018(MoHFW 2018).Out of the EAG states, Uttarakhand had the highest decline of funds(20% i.e. form 21crores to 16 crores)(MoHFW 2018). Assam had highest MMR in 2015-16 followed by Uttarakhand; Assam along with Odisha had highest out of pocket spending in public health institutions. Jharkhand, one of the poorest states of India has the lowest rate of institutional delivery amongst all other Indian states(62%) and has the highest number of anaemic women in India(65%).The heavy cut down in spending on the provisions of the scheme signifies the unwillingness of the government in improving maternal health scenario particularly in these four states. The reduction in funds imply that lesser number of beneficiaries could avail benefits and therefore the boom created by institutional births might not sustain longer,as money was seen as the motivator for institutional deliveries. The other EAG+ A states have seen marginal increase in existing JSY funds between 2015-16 and 2018. In the absence of funds coupled with shortage of infrastructure and in sufficient health staff, the maternal health of women continue to suffer.

Conclusion

The idea of implementing a single uniform policy in all states differs from state to state irrespective of the fact that the capacity of state actors, health infrastructure and political commitment. The overall health status, nutrition intake and healthcare seeking behaviour of a woman differs based on the socio-economic status, place of residence, cultural ethos as well as it differs due to accessibility of health institutions. Therefore, a uniform policy in all states to curb the menace of maternal mortality may not be effective. For instance, in a state such as Assam and Odisha the accessibility to the health facility is the major barrier, whereas in states such as Bihar, Jharkhand and Uttar Pradesh the ante-natal and post-natal care has been one of the lowest; indicating the low use of health facilities and JSY policy by eligible women. Nonetheless, there is insufficient data on social awareness of the scheme. It could be further probed whether people were aware of the components of the scheme, and if so was it translating into behaviour change? The third important factor is the accessibility of health facilities. The referral transport plays a major role followed by identification of health points during obstetric complications and emergency. Absence of health service providers, shortage or unavailability of necessary medicines and surgical equipments along with shortfall in blood units is bound to lead into inconvenience as well as high OOPS and the nonetheless increased risk to the life of a woman and her infant. Is it too much to expect from public healthcare facility?

The overall rate of institutional deliveries has increased which also led to increase in deliveries of marginalized women such as women from SC,ST,OBC and poor households,yet the women left out or unable to avail scheme benefits are largely the marginalized women. JSY, one of the largest conditional cash transfer schemes in the world cannot afford to let women suffer due to inaccessibility of the scheme. The socio-cultural and other barriers if planned properly could be tackled in appropriate manner. For instance, the eligible women under JSY refrained from visiting health centres where female medical officer was unavailable. This has been a long-lasting cultural practice where a woman is conditioned to minimize the interactions and contact with the opposite gender, even in emergency situations such as seeking healthcare. The AYUSH doctors often lacked skills in conducting deliveries especially surgical deliveries. Thus, this awkward mismatch pushed women to seek care elsewhere. Apart from this one we also need to look into the divergence in the scheme even at micro levels such as PHC and CHC levels. Why do JSY has poor indicators in some pockets for instance in Tea Estates of Assam or in Purnea, Bihar? Diving deep into the root-cause of the issue, one would notice that beyond numbers there is requirement of participation of people in decision making who can rightly demand and put forward their needs, which is not the possibility at the top.

Can we have robust infrastructure and health facilities in rural and adversely connected locations too? Often the argument given is that these facilities would not be able to generate enough demand and revenues and secondly the doctors would not serve in such 'punishment' postings. Isn't saving the life of a woman more important than any profits that public sector would like to earn? This is a question that remains to be answered by policy makers. Can't we aspire to not only reduce MMR down to zero, saving every single life of a mother and her child, but also to improve their overall health. It can be done by focusing on the weak links in the chain i.e. the underperforming states followed by all the underperforming districts and further moving to the CHC, PHC and sub-centres. Every district requires attention and should plan in a distinct way, which could be carved out with the democratic participation of all the stakeholders.

Bibliography

1. Brown, Carolyn Henning. 1984. "The forced sterilization program under the Indian emergency: Results in one settlement." *Human Organization* 43 (1): 49-54. https://www.jstor.org/stable/44125646.
2. Campbell, Oona M R, and Wendy J Graham. 2006. "Strategies for reducing maternal mortality: Getting on with what works." *Lancet* 388: 1284-99. doi:10.1016/S0140-6736(06)69381-1.
3. Carvalho, Natalie, and Slawa Rockicki. 2018. "The impact of India's Janani Suraksha Yojana conditional cash transfer programme: A replication study." *The journal of development studies* 989-1006. doi:doi.org/10.1080/00220388.2018.1506578.
4. Deshpande, R.V. 2011. "Is Janani Suraksha Yojana (JSY) contributing to the reduction of maternal and infant mortality? An insight from Karnataka." *The Journal of Family Welfare* 57 (1): 1-9.
5. Dongre, Ambrish, and Awani Kapur. 2013. "How is Janani Suraksha Yojana Performing in Backward Districts of India?" *Economic and Political Weekly* 53-59.
6. Garg, Charu C, and Anup K Karan. 2009. "Reducing out of pocket expenditures to reduce poverty: A disaggregated analysis at rural-urban and state level India." *Health Policy and Planning* 24 (2): 116-128.

7. Goli, Srinivas, Moradhvaj, Anu Rammohan, Shruti, and Jalandhar Pradhan. 2016. "High spending on maternity care in India: What are the factors explaining It?" *Plos one* 11 (6). doi:https://doi.org/10.1371/journal.pone.0156437.
8. Green, Hannah Harris. 2018. "Why is the burden of sterilisation on women in India? The answer lies in the Emergency era." *Scroll.in*, October 10. https://scroll.in/article/896925/why-is-the-burden-of-sterilisation-on-women-in-india-the-answer-lies-in-the-emergency-era.
9. Gupte, Prajakta R. 2017. "India:The emergency and the politics of mass sterilization." *Education about Asia* 22 (3): 40-44.
10. IIPS, and ICF. 2018. *National Family Health Survey (NFHS-4) 2015-16 Assam.* Mumbai: IIPS.
11. IIPS, and ICF. 2017. *NFHS IV: Rajasthan 2015-16.* Mumbai: IIPS. http://rchiips.org/nfhs/NFHS-4Reports/Rajasthan.pdf.
12. IIPS, and ICF. 2017. *NFHS: IV 2015-16.* Mumbai: IIPS. http://rchiips.org/NFHS/NFHS-4Reports/Odisha.pdf.
13. IIPS, and ICF. 2017. *NFHS: IV Bihar 2015-16.* Mumbai: IIPS. http://rchiips.org/NFHS/NFHS-4Reports/Bihar.pdf.
14. IIPS, and ICF. 2017. *NFHS: IV Chattisgarh 2015-16.* Mumbai: IIPS. http://rchiips.org/nfhs/NFHS-4Reports/Chhattisgarh.pdf.In.
15. IIPS, and ICF. 2017. *NFHS: IV Jharkhand 2015-16.* Mumbai: IIPS. rchiips.org/NFHS/NFHS-4Reports/Jharkhand.pdf.
16. IIPS, and ICF. n.d. *NFHS: IV Madhya Pradesh 2015-16.* Mumbai: IIPS. rchiips.org/NFHS/NFHS-4Reports/MadhyaPradesh.pdf.
17. IIPS, and ICF. 2018. *NFHS: IV Uttarakhand 2015-16.* Mumbai: IIPS. http://rchiips.org/nfhs/NFHS-4Reports/Uttarakhand.pdf.
18. Jat, T.R, N Ng, and M.S Sebastian. 2011. "Factors affecting the use of Maternal Health Services in Madhya Pradesh state of India:A multilevel analysis." *International Journal for Equity in Health* 10(1) (59). http://umu.diva-portal.org/smash/record.jsf?pid=diva2%3A489566&dswid=7705.
19. Kumar, Virendra, and Pushpenrdra Singh. 2016. "Access to healthcare among the Empowered Action Group (EAG) states of India: Current status and impeding factors." *The national medical journal of India* 29 (5): 267-273. http://www.nmji.in/article.asp?issn=0970-258X;year=2016;volume=29;issue=5;spage=267;epage=273;aulast=Kumar.
20. Lim, S.S, L Dandona, J.A.,James,S.L Hoisington, M.C Hogan, and E Gakidou. 2010. "India's Janani Suraksha Yojana, a conditional cash transfer programme to increase births in health facilities: An impact evaluation." *Lancet* 375 (9730): 2009-23. doi:doi.org/10.1016/S0140-6736(10)60744-1.
21. Lingam , Lakshmi, and Vaiedhi Yelamanchili. 2011. "Reproductive Rights and Exclusionary Wrongs: Maternity Benefits." *Economic and Political Weekly* 46 (43).
22. Mathew, C.K, Lalita Pulavarti, Udita Dutta, Udita Nikam, Devika Kannan, Sukriti Bharadwaj, Stuti Goswami, Nikhila Vijay , and Mahadevan Nambiar. 2018. *Public affairs index: Governance in the states of India.* Banglore: Public Affairs Centre. pai.pacindia.org/#/2018/public-affairs-index.
23. Mathur, Kanchan. 2008. "Gender hierarchies and inequalities:Taking stock of women's sexual and reproductive health." *Economic and Political Weekly* 43 (49): 54-61.

24. MoHFW. 2009. *Coverage Evaluation Survey.* New Delhi: HMIS,MoHFW. https://nrhm-mis.nic.in/SitePages/Pub_CoverageEvaluation.aspx#.

25. MoHFW. 2007-08. *District level household and facility survey factsheet India.* Mumbai: IIPS.

26. MoHFW. 2005-06. *National Family Health Survey-III.* Mumbai: IIPS. http://rchiips.org/NFHS/pdf/India.pdf.

27. MoHFW. 2015-16. *NFHS-IV.* Mumbai: IIPS. http://rchiips.org/nfhs/pdf/NFHS4/India.pdf.

28. —. 2018. "Rajya Sabha starred question no. 62." *Rajya Sabha.* July 24. https://pqars.nic.in/annex/246/As62.pdf.

29. MoHFW. 2015. *Rural Health Statistics 2014-15.* MoHFW. https://wcd.nic.in/sites/default/files/RHS_1.pdf.

30. Ng, Marie, Archana Misra, Vishal Diwan, Manohar Agnani, ALison Levin-Rector, and Ayesha De Costa. 2014. "An asseement of the impact of the JSY cash transfer program on maternal mortality reduction in Madhya Pradesh,India." *Global Health Action* 1-10.

31. Peel, Alison, Abhishek Bhartia, Neil Spicer, and Meenakshi Gautam. 2018. "If I do 10–15 normal deliveries in a month I hardly ever sleep at home.' A qualitative study of health providers' reasons for high rates of caesarean deliveries in private sector maternity care in Delhi, India." *BMC Pregnancy and Childbirth* 18 (470). doi:10.1186/s12884-018-2095-4.

32. Rajagopal, S, Sandhya Barge, Nayan Kumar, Nupur Mukherjee, Wajahat Khan, Rashid Pervez, and Vasant Uttekar. 2000. *Attitudes towards male and female sterilization in Uttar Pradesh.* Vadodara: Centre for Operations Research and Training (CORT).

33. Randive, Bharat. 2016. *Study of the conditional cash transfer programme Janani Suraksha Yojana for the promotion of institutional births:Studies from selected Indian states.* Umea: Umea University.Sweden.

34. Randive, Bharat, Vishal Diwan, and Ayesha De Costa. 2013. "India's conditional cash transfer programme (the JSY) to promote institutional birth : Is there an association between institutional birth proportion and maternal mortality?" *Plos One.* doi:https://doi.org/10.1371/journal.pone.0067452.

35. Registrar General. 2011. "Annual Health Survey (AHS) in 8 EAG States and Assam – Release of AHS Bulletin: 2010-11." *A MoHFW Website.* August 10. http://censusindia.gov.in/vital_statistics/AHSBulletins/files/AHSpr.pdf.

36. Sageer, Rabiatu, Eugene Kongnyuy, Wasilu Olaken Adembimpe, Omolaso Omosehin, Elijah Ayowole Ogunsola, and Bola Sanni. 2019. "Causes and contributory factors of maternal mortality: Evidence from maternal and perinatal death serveillance and response in Ogun state,Southwest Nigeria." *BMC Pregnancy Childbirth* 19 (63).

37. Scott, B., D Alam, and S Raman. 2011. *Factors affecting acceptance of vasectomy in Uttar Pradesh: Insights from community-based,participatory qualitative research.* The RESPOND Project Study Series:03, New York: The RESPOND Project EngenderHealth.

38. Shahrawat, Renu, and Krishna D Rao. 2012. "Insured yet vulnerable : Out of pocket payments and India's poor." *Health Policy and Planning* 27 (3): 213-221.

39. Sidney, Kristi, Vishal Diwan, Ziad El-Khatib, and Ayesha De Costa. 2012. "India's JSY cash transfer program for maternal health: WHo particpates and who doesn't- a report from Ujjain district." *Reproductive Health* 9 (2).

40. Singh, Aditya. 2019. "Shortage and inequalities in the distribution of specialists across community health centres in Uttar Pradesh,2002-2012." *BMC Health Services Research* 19 (331).
41. Singh, Prashant Kumar, Rajesh Kumar Rai, Shalini Singh, and Lucky Singh. 2018. "Rising caesarean births a growing concerns." *Economic Political Weekly* 53 (26-27). https://www.epw.in/journal/2018/26-27/commentary/rising-caesarean-births.html.
42. Singh, Pushpendra, Virendra Kumar, and Sonia Verma. 2016. "How affordable is childbearing in India? An evaluation of maternal healthcare expenditures." *Newborn and infant nursing reviews* 16 (4): 175-183. doi:doi.org/10.1053/j.nainr.2016.09.012.
43. Smith, G L, G P Taylor, and K F Smith. 1985. "Comparative risks and costs of male and female sterilization." *American Journal of Public Health* 75 (4): 370-374. doi:10.2105/ajph.75.4.370.
44. UNFPA. 2009: *Concurrent Assessment of Janani Suraksha Yojana in Selected States Bihar, Madhya Pradesh, Orissa,.* New Delhi: UNFPA. https://india.unfpa.org/sites/default/files/pub-pdf/JSYConcurrentAssessment.pdf.
45. WHO. 2018. "India has achieved groundbreaking success in reducing maternal mortality." South East Asia, WHO. https://www.who.int/southeastasia/news/detail/10-06-2018-india-has-achieved-groundbreaking-success-in-reducing-maternal-mortality.
46. WHO. 2011. *WHO guidelines on preventing early pregnancy and poor reporductive health outcomes among adolscents in developing countries.* Geneva: WHO. who.int/immunization/hpv/target/preventing_early_pregnancy_and_poor_reproductive_outcomes_who_2006.pdf.
47. WHO. 2015. *WHO statement on caesarean section rates.* Geneva: Department of Reproductive Health and Research ,WHO. https://apps.who.int/iris/bitstream/handle/10665/161442/WHO_RHR_15.02_eng. pdf; jsessionid= 6E9CA6D70AFDB4E 31653572890803963?sequence=1.

+++

Chapter Eleven

Community in Public Policy: A Reflection On North-east India

Ningthoujam Irina[12]*

Abstract

Communitarian perspective came as an ideology in the 1980s and 1990s that seeks to lessen the focus on individual rights and increase the focus on community responsibilities. Along with this idea, came the new form of governance linking governance structures and processes to civil society organizations, mass organizations, community organisations etc. Among all complementary work to the state, an important role as 'mediating institution' is now given to community and its local community organisation as the negotiating and collaborating agency between the citizen and the state. Thus understanding how the community forms collective associations and how gathering takes place expands the understanding of democracy and civic participation in a number of ways, a task that has become more relevant as participatory approach of public policy grow in popularity, particularly in the developing world.

In this background it has been observed that the society in the North East region of India, have been living in a closeknit community. The communities regardless of being tribal or non-tribal have not been able to entirely discard their traditional self governing institutions and have continued to function side by side with the modern state instituted institutions. In fact the Indian Government vision document 'North Eastern Region Vision 2020', acknowledges the presence of a strong tradition of local self-governing institutions in the region through 'Traditional Institutions. These include Syiemships, Dorbars and Rangbah Shnong of the Khasi Hills, the Dolois of the Jaintia Hills and the Nokmas of the Garo Hills of Meghalaya as well as other groups such as the Kuki-Impis, various clubs, associations and peoples' organizations of Manipur, Nagaland and other States. It is through these institutions that people participate in the democratic governance of their own life by actively engaging in

12. *Assistant Professor, Public Administration Mizoram University, Mizoram, India

the decision-making processes of making choices and implementation of those decisions.

Conclusive Comment

The present paper will attempt to interrogate the history of 'community' through traditional institutions of the northeast region and how the resultant impact of an intersection between informal traditional institutions with that of modern formal system has taken place in the public policy framing. The paper concludes with some suggestions for an effective and efficient deployment of these social capital institutions in ushering peace and wellbeing for the people of the state.

Keywords: *Community, traditional institution, local self-governing institution, social capital, participatory democracy*

Governance and Community

The contemporary discourse on 'Governance' embraces the 'participation' of all relevant stakeholders in a society cutting across the divide between state actors and non-state actors as public service delivery remains the greatest challenge. Since the early 1990s the government innovations revolving around the neo-liberal based - 'New Public Management' model has been criticized for being individualistic; consumer oriented and market centric[1]. In contrast to view Janet and Robert Denhardt (2003) proposed a "New Public Service', a set of ideas about the role of public administration in the governance system that places "public service, democratic governance, and civic engagement at the centre" (ibid. p. 24). Within this paradigm the people are seen as citizens, and the public interest is realized through a dialogue about shared values. Here citizenship is concerned more with general issues related to the nature of one's membership in a political community, including such issues as the rights and responsibilities of citizens, regardless of their legal status (Turner 1993:3).

Such a model of governance brings back the importance of 'community' and traces its roots to the wider debates on communitarianism. It attempts to bring governance innovation through collective radical localism promoting the ideals of community governance and grassroots democracy from below. The idea of 'community' goes back to its normative sense as explained by the German sociologist Ferdinand Tönnies (1887) as - '*Gemeinschaft* as life based on the bonds of kinship, geographical location and the sentiment of belonging to a group.' Though a pre modern, social construct, this concept of "community' has survived beyond the temporal dividing line between modern and premodern. The outcome of living with a sense of community (embedded self in a community) is the collective well-being, popularly translated as social capital. Here I conveniently take Perkins and Long's (2002) definition of social capital in terms of four distinct components: These are as under:

1. trust in one's neighbours and
2. in the efficacy of organized collective action (empowerment),
3. informal neighbouring behavior, and
4. formal participation in community organizations. This *social structural* approach to social capital may be contrasted with the more individualistic-based approach. In fact the potential for social capital to make a positive contribution in diverse areas of social concern such as health, community safety and education has captured the interest of policy makers, social analysts and researchers.

This also pushes scholars to pay greater attention to the non-formal aspects of 'politics' and its power relation in social structure towards informal governance[2]. In defining the meaning of the concept of 'informal governance' an important proposal was made by Helmke and Levitsky who define informal institutions as 'socially shared rules, usually unwritten, that are created, communicated and enforced outside the officially sanctioned channel' (2004 p 727). There has been enormous diversity in the definitions and instances of informal governance globally. With respect to Indian scholars we have Ananth-Pur (2004, p11) who sees informal governance as being outside the structure of the state, by referring to the 'non-governmental organization of social life in local setting which includes tribal or other indigenous structures for dispersion of power'. These institutions are not always acknowledged by formal government institutions assuming them to be conflicting with the modern liberal state.

In many conflict states and in developing countries such organizations are found to have an appealing form of self-expression and is potentially an attractive and effective strategy in strengthening service delivery. It also underlines the self-development and voluntary societal problem solving mechanism in a neighbourhood. A critical reappraisal of existing community-based organisations become more important to understand along with the nuances of the participatory process of democratization, particularly the ones that remain active under the contemporary system of governance. Helmke and

Levisky (2004) offered a fourfold typology of the relationship between informal governance and formal institution as -complementary, accommodating, competing and substitutive depending on the relationship and arrangement. Accordingly policy reforms are recommended towards such institutions.

On the other hand to meet the challenge of inefficiencies in public service delivery, governments are now increasingly adopting the new mode of innovative service delivery. Among the innovations, public administrators and government reformers are keen to understand the participatory governance notion through the perspective of collaborating with the vibrant community social capital. In fact with the failure of the state and the market to reach out to people, many small communities have collectively supported to serve their public goods. The lives of a community which evolve harmoniously - same identity, history and culture with a sense of solidarity and significance – has never been invaded by the state and market institutions in the allocation of resources and local service provisions.

Based on such a background, this paper is an investigative attempt at bringing together some of the existing literature on informal governance institutions and their role in the northeastern region of India. Some of the questions which I attempt to explore are-Is active support for and cooperation with 'traditional' authorities a sensible policy? Does it help create effective, legitimate and accountable public authority? How do the current new forms of participation and consultation articulate with existing institutions of informal governance? My attempt has not been on the question whether the traditional and "modern" systems of governance are competing against each other but more on to understand how the two systems can integrate more effectively in order to better serve citizens in terms of representation, participation, service delivery and access to justice.

Community institutions and capacities in North-east India

The region of North-east India comprises of eight states of the Indian Union namely Arunachal Pradesh, Assam, Manipur, Meghalaya, Mizoram, Nagaland, Sikkim and Tripura with a population of 41,91,6950 (as per 2011 census) comprising of 3.463 percent of India's population and geographically covering 8.05 percent of the country's total geographical area. Connected physically to the rest of India by a narrow strip of 27 km Siliguri corridor. Besides its alienation from the rest of India the region is home to294 communities, of which 156 communities are recognised by the constitution of India as 'scheduled tribes'[3]marked by diversity in customs, cultures, traditions and languages. A large number of inhabitants speak Tibeto-Burmese languages and have cultural similarities with South-East Asia.

This part of the region got merged with the Indian Union after an end of the British colonial rule and thus, introduced to the Indian system of governance as per the Constitution of India in 1950. Though the region is one of the richest in terms of natural resources and in its scenic beauty in India but it represents one of the poorest regions dotted with issues of unemployment, political violence, ethnic crisis, insurgency, etc. This broad socio-economic underdevelopment and state building crisis of Northeast Indian states has been explained by Indian policy framers through various notions of 'lack' in development. The Indian state identifies this lack because of various deficits as –infrastructure, basic needs and resource deficits. The region is henceforth officially recognized as 'special category' to receive special attention for socio-economic development.

However scholars like Prasenjit Biwas (2008) of the region have also acknowledged the lack of 'governance' deficit. In fact the region is one of the most challenging regions of the country in terms of delivery of services and access to growth opportunities. A corruption study survey by the Centre for Media Study and Transparency International India (2008) found that people in the region give bribes not to gain any personal benefits for unlawful activities but rather for services legally guaranteed to the citizens through the public institutions. For example people paid bribes to get beds in hospitals and to avail diagnostic services and for medicine. The same goes for any other public service. Now the question is how do individuals and communities sustain themselves in all these conflicts? In such situations, people often fall back on the community based informal network substitute systems which form the basis of coping strategies[4].

Regardless of tribal/non tribal distinctions, the communitarian form of life is the dominant characteristic of each community. A cohesive social entity and its presence of a "unity of will" are visible in most local neighbourhoods, which express the positive sentiments of identity and solidarity evaluated positively as something good. Individuals are bound by social obligation in terms of behaviour and etiquette in each community. For example, the Mizo community in Mizoram are guided by the social moral value of '*Tlawmngaihna*' and the institution of '*Zawlbuk*' which would mean self sacrifice for the service and well being of the community. Based on such an ethos, contemporary Mizo society has various social collectivities and associations working in various capacities for upholding the socio-political goods of the community. Of late the most appreciated innovative conduct is the formation an of election watchdog called Mizoram People's Forum (MPF) in June, 2006 jointly led by the local youth based organization, Young Mizo Association and the church to promote a good practice of sanitizing election processes following the Indian election conduct rules. The formation of MPF can be seen in the wake of the growing dissatisfaction on how election systems function and the growing awareness of the cost of such processes. Therefore MPF came in to strengthen and institutionalize the election process assuming their moral and social responsibility towards political institution building. The state has henceforth observed the most disciplined campaigning and peaceful elections in India.

The concept of '*Khullang Lamman*" among the Meitei Society in Manipur means reciprocity of service by one another in times of need, shapes the behavior of self in community living. And this very 'sense of community' is the foundation of every other social institution in Meitei society like *"Marup, Potyeng-lamman, singllup, etc'* and even the growth of modern neighbourhood organizations like *'local Club'* in contemporary Meitei society. In every *leikai* (locality/hamlet), it is now a norm to form a *leikai-club* (neighbourhood association) with its office building, library, halls, sport ground, etc. The space of a *leikai-club* is now made mandatory through the invocation of a consensus among the people and preserved for every *leikai*as their site of power. It works on the norm of a bureaucratic structure-written rule, hierarchy, division of work, commitment and neutrality, yet flexible on social norms and cultural morality. In Manipur, there are as many *leikai clubs* as neighouboods of leikai among the meitei community. They are known for active participation and promotion of various fields like sports, cultural, social and political issues of the community.

Besides these most of the communities in this region have self-governing village councils and organised tribal chief-doms till today continued from the late British period. The state of Meghalaya has traditional institution like DorbarsShnongs for Khasi under Syiemships, the Dolois of the Jaintias and the Nokmas of the Garos. Many studies have reported the work of Durbar Shnong in several contemporary urban areas, where they have collaborated together with government agencies, functionaries and NGOs on local issues such as water supply, electricity, roads, schools, as well as tackling anti-social elements such as bootleggers and drug peddlers. It also collaborates with Church organizations to construct Churches and cremation grounds. The success story of such community collective problem solving practice continues in The Northeast region.

Thus, we see that in most of these societies, informal institutional arrangements of the pre-constitutional and, therefore, pre-liberal democratic era, continue to function along side the government of the democratic republic, established since 1950. This implies that power is to a large extent in the hands of these community institutions besides exhibiting its legitimacy and acceptance in the region. These community based traditional organisations are largely autonomous in relation to the formal state structures; in other cases the two are deeply intertwined. To the extent that we can penetrate the ever-present discourse of 'traditionality', we judge that some informal local governance practices have changed little over many decades, while others seem remarkably recent like *Local clubs* and Young Mizo Associations which are registered bodies under the state legal norms. However these community organizations can be seen to be a modern evolutionary version of these socially embedded traditional institutions with the emergence of modern democratic norms and their demands to gain legitimacy from the state.

The greatest achievements of such community social capital, came with the state recognizing local community capacity by state legislation as local governance is a state subject. The state of Nagaland pioneered with the "Communitization Act" from 2002 to undertake developmental activities in harmony with the traditional institutions. The Act was introduced to institutionalize community participation by entering into a legal institutional partnership of the community with the state. This was connected in matters related with the management of local public utilities, public services and other developmental schemes to be transferred in the hands of 'User communities'. The user committee includes representation of the traditional institution and other stakeholders, which will ultimately own and control the services. As a result service delivery in education, health care and in the electricity sector have received encouraging outcomes, based on the study conducted a few months after the Communitisation programme was launched. Nagaland is now in a stronger position to monitor and ensure accountability of services in the post communitisation era.

Many communities of North, East India have been demanding constitutional recognition of their traditional institutions for its increase in exhibiting collective goods and well being for all time; but any legislation or tradition by them that discriminates is undemocratic and unacceptable in today's society. Critiques have raise issues over politics in these community organisations of this region, which have peculiar problems, at times that generate situations of crisis. There have been cases of traditional local government organisations, like *Dorbars* (in Meghalaya) and *Young Mizo Association* (in Mizoram) and *leikai Club* (in Manipur), created vigilante groups, which physically punished people in their kangaroo court trials. This had even resulted in the deaths of people who did not belong to the indigenous ethnic community and damage of private properties.

A Vision Democratic

Recognizing the potential of such community social capital in service delivery systems, the Indian Government vision document 'North Eastern Region Vision 2020'[5], acknowledges the presence of these strong traditions of local self-governing institutions in the region through `Traditional Institutions (TI) besides the formal institutions of Local Government[6]. The document emphasizes that it is through these institutions that people participate in the democratic governance of their own life by actively engaging in the decision making processes of making choices and implementation of those decisions:

> *"While designing local planning approaches, care must be taken to harmonize the functions and rights of traditional tribal self-governing village institutions such as the Syiemships and Dorbars of the Khasi hills of Meghalaya, the Kuki-Impi of the Kukis in Manipur, the Clubs of the Manipur valley and peoples' organizations of various tribes in Nagaland, with institutional mechanisms designed for modern development and service delivery".* (North Eastern Region Vision 2020 Vol.1 page 18-19)

The NER document, consequently, expresses the desirability and the necessity to ensure a harmonious relationship between the constitutional institutions of local governance and the Traditional Institutions for better governance of the people and for the region at large. However attention must be paid to the democratization of the functions of traditional Institutions, especially with gender representation. The vision document acknowledge that TIs have varying levels of influence in different states although they are not recognized constitutionally and their demand for such recognition may be considered if these institutions are democratized and representative of all groups, instead of being exclusive entities. They can not only as agents oversee the social order locally but also act as catalysts for local development. But the question is how a liberal sense of democratization will accommodate an existing community political life?

The document supports an active participation of people in the political processes and in grassroots planning to bring about the desired transformation of the region by helping to establish peace and set in motion the wheels of progress towards prosperity. The selection of various projects and their prioritisation, adaptation of central and state schemes to meet the priorities of the people, ensuring untied funds for implementation, and compilation of an information system required for planning and creation of a system of social accountability that would empower people to determine their own economic destiny. However, one must be critical towards such broad assumptions in paper and in practice. The following para will discuss how the recent governance and administrative reform towards community participation and community capacity actually empowered or de-empowered the community and the cost of participatory practice in the region.

The missing-gap in the practice of community participation

As a part of domestic national policy towards participatory governance and under the influence of international donors towards local resource management and cost recovery into the routine of policy implementation agencies, these states in the region are also going through governance reforms. In the year 1999, North Eastern Region Community Resource Management Project (NERCORMP) was initiated by the North Eastern Council, which is implemented jointly by the International Fund for Agricultural Development and the Government of India to unleash the potential for development tapped in the community capacity in two districts each of Meghalaya, Assam and Manipur. The first phase of the project has been documented as best practices by using 'community participation' as an agent in the planning and implementation processes.[7] However the main focus areas of the project has been reduction of shifting cultivation, commonly known as Jhum andpromotion of cash crops and perennial horticulture crops in jhum cultivating areas. Many scholars from the region have been apprehensive if the eradication of the age-old practice of jhum cultivation that has been the subsistence economy for the tribal people for years be wise[8]. To eradicate jhum cultivation would mean that many cultures and equalitarian social structures associated with promoting collective community living would go away. Therefore any effort to find a solution to this vexed problem must involve the Jhumias and approach must be Jhum centered[9]. The state has to be careful with the cost of such a capitalist mode of production and monetization of economy and relations which is being introduced through the use of community. There has been a failed case of Jatropha bio-fuel plantation—a supposedly green gold cash crop that was introduced in the region to enhance the supposedly stagnant economy. It proved to be a total failure as there is no processing factory or market to sell. Both the Government and the Company who encourage farmers to cultivate Jatropha is refusing to compensate the growers

The recent national programmes and missions, under United Nations Millennium development Goals (UNMDG) emphasise community participation. And indeed the opportunity of recognising and institutionalising the roles of these community institutions could have taken place in this recently enacted "Municipality Community Participation Act" which come as mandatory reform in urban governance[10]. But sadly, the enactment of such an Act astonished everyone. One of the objectives is to promote community participation in the identification, planning and delivery of services for the community. The very nature of social roles which have been contributed by *leikai-clubs* in Manipur as community representatives was acknowledged and given due partnership roles is Sarva Siksha Abhiyan, Total Literacy Campaign of the National Literacy Mission, National Health Mission, Total Sanitation Campaign and Bharat Nirman initiated by the Government to achieve the MDGs. However, such partnerships were observed only on paper and the use of leikai club has been mostly a one day affair to reach expenditure targets in implementation. There was no surprise when national programmes under UNMDGs promoting community participation fail in the state. The policy in fact promotes more of adhocism and the growth of corrupt elites classes to capture the funds received from such projects.

Such gap (supra) between the normative prescription and the functional aspect of community participation in the state governance strategy remains a bigger challenge. Similar finding of such experiences of participatory governance clothed in the language of the exclusive nature of 'participation' had also been already found and documented in India (D Mosse, 2004).

Conclusion

This tendency to revive traditional values and institutions remains strong, despite inroads of western values throughout colonial intervention in this region. Rather than dismissing non-western cultures as anti-democratic and authoritarian, there is a need to engage and work with existing institutions and practices to promote development and enhance choice and freedom for individuals and groups. In this context, the Asian Values debate has thrown little light while generating much noise. These problems therefore emerge from inadequate definitions of the nature and scope of the state and civil society, which exclude semi-autonomous and autonomous self-governing communities with their own institutional structures, laws and social security mechanisms The post-colonial State, on the other hand, essentially emulates western liberal institutions of governance, which are often at odds with traditional community cultural values and the region's contemporary socio-economic realities.

The traditional institutions in the region have also shown the capacity to adjust changes in order to represent the best interests of their communities and maintain overall social order. Public opinion is growing over the issue of the inclusion of women in the traditional institutions and in fact have included in certain institutions of *Dorbars* in urban Shillong. Growth of education, and scientific technology may not necessarily destroy the collective community living morals and culture but only improve its well being of being together. Provided with appropriate training, these community institutions have also proved willing and able to expand their traditional roles to become full partners in local development planning and implementation.

The potential of theosophical capital institutions as mechanisms for building a sustainable society in the region is not disputed. However, without the appropriate community capability building approach, the sustainability of such communitarian forms of life may be threatened by the neo-liberal based state policies. Rather such policy if continued can be seen as the neo-colonisation of community institutions by the International financial institutions and MNCs to capture the local resources and extend market policy of economy, manipulation of people's planning under the cover of community consent. In short, despite the rhetoric claim of participation, the status quo of top-down planning is maintained. Government backed by donor agencies are only seen in a hurry to adopt community participation with no sense of real ownership by this community. What role these institutions can play in partnerships in governance and development? and - how they can relate to the other institutions of governance and public administration has to be clearly sorted out? In fact, such existence of vibrant community institutions which have control over local knowledge and legitimacy of the community can further strengthen the governance and development of well being in a community. The strongest move in recent times is the mass public opposition of the New Citizenship Amendment Bill, 2019 in the northeast region to protect its indigenous communities. It had the fear that the migrants from outside could culturally and physically swamp the small communities.

End Notes

1. But NPM inspired innovation has brought innovation in western world and in some south Asian countries
2. Such discourse are strongly influenced by the new institutionalism theories that suggest that institutions help to formalize mutual expectation of cooperative behavior allow exercise of sanctions for non-cooperation and thereby reduce the costs of individual transactions.
3. The Constitution of India recognizes some communities as scheduled tribes because of their social and economic backwardness at the time of the adoption of the Constitution. For a list, see K. S. Singh, People of India An Introduction, Calcutta, presently Kolkata 1992.
4. The World Bank researcher observer, vol 15, no 2, august 2000, p 238
5. Launched by Indian Prime Minister, Manmohan Singh in 2007 in New Delhi
6. In the region there are many formal local governing institutions under (i) Sixth Schedule Frame (Meghalaya, parts of Assam, Mizoram and Tripura), (ii) State Legislation Frame (Nagaland and non-Council Areas in Mizoram), and (iii) National Frame (Arunachal Pradesh, Sikkim, Manipur excluding hill areas and non-Council areas in Assam and Tripura).
7. Case Study North Eastern Region Community Resource Management Project, 2011, http://indiagovernance.gov.in/files/gkc_oneworld_sustainable_development_north_east_india.pdf excessed on 3/09/2013
8. ZK Pahrü Pous', *'JHUM CULTIVATION MUST STAY WITH US!!!'* published on Manipuronline, February 25, 2011
9. G.Murtem, G.N.Sinha and J.Dopum JHUMIAS VIEW ON SHIFTING CULTIVATION IN ARUNACHAL PRADESH *Bulletin of Arunachal Forest Research 24 (1&2) : 35-40, 2008.* Vol242008
10. This Act has come through 'Jawaharlal Nehru Urban Renewal Mission (JNNURM)', to achieve the UNMDG by 2015. JNNURM is a programme for the development of urban infrastructure, which is funded by the World Bank, which demands the enactment, and modification of Municipalities Act institutionally and structurally.

References

1. Biswas Prasenjit, 2008, "Post Development, Democratic Discourse and Dissensus: A crique of Vision 2020, "Eastern Quarterly, Vol 4 (III &IV) p 178-88.
2. Crook, R. and J Manor, (1994) Enhancing Participation and Institutional Performance: Democratic Decentralisation in South Asia and West Africa. A Report to ESCOR, ODA of Phase Two of a Two-Phase Research Project
3. Denhardt, Janet V and Robert B. Denhardt (2003). The New Public Service: Serving, not Steering. M. E. Sharpe. Armonk, New York.
4. Human Development Report of North East States, (2011), Government of India
5. Michael Sandel (1996), Democracy's Discontent: America in Search of a Public Philosophy, Cambridge, Mass.: The Belknap Press of Harvard University Press
6. Mosse, D (2004) , Peoples' knowledge , participation and patronage :Operation and Representations in Rural Development' in B Cooke and U Kothari (ed) , Participation The new tryranny? P16-35, Zed Books
7. Newman, J. (2001) Modernising Governance: new labour, policy and society, London: Sage
8. Ostrom, V. (1973). The Intellectual Crisis in American Public Administration. CITY: University of Alabama Press.
9. Peace, Progress and Prosperity in the Northeastern Region Vision (2020), Vol 1
10. Peters, G. and Pierre, J. (2001) 'Development in inter-governmental relations: towards multi—level governance', Policy and Politics, 29.2., pp. 131-5
11. Pierre, J. and Peters, G. (2000): Governance, Politics and the State. London: St. Martin's Press.
12. Rhodes, R. A. W. (1996), The New Governance: Governing without Government. Political Studies, 44: 652–667.
13. Saegert, S., & Winkel, G. (1996). Paths to community empowerment: Organizing at home: American Journal of Community Psychology, 24, 517-550.
14. Thompson, G., Frances, J., Levacic, J. and Mitchel, J. (eds.), (1991) Markets, Hierarchies and Networks: The Co-ordination of Social Life. Sage Publications, London
15. Turner, Bryan S.., ed. (1993) Citizenship and Social theory, London Sage.

✦✦✦

Chapter Twelve

Rashtriya Madhyamik Shiksha Abhiyan: A Study

Zeba Fatima[13]*

Abstract

Democratic governance and socio-economic development depend on effective public policy. Education's role as a policy instrument is capable of instilling social change and economic advancement in developing countries by allowing communities the opportunity to take control of their destinies. It plays an important role in the progress of an individual's life and country.

Secondary education is the transitional phase in human life that is very important for the all-round development of a human being. It plays an important role in the overall education process because it provides a reforming tool in adolescent years before entering the bigger and serious part of education and career.

The Strategic framework by the Government of India towards the planning, implementation and universalization of secondary education in India is provided by the Rashtriya Madhyamik Shiksha Abhiyan- a centrally sponsored scheme of the Ministry of Human Resource Development, Government of India. This programme, launched in March 2009 for secondary education aimed at making quality education available, accessible and affordable to all young persons in the age group of 14-18 years. With this vision providing a secondary school within a reasonable distance of any habitation, ensuring universal access of secondary education by 2017 (Gross Enrolment Ratio of 100% universal retention by 2020) providing access to secondary education with respect to gender, socio-economic conditions, disability, economically weaker sections of the society, educationally backward girls and disabled children residing in rural areas and other marginalized categories like SC, ST, OBC and educationally backward minorities, RMSA was envisaged.

Keywords: *Education, Central Schemes, Aims and targets*

The education system takes students on the path of attaining the right knowledge, right belief, and right conduct. On very grounds, quality is the

13. *PhD Research Scholar, Department of Political Science, Jamia Millia Islamia, New Delhi

most important goal in human endeavour, especially in the field of education, which can be found with a proper analysis of a government program in a pre-determined area or analysing the impact of policy in the desired region over a period of time. The aim of education reflects the current needs and aspirations of the society and its lasting values. Role of education as a policy instrument, capable of instilling social change and economic advancement in developing countries by giving communities the opportunity to take control of their destinies needs to be analysed. Policy analysis is nothing more than finding out the impact of a policy. It is a technique that measures organizational effectiveness through the examination and evaluation of an effective program. An analytical study therefore, needs to be conducted.

Education is the foremost requirement of any civilization that allows human beings not only to distinguish between the civilized and the uncivilized but also to help them achieve targeted results. Education is a means to provide sophistication towards improving the socio- economic condition of a nation. It empowers citizens with probing abilities, leads to a better confidence level and secures one with racing and goal-setting abilities. Education does not involve only classroom learning but inculcates values, skills, and capacities. This helps individuals to plan their careers as well as play a part in building liberal values. Hence, education leads to changing both personal lives as well as the professional front for the better. India has seen exceptional development in education since independence. The overall literacy rate has moved up significantly during this era. However, the national goal of universalization of elementary education and eradication of illiteracy completely is yet to be achieved. There has been a significant increase in investment in education with the tremendous expansion of educational establishments in India. There has also been a significant and impressive increase in the acceptance of boys and girls, including scheduled caste and scheduled tribe students, particularly at the elementary level of education. The dropout rate at different stages of school education has been declining steadily. However, these rates are still very high and need sustained efforts to reduce them sharply.

The Right to Education has also been laid down as a fundamental right by the constitution of India by the Constitution (Eighty-sixth Amendment) Act, 2002, by inserting Article 21-A in the Constitution of India. According to very Article, it has become the responsibility of the state to provide free and compulsory education to all children of six to fourteen years of age as a Fundamental Right in such a manner as the State may, by law, determine. This article states that every child has a right to full-time elementary education of satisfactory and equitable quality in a formal school that satisfies certain essential norms and standards.

Armoogum Parsuramen said, "This act is an essential step towards improving each child's accessibility to secondary and higher education, bringing India closer to achieving national educational developmental goals, as-well-as the Millenium Development Goals and Education for All".

The Right of Children to Free and Compulsory Education became an Act, to enable the implementation of the fundamental right, after it was passed by the parliament in 2009. Article 21-A and the RTE Act came into effect on 1 April, 2010. The title of the RTE Act incorporates the words "free and compulsory". "Free education" means that no child, other than a child who has been admitted by his or her parents to a school which is not backed by the appropriate Government, shall be subject to pay any kind of fee or charges or expenses which may prevent him or her from pursuing and completing elementary education.

The 11th Fundamental Duty, which states that every citizen "who is a parent or guardian, to provide opportunities for education to his child or, as the fact may be, ward between the age of six and fourteen years" was also added by the 86th constitutional amendment in 2002.

"Compulsory education" casts an obligation on the Government and local administration to provide and ensure admission, attendance and fulfilment of elementary education to all children in the 6-14 age group. With this, India has advanced to a rights- based framework that casts a legal obligation on the Central and State Governments to implement this fundamental child right as consecrated in Article 21A of the Constitution, by the provisions of the RTE Act. It drastically helped in the reduction of dropout rate, improvement in the literacy rate, reduction in the gap of gender literacy rate, etc.

Public-Policy

Democratic governance and socio-economic development depends on effective public policy. In this process, the legislature, executive, judiciary, administration and political parties contribute to the development of such policies.

A policy is a deliberate system of principles to-guide resolutions and achieve rational outcomes. In short, it is a statement of purpose and is implemented as a procedure or protocol. Policies are a part and parcel of almost all countries across the globe. India is one of the countries that have been working on many education policies for long.

Public-policy is formed by the combination of two words that is "public" and "policy". The public dimension here indicates „public ownership or control for a public purpose. The public sector comprises the domain of human activity regarded as requiring governmental intervention, Contrary to it, policy indicates guidance for action, declaration of goals, course of action and declaration of general-purpose or an authoritative decision.

Public-Policy is a frequently used term in our day-to-day life and our academic literature, where we often refer to national health policy, education policy, wage policy, agriculture policy foreign policy and so on.

Education policy consists of the principles and government policies in the educational sphere as well as the collection of laws and rules that govern the operation of education systems.

Education's role as a policy instrument is capable of instilling social change and economic advancement in developing countries by allowing communities to take control of their destinies. It plays an important role in the progress of an individual's life and country. People are made aware of what is going on in the world and can understand these issues and take necessary measures if they are educated. Education tames the astray mind, nurturing its capabilities the same way as training builds a clever dog. Education is the means through which the aims and habits of a group of people sustain from one generation to the next. It encompasses the complete development of knowledge, skills, and character of an individual. It is the process of facilitating learning or acquisition of knowledge, skills, values, beliefs, and habits.

The education sector is fully integrated into society, through interactions with a large number of stakeholders and other sectors. These include (i) parents, (ii) local communities, (iii) religious leaders, (iv) NGOs, (v) stakeholders involved in health, child protection justice and law enforcement (police), (vi) media and (vii) political leadership. The education sector or education system is a group of institutions like ministries of education, local educational authorities, teacher training institutions, schools, universities, etc. whose primary purpose is to provide education to children and young people in educational settings. It involves a wide range of people like, curriculum developers, inspectors, school principals, teachers, school nurses, students, etc.

These institutions can vary according to different contexts. Schools deliver education, with support from the rest of the education system through various elements, such as education policies and guidelines – to which school policies can refer – curricula and learning materials, as well as pre- and in-service teacher training programs. The school environment – both physical (infrastructures) and psychological (school climate) – is also guided by school policies that should ensure the well-being of students when they are in school.

The structure of the school system in India has four levels, namely: Lower primary (age 6 to 10 yrs.),

Upper primary (11 and 14),

Secondary (15 to 16) and -

Higher secondary level (17 and 18 yrs.).

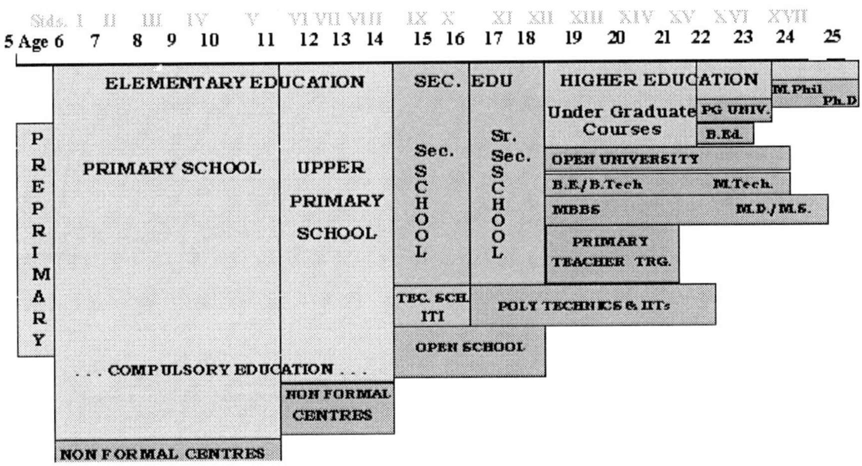

Secondary Education

Secondary education in India starts from class VIII or IX depending upon the states or union territories. The Secondary Stage consists of Classes IX-X in 19 States/UTs. Viz., Arunachal Pradesh, Bihar, Haryana, Himachal Pradesh, Jammu & Kashmir, Madhya Pradesh, Manipur, Nagaland, Punjab, Rajasthan, Sikkim, Tamil Nadu, Tripura, Uttar Pradesh, West Bengal, Andaman & Nicobar Islands, Chandigarh, Delhi and Karaikal region of Pondicherry. The Higher Secondary/ Senior Secondary stage of school (classes XI-XII) which comes under the 10+2 pattern is available in all the States/UTs through in some States/UTs. These classes run in Junior colleges or are attached to universities.

Secondary school plays an important role in the overall education process because those are the years before entering the bigger and serious part of education. It is extremely important to focus during these years. Students get into their teenage and are excited about so many things. The secondary school gives the student a wider scope and perspective about education and what career choices to make in the future. It is basically a connecting link between upper primary and higher education. It is a transition phase between childhood and youth.

Aims and Objectives of Secondary education

General Aims of Secondary Education: John Dewey has said that "An aim is a foreseen end that gives direction to an activity or motivates behavior." It is essential to formulate the aims and objectives of education with special reference to the needs of society and its people. The needs of society change from time to time and hence it becomes essential to reconstruct the following aims and objectives of education:

Aim of Physical Development

1. Aim of Spiritual Development
2. Aim of Cultural development
3. Aim of Moral/Religious development
4. Aim of Intellectual development
5. Aim of Emotional development
6. Aim of Social development
7. Aim of Education for Vocation

Objectives of Secondary Education

1. To acquire necessary knowledge, skills, and attitude for the development of the self and the nation.
2. To develop socially, morally, intellectually, physically and emotionally.
3. Enhance understanding and respect for own and other people's cultures and their place in contemporary society.
4. Develop into a responsible and socially well-adjusted person.
5. Enhance enjoyment in learning.

6. Identify individual talents and develop them.
7. Build a foundation for technological and industrial development.

At present, the following schemes targeted at the secondary stage (i.e. class IX to XII) are being implemented in the form of Centrally Sponsored Schemes:

1. Rashtriya Madhyamik Shiksha Abhiyan
2. Girls Hostel Scheme
3. National Scheme of Incentives to Girls for Secondary Education
4. Inclusive Education for Disabled at Secondary Stage
5. Scheme of Vocational Education
6. National Merit-cum-Means Scholarship Scheme
7. Scheme for construction and running of Girls' Hostel for students of secondary and higher secondary schools
8. Scholarship schemes for Minority students
9. National Scholarships

Here we are focusing our studies on Rashtrita Madhyamik Shiksha Abhiyan(RMSA). What is RMSA?

Background of Rashtriya Madhyamik Shiksha Abhiyan (RMSA)

Since the initiation of the National Policy on Education (NPE), 1986, there have been no major changes in the structure and organization of the secondary and higher secondary school systems under the Ninth Plan period.

The goal of universal secondary education cannot be achieved unless the efficiency of the primary education system is improved. Even the goal of Universal Elementary Education (UEE) cannot be achieved without very achievement. Therefore, Sarva Shiksha Abhiyan (SSA) was launched in 2001 in order to achieve this target for elementary education. Sarva Shiksha Abhiyan (SSA) is Government of India's flagship program for the achievement of Universalization of Elementary Education (UEE) in a time-bound manner, as mandated by 86th amendment to the Constitution of India making free and compulsory Education to the Children of 6-14 years age group, a Fundamental Right. SSA is being implemented in partnership with State Governments to cover the entire country and address the needs of 192 million children in 1.1 million habitations. The program seeks to open new schools in those habitations which do not have schooling facilities and strengthen existing school infrastructure through provision of additional classrooms, toilets, drinking water, maintenance grant, and school improvement grants.

In already existing schools the inadequate teacher strength was provided with additional teachers, while the capacity of existing teachers is being strengthened by extensive training, grants for developing teaching-learning materials and strengthening of the academic support structure at a cluster, block and district level. SSA seeks to provide quality elementary education including life skills. SSA has a special focus on girl's education and children with special needs. SSA also seeks to provide computer education to bridge the digital divide.

Once the goal of Universal elementary education (UEE) is achieved, only then, one can think of universalization of senior secondary education (USSE). On the recommendations of the Central Advisory Board on Education (CABE), the Government of India has prepared a centrally sponsored plan for universal access at secondary education known as Rashtriya Madhyamik Shiksha Abhiyan (RMSA) during the 11th plan with the total cost of Rs. 20,120 crore.

Sentient Features of RMSA

This scheme was launched in March 2009 with the objective to enhance access to secondary education and to improve its quality. The implementation of the scheme started from 2009-10. It is envisaged to achieve an enrolment rate of 75% from 52.26% in 2005-06 at the secondary stage of implementation of the scheme by providing a secondary school within a reasonable distance of any habitation by subsuming other centrally sponsored schemes of secondary education- Information and Communication Technology (ICT) at school, girls hostel, Inclusive Education for Disabled at Secondary Stage (IEDSS) and Vocational Education (VE) in their existing forms, under the umbrella of RMSA in 2013. The pattern of assistance as well as coverage of schools as per the existing norms of all subsumed schemes will continue for the 12th Five Year Plan, improving quality of education imparted at secondary level through making all secondary schools conform to prescribed norms, removing gender, socio-economic and disability barriers, providing universal access to secondary level education by 2017, i.e., by the end of 12th Five Year Plan and achieving universal retention by 2020.

The funding from the central ministry is provided through state governments, which establish separate implementing agencies. Under RMSA the responsibility to develop Secondary Education Management Information System (SE-MIS) is given to the Department of Educational Planning, National University of Educational Planning and Administration (NUEPA), New Delhi.

Four major heads for classification

Quality improvement

In school, there was the promotion of the science laboratories, environmental education, promotion of yoga, as well as centrally sponsored schemes of population education project, international mathematics and science olympiads. The state governments provide in- service training for the teachers and provide infrastructure and research inputs.

Information communication technologies (ICT)

The Information and Communication Technology (ICT) in schools have been subsumed in the Rashtriya Madhyamik Shiksha Abhiyan (RMSA). Now ICT in Schools is a component of the RMSA. The Scheme is a major catalyst to bridge the digital divide amongst students of various socio-economic and other geographical barriers. The Scheme provides support to States/UTs to establish computer labs on a sustainable basis.

ICT comprises centrally sponsored schemes like computer education and literacy in schools (CLASS) and educational technology (ET) which familiarizes the student with Information technology (IT). Due to the rise in IT demand in today's world, a major importance is given on it. Components of a merged scheme ICT in school include:

1. Funding support for computer education plans;
2. Strengthening and reorientation of the staffs of SIETS - state institutes of education and training;
3. There is the digitalization of SIETs audio and video cassettes with the partnership of NGOs, and-
4. Management of internet-based education by SIETs.

Access and equity

RMSA not only emphasizes on providing secondary education for the special focus groups that include scheduled tribe and scheduled caste groups, minority girls and CWSN children, but it also gives importance on removing the existing disparities in socio-economic and gender background in the secondary level of education. They are termed as the vulnerable/ disadvantaged group. Certain strategies were implemented to provide free access towards secondary education and they are given as following steps:

1. Identification of the disadvantaged groups: For this purpose, educational indicators like gross enrolment ratio (GER), net enrolment ratio (NER), drop-out rate, retention rate, gender parity index (GPI), gender gap etc. were analyzed.
2. Need assessment: This is the critical step to prepare for the equity plan where the factors affecting the education of this group of children were evaluated with the involvement of the community members, teachers, civil society, etc.
3. Strategizing for the addressing gaps: Since there are multiple interwoven factors that cause the un-equitable condition in this scenario, the strategy was called to have a set of multi- dimensional activities.
4. Project-based proposal: Development of a project-based strategy enables the RMSA to call for an evidence-based and outcome-oriented strategy.

Integrated education for disabled children (IEDC)

Inclusive education has been highlighted to bring about an expansion in terms of meeting/catering to the needs of the mentally and physically disadvantaged children. This scheme continues to be a separate centrally sponsored scheme. It includes several components for convergence with integrated child development services for early interventions, Sarva Shiksha Abhiyan (SSA) for the particular group at the elementary level, and special schools.

Goals And Objectives

- Establishing Secondary School within a radius of 5kms.
- Achieving 75% access by 2012-13 and 100% access by 2017-18.
- Achieving 100% retention by 2020.
- Providing necessary physical facilities, teaching and non – teaching staff for every secondary school
- To see that no student shall be deprived of secondary education because of gender disparity, socio-economic reasons, disability

- Improving the quality of education imparted at the secondary level.
- Eradicating gender differences.
- Removing Socio-economic and disability barriers.
- Enhancing the funds of Management, Monitoring Evaluation and Research (MMER) from 2.2 percent to 4 percent of the total outlay.
- Extending all the benefits of RMSA to aided secondary schools excluding infrastructure support / core areas.
- Authorizing the RMSA, Project Approval Board (PAD) of Ministry of Human Resource Development to consider for approval of the integrated plan of the umbrella scheme of RMSA, including the subsumed four centrally sponsored schemes of secondary education and release of funds to the RMSA state implementation society directly.

Important physical facilities provided under the scheme are

1. Laboratories,
2. Libraries,
3. Additional Class Rooms
4. Art and crafts room,
5. Toilet blocks,
6. Drinking water provisions and-
7. Residential Hostels for Teachers in remote areas.

Important quality interventions provided under the scheme are

1. Appointment of additional teachers to reduce PTR to 30:1, (ii) focus on Science, Math, and English education,
2. In-service training of teachers,
3. Science laboratories,
4. ICT enabled education,
5. Curriculum reforms; and
6. Teaching-learning reforms.

Important equity interventions provided in the scheme are

1. Special focus in micro-planning

2. Preference to Ashram schools for up-gradation
3. Preference to areas with a concentration of SC/ST/Minority for the opening of schools
4. Special enrolment drive for the weaker section
5. More female teachers in schools; and
6. Separate toilet blocks for girls.

Funding method

The Ministry of Human Resource Development directly provides funds to the state governments. Each state government then releases the funds to the approved implementing agencies or institutions. During the XI Five Year Plan, the Central Government provided 75% of the total fund for each state, while 25% was borne by the state as a matching share.

However, in the remote northeastern states and Sikkim, the matching share was waived to 10%.

Implementation Mechanism of RMSA

The scheme is being implemented by the State government societies established for the implementation of the scheme. The central share is released to the implementing agency directly. The applicable State share is also released to the implementing agency by the respective State Governments.

Ministry of Human Resource Development (MHRD) is the nodal central government ministry to coordinate RMSA with the help of RMSA State Implementation Societies (SIS) in each state. However, there are a lot of support arrangements and institutions available for better implementation of RMSA. The Technical Support Group (TSG) supported by MHRD, is a constituent of the NRG and has a direct reporting relationship with the ministry. TSG provides technical and operational support and expertise to national and state-level teams. A National Resource Group (NRG) provides guidance for bringing about reforms in (i) teaching- learning processes, (ii) curriculum, (iii) teaching-learning material, (iv) ICT education and (v) mechanisms of monitoring and evaluation.

Besides this, various sub-committees have been constituted under NRG. These subcommittees comprise members from the TSG and meet thrice a year to apprise themselves of the progress made on mutually set goals and commitments.

In addition, NCERT and NUEPA support through dedicated RMSA units. RMSA-TCA has also been set-up for capacity building support with the assistance of DFID. In terms of financial inputs, the central share is released to the implementing agencies directly, whereas the applicable State share is also released to the agencies by the respective State Governments. various sub-committees have been constituted under the National Review Group includes Curriculum Reform Subcommittee, Teacher and Teacher Development Sub-committee, ICT Sub-committee and Planning and Management Sub-committee, etc.

Project Monitoring System (PMS)

In a significant step towards leveraging technology to enhance efficiency and manage the implementation of RMSA, a Project Monitoring System (PMS) has been enabled in the website, in which States/UTs may view the status of all components' (RMSA, ICT, IEDSS, GH & VE) GoI Releases, approved outlays, coverage as per UDISE, status of teachers, school wise list of approvals, school wise gaps, etc. under Integrated RMSA. In addition, online submission of Monthly Progress Reports, physical as well as financial, can also be made by the respective State/UTs in the PMS.

The core objective for implementation of Project Monitoring System is:

1. To obviate the need for submitting hard copies, except where it is mandated otherwise.
2. To have transparency and accuracy in the System w.r.t Approvals, Releases, Financial Status.
3. To streamline the Financial Management system.
4. To facilitate Just in Time movement of funds to lower levels of Program Implementation.
5. To help in better financial management, more accurate assessment of the actual requirement for implementation.

Revision of certain norms of the Scheme

Achievements and allocation State/UT-wise status of Habitations Covered with Primary, Upper Primary & Secondary Level Schools RMSA Programme (in reply to Unstarred Question on 07.02.2019) (From: Ministry of Human Resource Development)

Table 1:

Sl. No.	States/UTs	Primary Level in %	Upper Primary Level in %	Secondary Level in %
1	A & N Island	86.36	39.14	100
2	Andhra Pradesh	96.49	94.82	84.8
3	Arunachal Pradesh	86.7	79.46	60.08
4	Assam	99.6	99.72	97.02
5	Bihar	96.68	97.52	90
6	Chandigarh	100	100	100
7	Chhattisgarh	97.91	97.07	90.87
8	Dadra & Nagar Haveli	100	100	90.83
9	Daman & Diu	100	100	100
10	Delhi	100	100	100
11	Goa	100	100	100
12	Gujarat	100	100	89.75
13	Haryana	97.94	93.4	88.95
14	Himachal Pradesh	95.52	94.29	93.89
15	Jammu & Kashmir	87.67	87.35	79.88
16	Jharkhand	99.78	98.89	85.82
17	Karnataka	96.21	95.43	94.1
18	Kerala	97.74	96.84	94.27
19	Lakshadweep	100	100	100
20	Madhya Pradesh	99.45	99.69	83.92
21	Maharashtra	95.51	84.84	94.08
22	Manipur	85.42	43.19	56.6
23	Meghalaya	91.92	87.09	55.05
24	Mizoram	97.99	95.59	45.54
25	Nagaland	87.12	70.91	45.72
26	Odisha	96.71	97.78	96.12
27	Puducherry	100	100	100

Sl. No.	States/UTs	Primary Level in %	Upper Primary Level in %	Secondary Level in %
28	Punjab	99.71	99.76	99.39
29	Rajasthan	96.36	97.36	84.76
30	Sikkim	100	100	91.18
31	Tamil Nadu	97.52	98.71	94.61
32	Telangana	98.24	87.68	90.44
33	Tripura	92.54	92.68	67.04
34	Uttar Pradesh	96.08	97.64	80.06
35	Uttarakhand	97.7	98.48	91.62
36	West Bengal	99.52	99.41	99.22
Total	Total	97.15	96.49	88.24

Source: ***RAJYA SABHA SESSION - 248 UNSTARRED QUESTION No 526;***

RMSA: Rashtriya Madhyamik Shiksha Abhiyan.

Achievements of RMSA listed in its 2015-2016 report include:

1. 11,577 new secondary schools approved; 10,082 functional
2. 52,750 additional classrooms approved; 20,839 completed; 16,774 in progress
3. 25,948 science laboratories approved; 10,107 completed, 8,532 in progress
4. 21,864 computer rooms approved; 6,920 completed, 6,297 in progress
5. 27,428 libraries approved; 10,133 completed, 8,929 in progress
6. 31,453 art and craft rooms approved; 12,062 completed, 9,686 in progress
7. 12,327 drinking water facilities approved; 7,096 completed, 2,507 in progress
8. 5,408 teachers' quarters approved; 623 completed, 509 in progress
9. 2,975 major repairs approved; 1,313 completed, 271 in progress

As per Annual report 2017 of Ministry of Human Resourse Development Latest Developments under the scheme are:

During the financial year 2016-17:

1. 3798 schools have been approved for implementation of component of vocational education across 27 states /UT's.

2. 100 National Skills Qualification Framework (NSQF) are selected to compliant job roles to be taken up in the schools under vocationalisation of secondary and higher secondary education.
3. Sensitisation of states and UT's about the concept of job roles and review the implementation
4. The Ministry has approved 259 new girls hostels in 2016-17(58 in Andhra Pradesh,10 in Arunachal Pradesh, 93 in Bihar, 31 in Jharkhand, 1 in Kerala, 43 in Odisha and 23 in Telangana)
5. Under National Merit-cum-Means Scholarship Scheme (NMMSS), during the year 2016-17, 64426 scholarships have been sanctioned in accordance with the proposals received from the state/ UT's.
6. Under National Scheme of Incentive for Girls for Secondary Education (NSIGSE), during 2016-17 , an amount of Rs 44.65 crores has been sanctioned covering 1,47,577 girl students.
7. Direct Benefit Transfer (DBT) System envisages direct transfer of funds to beneficiary account through Aadhaar Payment Bridge (APB). Both National Merit-cum-Means Scholarship Scheme (NMMSS) and National Scheme of Incentive to Girls for Secondary Education (NSIGSE) are covered under DBT. Under this scheme, a national scholarship portal(NSP) has been made operational for submission of proposals/ list of beneficiaries by the states governments for NMMSS and NSIGSE.

Conclusion

Rashtriya Madhyamik Shiksha Abhiyan (RMSA) launched in 2009 for secondary education produced great results in the educational development of secondary education by making all secondary schools conform to prescribed norms, removing gender, socio-economic and disability barriers, and providing universal access to secondary level education, but still there is a gap between target and results achieved. As we know Secondary education in India constitutes standards IX and X, whereas standards XI and XII are designated as the higher (senior) secondary stage. The normal age group of the children in secondary classes is 14–16 whereas children in the age group of 16–18 are in higher secondary classes. The population in the age group 14–18 was 9.6 crore in 2011 as per census data and the total number of government secondary schools was 73,825 in 2013–14 whereas the number of government elementary schools stood at 10,93,969. Thus, the ratio of elementary and secondary schools is 15:1 at the national level. After five years of the RMSA scheme of the central government, access to secondary education remains a serious concern. The onus of providing education rests largely with the government and the share of government schools at the elementary and secondary levels (including aided schools) is 75% and 63% respectively. The RMSA project approval board (PAB) granted permission to upgrade about 10,400 schools up to 2013–14, which is akin to a seed of cumin in a camel's mouth. This also reflects the improvidence and lackadaisical approach of the Ministry of Human Resource Development (MHRD) officials.

Future prospects

As per The Union Budget, 2018-19, three schemes of the government of India, Sarva Shiksha Abhiyan (SSA), Rashtriya Madhyamik Shiksha Abhiyan (RMSA) and Teacher Education (TE) is going to be subsumed under the Samagra Shiksha Abhiyaan

This scheme has proposed to treat school education holistically without segmentation from pre-nursery to Class 12. Samagra Shiksha - an overarching programme for the school education sector extending from pre-school to class 12 has been, therefore, prepared with the broader goal of improving school effectiveness measured in terms of equal opportunities for schooling and equitable learning outcomes. An allocation of Rs 75,000 crore over the period 1st April, 2018 to 31st March, 2020 has been approved for the Scheme which is a 20% increase over the current allocations. Its main features, inter alia, are as follows:

1. Annual Grant of Rs. 5,000 to Rs. 20,000/- per school for strengthening of Libraries.
2. Composite school grant increased from Rs. 14,500-50,000 to Rs. 25,000-1 Lakh and to be allocated on the basis of school enrolment.
3. Annual Grant for sports equipments at the cost of Rs. 5000 for Primary Schools, Rs. 10,000 for upper primary schools and up to Rs. 25,000 for secondary and senior secondary schools.
4. Allocation for Children with Special Needs (CwSN) increased from Rs. 3,000 to Rs. 3,500 per child per annum including a stipend of Rs. 200 per month for CWSN girls to be provided from Classes I to XII. – earlier it was only for classes IX to XII.

5. Allocation for uniforms enhanced from Rs. 400 to Rs. 600 per child per annum.
6. Allocation for textbooks enhanced from Rs. 150/250 to Rs. 250/400 per child per annum.
7. Upgradation of existing schools.
8. Upgradation of Kasturba Gandhi Balika Vidyalayas (KGBVs) from Class 6-8 to Class 6-12.
9. Strengthening Teacher Education Institutions like SCERTs and DIETs to improve the quality of teachers with SCERT as the nodal institution for in-service and pre-service teachers' training
10. Enhanced use of digital technology in education through smart classrooms, digital boards and DTH channels.

As the Scheme expands support for school education at pre-school and senior secondary levels, it provides for additional job opportunities for teachers, part-time teachers, support staff in schools, resource persons for academic support to teachers, teacher educators and administrative personnel. Further, the matters related to requirement of manpower to administer the Schemes, recruitment and the terms and conditions of service fall within the purview of the States and Union Territories.

References

1. Resolution of the GoI dated 26th June, 2009 for setting up the National Mission on the RMSA.
2. Press released of the GoI dated 7th June, 2011, and 2nd may 2013.
3. Aide Memoire of the First Joint Review Mission of the RMSA held during January 14 and 18, 2013.
4. Press release of the World Bank (W.B.) dated October 5, 2012. 5. Business case of the DFID, dated March 2012.
5. Framework for implementation of RMSA- GoI- document undated.
6. Promoting innovations under RMSA-Guideline – dated 27 January, 2012 GoI document
7. Draft Frequently Asked Questions on Quality-GoI document –undated.
8. Statement on state-wise release of funds and their utilization- GoI document – undated. 10. IIM press release in The Hindu 16th October, 2006.
9. "Rashtriya Madhyamik Shiksha Abhiyan". EdCIL (India) Limited. Retrieved 2 February 2014.

10. "Rashtriya Madhyamik Shiksha Abhiyan". Indian Yojana. Retrieved 2 February 2014.
11. "Rashtriya Madhyamik Shiksha Abhiyan (RSMA)" Retrieved 2 February, 2014 Bihar Madyamik Siksha Parishad..
12. http://rmsaindia.org/administrator/components/com_pdf/pdf/Planning%20for%20 Seconda ry%20Education.pdf
13. http://rmsaindia.org/administrator/components/com_pdf/pdf/Equity_Action_ Plan_201 4.pd
14. Parveen Kaswan (4 May 2013). "Rashtriya Madhyamik Siksha Abhiyan (RMSA)". Simply Decoded. Retrieved 2 February 2014.
15. "Union cabinet approves Rashtriya Madhyamik Shiksha Abhiyan proposal". Indian Education Review. 3 May 2013. Retrieved 2 February, 2014.
16. Research Pape Education 2017 CRITICAL REVIEW ON EDUCATION MANA GEMENTSYS TEM OF SECONDARY SCHOOL EDUCATION
17. Research Paper Education Nov 2016 Volume : 2 | Issue : 11 |
18. GUIDANCE AND COUNCILING IN INDIA INITIATIVE SUNDER RASHTRIYA MADHYA MIKSHIK SHAABHIYAN (RMSA)
19. INDIA Handbook 2018 for Competitive Exams - Schemes, Yojanas, Policies, Bill .By Disha Experts

Websites

1. https://pib.gov.in/newsite/PrintRelease.aspx?relid=95477 mhrd.gov.in/overview-secondary-education wikipedia.org/wiki/Rashtriya_Madhyamik_Shiksha_Abhiyan rmsaindia.org
2. www.apteacher.net/RMSA_information.php http://www.aicte-india.org
3. http://www.ssa.nic.in https://www.apteacher.net/RMSA_information.php
4. Ministry of Human Resource Development. "Rashtriya Madhyamik Shiksha Abhiyan". National Informatics Centre. Retrieved 2 February 2014.
5. http://samagra.mhrd.gov.in/https://pib.gov.in/PressReleaseIframePage.aspx?PRID=1540333https://www.india.gov.in/spotlight/rashtriya-madhyamik-shiksha-abhiyan#tab=tab-1
6. https://data.gov.in/resources/stateut-wise-status-habitations-covered-primary-upper-primary- secondary-level-schools-rmsa

+++

Chapter Thirteen

Enactment of Muslim Women (Protection of Rights on Marriage) Act, 2019 Omitted Discussion

Meena Kumari[14]

Abstract

The Supreme Court in Shayara Bano v. Union of India (2017) 9 S.C.C. 1 (India) declared the talaq-a-biddat unconstitutional and void. Thereafter, the government after a long wrangle on July 30, 2019 passed the Muslim Women (Protection of Rights on Marriage) Bill, 2019 (also known as triple talaq law).

The government identifies the problem, competing interests and prevailing reality before the enactment of any law and there is always a public policy behind it. Legislators are the policy makers owing great responsibility towards the people they represent. Legislative debate is an important tool to identify the public policy behind the enactment of any Act. It also constitutes external aid to an interpretation of the statute to discover the intention of the legislature.

This article insights into one of the important missing discussions in the legislative debate on - Muslim Women (Protection of Rights on Marriage) Bill, 2019-comparison of law of talaq with other countries. The comparison might throw light on different aspects like whether the ban in other countries was express or implied, whether the law in other countries provide any procedure, whether that law creates any confusion, what were the issues regarding the law in other countries before their courts and how their courts address those issues. This discourse might help in clarifying doubts and enrichment of policy. Thus, this article sheds light on missing discourses and provides a comparative overview of law of talaq prevailing in Pakistan and Bangladesh.

Keywords : *Triple Talaq Law, legislative debate, comparative overview, Talaq Laws, Pakistan and Bangladesh.*

---

14. Assistant Professor, Faculty of Law, University of Delhi, New Delhi

Introduction

On August, 2017; the apex court of India held triple *talaq* as violative of Article 14 of the Constitution. It is not that the issue of triple *talaq* came to the judiciary for interpretation for the first time, before that also there were high court and apex court judgments regarding the interpretation and validity triple *talaq*. What is new in the current judgment was the direction, although by minority judgment, to legislature to enact a law regarding this.

The government abided by the direction of the Supreme Court and brought the bill to regulate the practice of triple *talaq* among Muslims. The government wrangled to pass the bill in both houses of Parliament and also brought Ordinances. Ultimately after some amendments, the bill was passed in both houses of Parliament and declared triple *talaq* void and illegal.

Whenever legislators introduce a new bill or a law, it always contains public policy. The objective and reasons of the bill and the debate on the bill unlocked the policy behind the introduction of that bill by the legislature. Both the objectives and reason of any law and the debate is also to form an important aid for interpretation of statutes by the judiciary when the case comes before it. Thus the legislative debates during the passing of any bill is very important for the knowledge and information of the public, as it is the public, who have elected and send the legislators to represent them. The article tries to examine the omitted discussions on important points in the enactment of the law.

Triple *Talaq* and Judicial Interpretation

Under the Muslim Personal Law there are various modes of dissolution of marriage:- 1. By the death of one of the parties to marriage, marriage is automatically dissolved. 2. At the instance of the party, 3. Dissolution of marriage through the court. *Talaq* is one of the modes to dissolve the marriage at the instance of the husband.

In Pre-Islamic era the husband had an unlimited power to dissolve a marriage by pronouncing talaq without any reason and for any number of times. Moreover, they also had the power to resume the marriage relation at any time; thus the position of the Muslim married women was terrible. After the advent of Islam, Prophet Muhammad introduced some reforms and limited the power of the husband to pronounce the *talaq* for three times only.

There are two main forms of *talaq:- (i) talaq-e-sunna and (ii) talaq-e-biddat. Talaq-e-sunna* further has two forms of *talaq- i.e. (i) talaq-e-ahsan* and *(ii) talaq-e-hasan. Talaq-e-biddat* is called triple *talaq. Talaq-e-ahsan* is considered as the best form of *talaq*. In this form the husband pronounces the single revocable *talaq* during the *tuhr* period and abstains from the cohabitation with wife for two more *tuhr* periods in sequence. The *iddat* period for wife also begins with the pronouncement of the husband. As soon as the third *tuhr* period completes, *iddat* period as well *talaq* becomes complete and irrevocable. This amounts to a single irrevocable *talaq*. The couples are prohibited to resume the cohabitation or marital relationship unless they contract a fresh marriage with fresh *mehr*. If the husband and wife want to marry again they can enter into a fresh *nikah* without any restriction of performing an intervening marriage by the wife, but if the husband pronounced the *talaq* three times the couple cannot remarry again without the intervening marriage of wife with someone else.

Talaq-e-hasan is called as a good form of *talaq*. The husband pronounces three successive *talaq* in each three *tuhr* period and refrains himself from cohabitation during the period. The *iddat* period commences as soon as third *tuhr* period concludes. It is significant to note that the first and second pronouncement may be revoked by the husband by resuming the marital relationship but the third pronouncement of *talaq* becomes irrevocable. As soon as the third declaration of *talaq* is made *talaq* becomes irrevocable and marriage stands dissolved. The couple cannot remarry unless the wife contracts an intervening marriage with a other person.

Talaq-e-biddat is also called triple *talaq*. This may be effected by single definitive *talaq* like 'I *talaq* you irrevocably' or three pronouncements at the same time simultaneously, marriage is dissolved immediately on the pronouncement. Although this form of *talaq* is considered irregular among Muslims and followed in *Hanafi* school of *Sunni* sect. it has been described as 'bad in theology, but good in law'

1. In *Rashid Ahmed v. Anisha Khatun* Privy Council held that the pronouncement of triple *talaq* constituted immediately effective divorce. Even a *talaq* pronounced under compulsion or jest is valid and effective. Thus, the Privy Council upheld the triple *talaq* pronounced by the husband in absence and without the knowledge of the wife.
2. In *Jiaudin Ahmed v. Anwara Begum* High Court of Gauahati held that the

correct law of *talaq* as ordained by the Quran is that the *talaq* must be for a reasonable cause and be preceded by attempts at reconciliation between husband and wife with two arbiters, one from wife's family and a other from the husband's family. If attempt of reconciliation fails only then *talaq* may take place. In *Rukia Khatun v. Abdul Khalique* high court quoted the Muslim authorities like Muhammad Ali, Yusuf Ali, Ameer Ali and Fyzee to rule out the observation made by Macnaghten that 'there is no occasion for any particular cause for divorce, and mere whim is sufficient' and held that *talaq* must be for a reasonable cause and be preceded by attempts at reconciliation between the husband and wife by two arbiters- one from husband's side another from wife's side. If attempt fails *talaq* may take place.

3. In *Masroor Ahmed v. State (NCT of Delhi)* the Court held that triple *talaq* even for Sunni Muslims be regarded as one revocable *talaq*. This would enable the husband to think and get an oppurtunity to revoke the same during the *iddat* period; meanwhile family members of both husband and wife make efforts for reconciliation. On expiration of *iddat* period *talaq* becomes irrevocable. Couple can remarry by contracting fresh *nikah* with fresh *mehr* without any intervening marriage of wife with other person.

Even in some cases, judges alert the state that justice has become elusive to Muslim women and the remedy therefore lies in codification of the divorce. The court could not grant any relief to the petitioner.

Thus, the judiciary in India took an initiative to disapprove and criticize the triple *talaq* and provide justice to Muslim women. It is judicial activism of judiciary which facilitates the Muslim women to ascertain their rights. The judiciary may more actively and stunningly strike out the triple *talaq* by way of substantive equality as laid down by CEDAW convention and by following the feminist approach of equality; but the concept of patriarchy and difference between sex and gender are conspicuously missing from the judgments or interpretation of the triple *talaq*. The judiciary interprets it by way of holy Quran, authorities of Islam, by article 25, freedom of religion but not through patriarchy concept or through lens of feminism.

Shayra Bano vs. Union of India and others

The latest judgment on the validity of triple *talaq* is the *Shayra Bano* judgment.

The case comprised of six writ petitions dealing with the very issue. Supreme Court comprehensively described various modes of *talaq*, Quran with reference to *talaq*, legislation in the field of Muslim personal law in India, abrogation of tripe *talaq* by legislation in other countries in the world, judicial decisions on triple *talaq*, article 25, constitutional morality etc; although the highest court did not consider the feminist theory, substantive equality, concept of patriarchy to contrast the triple *talaq*. The court gave very brief regard to the provision of the CEDAW; although any discussion on the equal rights of women is incomplete without the CEDAW.

The court held that the triple *talaq* is manifestly arbitrary as marital relationship can be dissolved capriously and whimsically by Muslim husband without any effort of reconciliation. Triple *talaq* is a form of *talaq* which itself is considered as innovative and applying the test of manifest arbitrariness, this form of *talaq* is held to violate the fundamental right under article 14.

Legislative Debate on Muslim Women (Protection of Rights on Marriage) Bill, 2019

On June 21, 2019, the Muslim Women (Protection of Rights on Marriage) Bill was introduced by law minister *Ravi Shankar Prasad* for a second time in Lok Sabha, which was passed on July 25, 2019 and thereafter passed by Rajya Sabha on July 30, 2019 after a wrangle debate.

For the first time, 78 women members have been elected in the Lok Sabha; although the number is still small as per the total number of seats of Lok Sabha and as per the population of women. Likewise there are 26 women members in Rajya Sabha. These represents all the women in Parliament but less than ten shared their views on the sensitive matter. The main arguments against the bill in the debate in Lok Sabha and Rajya Sabha were as follows: that the bill conflated civil and criminal law by criminalizing the act of triple *talaq*, which is already declared null and void by the Supreme Court; thus framing a law for criminalizing Muslim husbands for a void act. It is a class legislation, which is pointed at one community or class thus violating Article 14 of the Constitution. Bill does nothing to improve the status of Muslim women; thus not come under the purview of Article 15 the Constitution. Thus, being absence of procedural safeguards it can be easily misused and thus, it is in violation of Article 21 of the Constitution. Bill is also in violation of Article 13(2) of the Constitution - as it is violating the fundamental rights of the citizen under Article 25 of the

Constitution. There are only 0.56 percent divorce incidents in Muslims which is negligible, so there was no need of any law. There are safeguards under section 498A I.P.C. 1860 and Protection of Woman from Domestic Violence, 2005, which are sufficient to deal with; Thus; no need of this is here. This bill was passed with the political intention to harass Muslim men. It provides punishment up to three years, how can a husband in jail provide subsistence allowance to wife?

The arguments in favor of the bill were as follows:

(i) that after the Supreme Court judgment in Aug. 17, 2019, 345 incidents of triple *talaq* came into light till July 24, 2019; thus, it is necessary to provide penal provision for deterrence. The Supreme Court urged that the government should legislate on it. Triple *talaq* causes injustice to Muslim women; thus, for gender justice and justice to women; law is imperative. Penalization was considered necessary as the idea of triple *talaq* symbolized the one-sided end of the marriage. The practice of triple *talaq* is the matter of oppression, exploitation and injustice to Muslim women.

Above analysis of the debate shows the missing discourse of feminism; although some women members declared that they are feminists but would not support the bill because it might be misused against Muslim husbands or it causes fear in the community (not able to understand whether this community includes women or not). Some talked about equality of the Muslim women but compared with women of other communities. Some calculated divorce rate and argued that it is negligible but forget that injustice to anyone is danger to justice everywhere. The basic themes of women's movement, patriarchy, difference between sex and gender are missing there also.

Legislative Debate as an Aid of Interpretation

There are various rules of interpretation. By applying these rules of interpretation the judiciary tries to find out the intention of the legislature to enact a law or the policy behind enacting a law, to apply that law in a particular situation. The legislative debate provides great help to find out the policy behind the law. It is the parliament or the legislative assembly debate where the policy behind any Act becomes manifest and clear. Court interprets law and evolves justice on such interpretation of law. It is in the domain of the legislature to make law. Justice has become elusive for Muslim women in India. It is for the law makers to correlate law and social phenomena relating to divorce through the process of legislation to advance justice in institutionalized form. It is imperative that to advance justice, law must be formulated without any repugnance to religious freedom guaranteed under the constitution of India. It is for the State to consider the formulation of codified law to govern the matter. The parliament codified the law of *talaq*; thus the debate opens the policy behind the enactment of the law.

Parliamentary debates are throwing light upon the meaning of statutory provisions. Willes J. stated that '*the sense and meaning of an Act of Parliament must be collected from what it says when passed into law, and not from the history of changes it underwent in the house where it took its rise*' in *Miller v. Tayler* [(1769) 4 Bum 2303] Although initially English courts and the Supreme Court of India did not consider the Parliamentary history of legislation, the bills presented, the debates on the bill as an aid to the construction because of the rule of exclusion; however this rule of exclusion of parliamentary history has been confined by the Apex Court and seek advice from legislative debates in resolving ambiguities.

Omitted Discourse: Comparison of Law on Triple *Talaq* with Other Countries

Debate on the bill of triple *talaq* draws attention that there are many countries, which codified the law of *talaq;* but not provide any detail of the law enacted by those countries, loopholes in that law and how the courts of those countries interpret such law. Such a discussion may throw light on different aspects of codified law of *talaq*- advantages as well as drawbacks. It also strengthens the policy related to the codification of the law of talaq.

Law of talaq in Pakistan: The Muslim Family Laws Ordinance 1961 provides the mechanism for dissolution of Muslim marriage by pronouncing *talaq* by husband. Section 7 permitted the Muslim man to pronounce *talaq* in any form, but laid down the procedure of reconciliation effort. According to section 7 of MFLO 1961 any man after pronouncing the *talaq* in any form must give Chairman a notice of *talaq* in writing and also give a copy of it to wife. Thereafter, the Chairman shall constitute an Arbitration Council within thirty days of receiving the notice to make efforts of reconciliation. The *talaq* already pronounced by the husband is not effective until the expiration of the ninety days or if wife is pregnant then until the termination of birth of the child from the date on which notice is sent to Chairman. On violation of this procedure on pronouncement of *talaq* the man shall be liable to punishment up to one year simple imprisonment or fine up to five thousand rupees or both. This section prohibits practice of *halala.* If both the parties wish to remarry, no intervening marriage of the woman with third person is required; although with condition that the *talaq* pronounced by the husband shall not be the third *talaq*.

This Ordinance tried to incorporate the *talaq-ahsan* form of *talaq-ul-sunna*; even though the man pronounces tale in any form, the tale will not be effective for ninety days from the date of notice to Chairman and it amounts to one tale. The man may remarry, the woman without any intervening marriage of the woman with any other third person.

Among different forms of talaq, the pronouncement of three *talaq* in one breath i.e. triple *talaq* was the most common form prevailing in Pakistan known as *talaq-i-bain*. It constituted the irrevocable *talaq*. Thereafter the woman followed the *iddat* period.

No Time Period Provided

One of the drawbacks of MFLO, 1961 is that it does not provide the time period within which husband must give notice of *talaq* to Chairman, it uses phrase 'as soon as possible', which is vague. Husband may play tricks to prolong the period of *iddat* as according to MFLO it commenced from the date of notice served on Chairman. Further, where husband fails to notify the *talaq* to Chairman, complaint can be filed by the Chairman and no right is given to wife. However in the province of Punjab by way of amendment the right to file complaint is also given to wife.

In 2005, Law and Justice Commission in its 74th report recommended certain reforms to remove the drawbacks and confusion create by conflicting judgments. The Commission proposed that notice to the Chairman should be given within 7 days of pronouncement of *talaq* by the husband, failure to which gives right to woman to give such notice to Chairman. However this recommendation has not been incorporated in MFLO, 1961

Where the man who has not followed the above procedure laid down by sec. 7, shall face the following consequence-

(i) The man shall be liable to punishment of simple imprisonment up to one year or fine up to five thousand rupees or with both.

In Pakistan the validity of triple *talaq* was never challenged, however the validity and legality of substantive reforms made by MFLO, 1961 was challenged frequently. Most of the judicial discourse revolves around the procedure laid down under MFLO 1961 and consequence of non-compliance. In *Sayed Ali*

Nawaz Gardezi v. *Lt. Col. Muhammad Yusuf,* the Supreme Court of Pakistan emphasized on the purpose of sec.7 of Ordinance that the main purpose is to prevent the hurried decisions of repudiation of marriage by pronouncing *talaq* unilaterally without any attempt of conciliation. Where the husband pronounced *talaq* and refrained from giving notice to Chairman under sec. 7, it was deemed to withdraw the *talaq* and marital status remained in existence. Thus, the requirement of notice under sec.7 was held to be mandatory for *talaq* in any form. In *State* v. *Taquir Fatima,* the court held that where no notice is given to the Chairman, the *talaq* could not become effective. In *Inamal Islam* v. *Hussain Bano,* the issue before the court was whether it is necessary to give a copy of the notice of *talaq* to wife under sec.7. The court held that the supply of copy of the notice to Chairman to wife is mandatory and considered a necessary part of the procedural requirement of sec. 7 for *talaq*.

However, Karachi High Court had taken a slightly different view with this regard in *Praveen Chaudhary* v. *Senior Civil Judge* that - it is necessary to give notice to the Chairman of *talaq* but absence of any notice or communication to wife before notice to Chairman is not necessary. There are two interpretations of this view, that (i) it is not necessary to inform the wife at all of the pronouncement of *talaq*, which is an essential requirement of Islamic law or (ii) it is not necessary to inform the wife of the supply of notice of *talaq* to the Chairman.

In Pakistan sec. 7 of MFLO, 1961 has been challenged on the ground that it was repugnant to Islamic law. The Federal Sharia Court (FSC), was initially of the view of excluding the personal laws including the MFLO, 1961 from the purview of its review powers; however in *Allah Rakha* v. *Federation of Pakistan* held that Federation *Sharia* Court has power to review the provisions of MFLO, 1961 and held that notice under sec. 7 of the MFLO, 1961 was not essential for effectuating *talaq*. The appeal against the decision of the Federal *Sharia* Court is still pending before the *Sharia* Appellate Bench of the Supreme Court of Pakistan since 2000, by which the decision remains in limbo.

The analysis of cases regarding requirement of notice of talaq to Chairman provides that the law is not settled on the validity of triple talaq and legal effect of husband's failure to serve a notice of talaq to chairman under MFLO, 1961. There were various contradictory judgments with judges interpreting in one or another way. Federal Shariat Court held that *talaq* is valid even when the husband failed to serve notice of *talaq* to Chairman. An appeal against this ruling is - still pending in Supreme Court. Thus, the law of *talaq* in Pakistan is still developing and further certain developments are expected in near future.

Law of talaq in Bangladesh: The Muslim Family Law Ordinance, 1961 was enacted when Bangladesh constituted the part of Pakistan, known as East- Pakistan before 1972. This Ordinance was enacted to give effect to the recommendations of the Commission on Marriages and Family laws. This Act applies to all citizens of Bangladesh. Section 7 of Ordinance codified the Islamic law of *talaq*. It laid down the scheme of *talaq*:

Firstly, the husband who pronounces *talaq* in any form shall give the Chairman of Arbitration Council - the notice in writing and also give a copy of this notice to wife.

Secondly, the Chairman, on receipt of the notice, shall constitute an Arbitration Council to make efforts to bring reconciliation between the parties by all effective means.

Thirdly, the *talaq* shall be effective only after expiration of ninety days from the day when notice is delivered to the Chairman. If wife is pregnant then *talaq* shall be effective after ninety days or till pregnancy ends, whichever is later.

The violation of this procedure attracts the punishment up to one year or fine which may extend to ten thousand *takka* or both. Clause (6) of section 7 derecognizes the practice of *halala*. It provides that the woman whose marriage is dissolved by way of *talaq* may again enter into marriage with the same man without solemnizing any intervening marriage; although with the condition that the *talaq* pronounced by the husband shall not be the third *talaq*.

It also imposes a condition that such termination of marriage shall not be for third time. It means that if already two times marriage was terminated by husband by pronouncing *talaq* following the procedure but every time both the parties enter into marriage again; and then if the *talaq* pronounced for the third time then the marriage be terminated accordingly. In such cases if both the parties again want to enter into marriage then intervening marriage and *talaq* with third person is essential i.e. practice of *halala* is essential.

The procedure laid down under section 7 shall also be applicable on *talaq-i-tafweez*, – whereby the right to *talaq* is delegated to wife or party dissolves the marriage by any other way. There is administrative differences in terms of the governmental bodies that apply the provisions of the MFLO, 1961 at the local level. Applications, appeals and conciliation procedures go to the Union Parishad or Municipal Corporation.

In Bangladesh, the constitutional validity of Muslim Family Law Ordinance 1961 is not challenged in court.

Conclusion

The debate in the Parliament on Muslim Women (Protection of Rights on Marriage) Bill, 2019 omitted a debate on the law of *talaq* as enacted by Pakistan and Bangladesh. It is also important because before independence and Partition, all these three countries shared the same history. There existed a cultural similarity; thus, the law enacted by these countries, drawbacks or loopholes of law, the issues before the court, problem in implementation of law etc. will helpful in making, explaining, implementing and anticipating the controversial issues beforehand.

The law enacted by other countries might be helpful to both who oppose the enactment of law as well as who support; as both can take the help of the provisions enacted by that law to explain their point of argument.

The debate in parliament is also helpful to the court to find out the policy of the government behind the enactment of the law, if any issue comes before the court related to the interpretation of the law.

References

A. Laws or Acts, International Conventions and Case Laws

1. Convention on the Elimination of All Forms of Discrimination Against the Women
2. Muslim Women (Protection of Rights on Marriage) Act, 2019
3. Muslim Family Law Ordinance 1961

B. Case Laws

1. *Inamal Islam* v. *Hussain Bano* 1976 PLD Lah 1466.
2. Jiaudin Ahmed v. Anwara Begum (1981) 1 Gau. L.R. 358.
3. *Masroor Ahmed v. State (NCT of Delhi)* 2008 (103) DRJ 137.
4. *Miller v. Tayler* [(1769) 4 Bum 2303
5. *Praveen Chaudhary* v. *Senior Civil Judge* 1976 PLD Kar 416.
6. *Rakha* v. *Federation of Pakistan* (2000) PLD FSC.
7. *Rashid Ahmed v. Anisha Khatun* AIR 1932 PC 25.
8. *Rukia Khatun v. Abdul Khalique* (1981) 1 Gau. L.R. 375.

9. Shayra Bano vs. Union of India and others W P (c) No. 118 of 2016
10. *Sayed Ali Nawaz Gardezi* v. *Lt. Col. Muhammad Yusuf* 1963 PLD SC 51.
11. *State* v. *Taquir Fatima* 1964 PLD (WP) Kar 306

C. Book

1. Mahmood, Tahir, 2016, *Muslim Law in India and Abroad*, New Delhi, ULP.
2. Mahmood, Tahir, 1987, *Personal Law in Islamic Countries: History, Text and Comparative Analysis,* New Delhi, Academy of Law and Religion.
3. Mulla, Sir Dinshaw Fardunji, 2016, *Mulla Principles of Mahomedan Law*, New Delhi, LexisNexis

D. Websites

1. https://scholarblogs.emory.edu/islamic-family-law/home/research/legal-profiles/bangladesh-people
2. http://www.prsindia.org/billtrack/muslim-women-protection-rights-marriage-bill.
3. http://rajyasabha.nic.in>home>debatesofficialdebate.aspx
4. http://loksabha.nic.in/debates/uncorrecteddebate,aspx

Chapter Fourteen

Public Policy and Nation-Building: A Critical Assessment of National Education Policy of India

Mohd Rashid Khan[15]

Abstract

Public policy is a purposive course of action in the pursuit of public interest. Once this course of action transforms from paper to the ground with the purpose of serving national interest, it shows the will and commitment of the government. Post independence India's biggest challenge was "nation building". Lack of education is the biggest developmental hurdle. Despite India's high GDP growth it has not been able to provide qualitative as well quantitative education to citizens. In this paper, there is an attempt to understand education policy and explore the various dimensions of policy aspects with regards to nation building.

Keywords: *Public Policy, Nation-building, National education Policy, Governance*

Introduction

Education is the pillar of development of human society and mankind. Human civilizational development is the finest example of manmade creation realized through the enhancement of education. India a country of billion plus population with so much diversity sustained political and social upheavals over a period of time. In the post-independence scenario, there were many challenges before the nation from poverty to illiteracy, economic depravity to political fragility, religious hatred to ethnic aspirations. In such a chaotic situation, our nation builders imagined an inclusive idea of India and became torch bearers towards the nation building goals. During Post Independence the major challenge was to educate the large illiterate population so as to bring them into the main-stream – India had to coup win many challenges. Among those one of the biggest goals was "nation building". It employed various methods to mainstream the marginalized

15. PhD, Research Scholar, Department of Political Science, Jamia Millia Islamia, New Delhi

section of societies. Though many policy initiatives were taken into consideration yet there are still large segments of society which remain unattended due to failure of governance. Lack of education is the biggest developmental hurdle. Despite India's high GDP growth it has not been able to provide qualitative as well quantitative education to citizens. Education is the panacea for all evils; it is the instrument of nation building. Our first education minister emphasizes the importance of education by saying that "Every individual has a right to an education that will enable him to develop his faculties and live a full human life" (Maulana Abul Kalam Azad). So, it is obvious that public policy making becomes very important. Public policy became the major instrument in realizing such goals.

In this study, an attempt will be made to understand what public policy is and how public policy transforms the development agenda on the ground. It has taken special consideration of India's national education policy where it explores the various dimensions of policy aspects with regards to nation building. The major thrust is on a critical analysis of the national education policy. The study employs both qualitative as well as quantitative approach in its method of inquiry in which it undertakes primary data as well as secondary data to collaborate in its analysis.

Public-Policy

Public policy is simply associated with legislation and regulation of various activities of government that encompasses all spheres of civil and, political life. Generally speaking public policy is what the government chooses to do, or not to do (Thomas R. Dye, p. 5). It is a decision made by government to either act, or not act in order to resolve a problem. Public policy is a course of action that guides a range of related actions in a given field. They rarely tackle one problem, but rather deal with clusters of entangled and long-term problems (Ibid). Public policy provides guidance to governments and accountability links to citizens (Melissa, Shaxton, p. 1). Public policy is a purposive course of action in the pursuit of public interest. Once this course of action transforms from paper to ground with the purpose of serving national interest, it shows the will and commitment of government (Anderson, p. 2).

Public-policy scope transcends all spheres of life. Public-policies are as old as governments. Whatever is the form, (oligarchy, monarchy, aristocracy, tyranny, democracy etc.,) whenever and wherever governments have existed, public policies have been formulated and implemented. To cope with the varied troubles and demands of the people the government has to create several policies, these policies are called public policies. Actually, the scope of public policy is determined by the kind of role that the State adopts for itself in a society. In the classical capitalist society, state was assigned a limited role and it was expected that the State would merely act as a regulator of social and economic activity and not its promoter. With the advent of planned view of development, the State began to be perceived as an active agent in promoting and shaping societies in its various activities. This was considered as a great change in the role of a State. Public-policies expanded their scope from merely one of regulation to that of development. Expansion in scope led to several other consequences like many more government affiliated institutions came into being in order to formulate and implement policies.

In India, the Planning Commission (now renamed NITI Ayog) and its attendant agencies came into being in order to formulate policies and develop perspectives that could define the direction which - the country would follow (K. Saigal, p. 3). So, the first major goal of public policies in our country has been in the area of socio-economic development. Wide ranging policies were formulated in the area of industrial and agricultural development. Many policies were converted into Statutes. Like Industrial Development and Regulating Act or Land Tenancy Act. Others were kept as directives in the various plan documents. For all policy directions, the Five Year Plans became the major source. These policies were of two types, one of regulation and the other of promotion. Laws laid down what could be done or not done by the entrepreneurs. This could be in the larger area like what goods can be produced by the public or whether certain goods can be delivered only by government agencies undertaking. Laws also specified how State agencies themselves were to provide goods and services like electricity, transport etc. The State undertook similar responsibility in the social sphere. Dowry Act, Divorce Act, etc., are examples of this. But socio-economic transformation was not the only problem when India became independent. There were also problems of national integrity, the external environment was a source of threat and the country had to develop suitable policies to defend itself.

Apart from this, there have been internal challenges. Regionalism has given rise to divisive tendencies that have to be countered in the long-term perspective These would include not only defence policies but also similar efforts at decentralisation that create greater nationhood cohesiveness. Thus, since independence, public-policies in India have been formulated with a view to achieve socio-economic development and maintain national integrity. These goals have been complex demanding coherent policies. This has been a difficult task because goals have had to be divided into sectors and sub-sectors. Many a time by its very nationalist policies has been contradictory. What may be rational for economic development; may not be so for national Integration. There is a need of a strong Centre to cope with external threats but it may go against the principle of decentralisation which provides for greater national cohesion of a heterogeneous society. This is the reason why ascertaining of the actual impact of public policy becomes a necessity (ibid, Pp.01-07).

Public-Policy in India (The bigger democracy of the world

India is a sovereign, socialist, secular, democratic republic having a parliamentary form of government. The institutions of legislature, executive, and judiciary play a significant role in policy making. Besides, some nongovernmental organizations perform a major part in the total process. The Indian system of governance is in accordance with some of the basic objectives having been laid down through the planners, of course, in the light of the Constitution of the country. Broadly, in the context of these objectives, the policies have been and are being framed. Some of these objectives contain elimination of poverty, elimination of illiteracy, initiating events of social justice, bringing in relation to the reduction of disparities in income and wealth, even sharing of economic power, helping weaker sections, establishing greater excellence opportunity, resisting inflationary pressures, utilization of manpower possessions to the fullest extent, boosting industrial productivity, achieving self-sufficiency in basic needs of shelter, clothing and health for all, augmenting agricultural production, achieving economic and technological self-reliance, promoting active involvement of all the sections of people in the process of development, developing the transport system, promoting policies for controlling the growth of population, etc. These are just some of the basic objectives which our development policies have been trying to achieve. The main thrust of the system has been on self-reliance, economic growth, industrialization, modernization, social justice and education. In the context of these major goals, the policies have been formulated and implemented. We would now be focusing on the national education policy of India (P. Sahni, p. 04).

The nature of the State's policy process and its importance will become clearer, if we take up the Indian experience in the field of policy formulation and implementation. This case, study is appropriate because we have accumulated very rich experience in making and carrying out many public policies. Since Independence, our Five Year Plans have been emphasizing on planned economic development. Planning is the base of all public policies. Theoretically, in a planned development, all the policies should enumerate from planning itself. A discussion on some of the crucial characteristics of public policy in a planned context would highlight public policy experience in India.

National Education-Policies

Education has always been given an important place in Indian society. The great leaders of the Indian freedom movement realized the fundamental role of education and, throughout the nation's struggle for independence, stressed its unique significance for national development. Immediately after independence, a major concern of the Government of India and of the States has been to give increasing attention to education, as a factor, vital to national progress and security but, simultaneously, it was, also, visible that the success rate of this objective was not sufficient and many problems prevailed at both levels- policy and practical. Problems of educational reconstruction were reviewed by several commissions and committees, notably the University Education Commission (1948-49) and the Secondary Education Commission (1952-53). Some steps to implement the recommendations of these Commissions were taken; and with the passing of the Resolution on Scientific Policy, under the leadership of Jawaharlal Nehru, the development of science, technology and scientific research received special emphasis. Towards the end of the third Five Year Plan, a need was felt to hold a comprehensive review of the educational system, with a view to initiating a fresh and more determined effort at educational reconstruction; and, then, the Education Commission (1964-66) was appointed to advise the Government on, " the national pattern of education and on the general principles and policies for the development of education at all stages and in all aspects." The Government was happy to note that a consensus on the national policy on education has emerged, in the course of these discussions.

Based on the report and recommendations of the Education Commission (1964–1966), the first National Policy on Education was announced in 1968, which called for a "radical restructuring" and equalizing of educational opportunities, in order to achieve national integration and greater cultural and economic development. The policy called for fulfilling compulsory education for all children up to the age of 14, as stipulated by the Constitution of India, and the better training and qualification of teachers. The policy called for focus on learning of regional languages, outlining the "three language formula" to be implemented in secondary education. Language education was seen as essential to reduce the gulf between the intelligentsia and the masses. The policy, also, encouraged the teaching of the ancient Sanskrit language, which was considered an essential part of India's culture and heritage. The NPE, of 1968, called for education spending to increase to six percent of the national income. According to the National Policy on Education-1968, the government of India had formulated certain principles to promote the development of education in the country.

These principles are enumerated as under:

Free and Compulsory Education- According to the Indian Constitution, education should be free and compulsory up to the age of 14. Steps should be taken to ensure that the child, enrolled in the school, should successfully complete the course.

Education of Teachers- The teacher is the most important person to determine the quality of education in the country. He/she should be honoured in society. His/her emoluments and service standard should be increased, with due regard to her responsibilities and qualifications. Proper attention should be given to quality teacher education. They should, also, get academic freedom to write, to study and to speak on national and international issues. The constitution of India (Article 19) mentions freedom of expression for all.

Language Development- The policy had, also, emphasized on the development of Indian, as well as foreign languages, in the country. The three language formula should be introduced, in which a student at the secondary level, should know Hindi, English and the regional language of his state. The language Sanskrit, has been included as an optional subject, at the secondary level.

Education Opportunity for all- Under this policy, every child of the country should get education, irrespective of caste, religion, region or whatever the case may be. Special emphasis should be laid on backward classes, minority children, girls and physically challenged children to avail the education facilities.

Uniform Education Structure- The structure of education should be made uniform throughout the country. It should be a 10+2+3 pattern from higher secondary to college level. During the course of study, each student should get to play sports and games i.e. co curricular activities. They should also develop the quality of work experience and should participate in programmes related to National construction and Community services.

To review the progress- The government should review the progress of education in the country, from time to time, and should present guidelines for its future development which provides a good and strong base for the education system. After this, a new policy on Education came into existence and was formulated in 1986, which, also, has most of the qualities of education policy 1968 and more than that. The main focus of the commission was on these three aspects, particularly, (NCT, 1983-85). First, measures to give to the teacher is the status he needs and deserves to help him do his duties at the highest possible level of performance, which implies a suitable salary that, in the prevailing economic conditions - will not only meet his economic needs, but be commensurate with his professional status and powerful enough to attract and retain 'talent' in the profession; Second, the evolution of a system of teacher preparation that would help the teacher develop skills and values, so as to make his teaching and efforts at character development, effective and go far; and third, to indicate the broad parameters of a code of conduct which would motivate and help the teacher give his best in the performance of his duties; and to point out other conditions that are necessary for such a code's effective enforcement.

The Report highlights the basic concerns that, until standards of school education improve; the university education will contribute only in parts. The Report raised issues regarding how higher education has to play a role in school education, as teachers in schools are from universities. The Report talks about the role of higher education, as having academic and moral leadership. If the university falters in this key function, there is little that can be done to save the school system from the deleterious effects of its dys-functionality.

Another important commission was constituted in 2005, the National Knowledge Commission (established on 13th June 2005 and given a timeframe of three years from 2nd October 2005 to 2nd October 2008). This significant commission has talked about the education system in India, at length. The main frame or reference of this National Knowledge Commission (NKC) was: to (i) build excellence in the educational system to meet the knowledge challenges of the 21st century and (ii) increase India's competitive advantage in fields of knowledge, promote creation of knowledge in Science and Technology laboratories, (iii) improve the management of institutions engaged in intellectual property rights, (iv) promote knowledge applications in agriculture and industry, (v) promote the use of knowledge capabilities in making government an effective, (vi) transparent and accountable service provider to the citizen and (vii) promote widespread sharing of knowledge to maximize public benefit.

The National Education-Policy, 2019

The Draft National Education Policy 2019 came into the public domain. It has taken inputs from the T.S.R. Subramanian Committee report and the K. Kasturirangan Committee with consultation of the Ministry of Human Resource Development (MHRD) - has produced the policy document. The Main features of National Education Policy (NEP 2019) are - to universalize the pre-primary education by 2025 and provide foundational literacy/numeracy for all by 2025. It proposes new Curricular and Pedagogical Structure, with 5+3+3+4 design covering the children in the age group 3-18 years. Under this, Pre-Primary & Grades 1-2 is considered as foundational Stage; Grades 3-5 as Preparatory Stage; Grades 6-8 as Middle Stage and Grades 9-12 as Secondary Stage. This is an academic restructuring only; there will be no physical restructuring of schools. NEP aims at equitable & inclusive education for every child in the country, with a special focus on Under-Represented Groups (URGs). It will also ensure Universal Access & Retention with 100% Gross Enrolment Ratio for all school education by 2030 (NEP, 2019).

Nation Building

Education is the most vital component for a nation. The education level of a country decides whether a country is developed or not because only the educated population can lead to better capital formation. Education is the pathway to any nation-building enterprise. Education plays a very important role in nation building. It is education that transforms the human being into an intelligent honest citizen towards its country. A proper or right education can make an independent citizen who leads to developed country (economic growth in for of increasing per capita income or GDP growth rate, political sensibility, enactment of his/her social responsibility towards society as well as nation). Education gives people, take the skills they need to help themselves out of poverty or in other words; live into prosperity.

Education, primarily, has been seen as a tool for social engineering. In the Kothari Commission, the vision of a desirable society presented in the report does contain glimpses of the ideals of equality and social justice. The NPE 1986/92 takes individuals more seriously and there is a definite shift (from the Kothari commission) towards critical thinking, but, still, the individual is regarded as a resource to be used to achieve national goals, rather than an active participant in defining these goals. The Kothari Commission derives the aims of education from the national goals, though the aims of education may contain elements of individual freedom and critical thinking, but the justification for these last two is sought in terms of national goals. That education in itself, has great goals, a demand and supply, needs to be acknowledged by the policies. We should try to promote 'equal understanding of and equal respect for all religions', through education. '*SarvadharmaSamabhava*' is the same thing as '*panthnirpekshata*'. Religion, in its basic form (devoid of myth, dogma and ritual), would draw the younger generation towards basic moral and spiritual values. Only education that leads to belief in God - can contribute to the service of the country and humanity as a whole.

A state-run education system should promote an equal understanding of all religions, without adhering to a particular religion or particular religious ideas. This is possible, if all the religions are, critically, analysed in the classroom and the students should be free to make their own choice. This would lead to the acceptance of the different religious ideas, as either true or with equal disbelief, in all the religious ideas. National education policy which stresses also on comparative religious education that it would enable harmonious interfaith in society and ultimately serve nation building purposes.

A Critical Assessment

Education is the foundation of human development and the creation of egalitarian society. Education helps to inspire our minds and provide a deeper understanding of society to form the very essence of our actions. It has transformative effects on society as well as help in realisation of nation-building goals. Education is a powerful tool by which economically and socially marginalised groups can lift themselves and can enjoy their life. It is a vital tool to exercise all fundamental rights enshrined in a modern constitutional state.

In the post liberalisation scenario, commercialisation of education creating avenues of disparities & exclusion. Though, it is filling the growing demand of professional technical education (i.e. technical know - how) but at the same time influencing educational policies of government at the cost of public education. It is important to allow the private players to enter in the field of education but under certain provisions so that the basic concept of the welfare state should be protected and it remains within the reach of every citizen.

India's education system is currently facing serious problems and challenges and there are no simple remedies that can solve them. Rampant unemployment, unstructured economic reform, shortages of public funding plague of public education. Government cannot escape from its responsibility to patronage education by adopting privatisation and market-oriented approach. It is a known fact that a majority of poor citizens are not capable of affording basic education. Government should see education as an avenue of homogenizing national identity. The government must continue to support education through national education policy so as to maintain fair quality and to attain certain socio-economic objectives and realize the nation building goals.

References

1. Anderson, James E. (1975), Public Policy Making. Praeger: New York, p. 2
2. Dye Thomas R. (1972), Understanding Public Policy, Prentice Hall: Englewoodcliff, p. 5
3. Ramirez, F.O. and J. Boli (1987), The Political Construction of Mass Schooling: European Origins and Worldwide Institutionalization, Sociology of Education, Vol. 60, Pp. 2-17.
4. Sahni Pardeep (1987), Public Policy: Conceptual Dimensions, Kitab Mahal: Allahabad, p. 04
5. Saigal Krishan, (1983), Policy Making in India: An Approach to Optimisation, Vikas Publication: New Delhi, Pp. 01-07
6. Smith, A. D. (1998), Nationalism and Modernism: A Critical Survey of Recent Theories of Nations and Nationalism, Routledge, London, p.4
7. M. Melissa, S. Louise (2012), Understanding and Applying Basic Public Policy Concepts,
8. University of Guelph, at- https://www.politicipublice.ro/uploads/understanding_public_policy.pdf, Accessed date, 12/12/2019.
9. The Mudaliar Commission (1952-53), Accessed date, 13/12/2019, at-https://www.educationforallinindia.com/1953%20Secondary_Education_Commission_Report.pdf
10. The Kothari Commission (1964-66), Accessed date- 13/12/2019, at- http://www.yourarticlelibrary.com/education/kothari-education-commission-1964-66/76816
11. The Curriculum Framework (1975), Accessed date- 13/12/2019, at- http://epathshala.nic.in/programmes/national-curriculum-frameworks/
12. The National Policy Education (1986), Accessed date- 13/12/2019, at- http://www.ncert.nic.in/oth_anoun/npe86.pdf

13. National Curriculum Framework for School Education-NCF 1998, Accessed date-13/12/2019, at- http://www.ncert.nic.in/rightside/links/pdf/framework/english/nf2005.pdf
14. National Curriculum Framework for School Education-NCF2000, Accessed date-13/12/2019, at- http://www.ncert.nic.in/rightside/links/pdf/framework/english/nf2005.pdf
15. National Curriculum Framework- NCF 2005, Accessed date- 13/12/2019, at- http://www.ncert.nic.in/rightside/links/pdf/framework/english/nf2005.pdf
16. National Education Policy 2019, MHRD, Government of India, Accessed date, 12/12/2019, at- https://mhrd.gov.in/sites/upload_files/mhrd/files/Draft_NEP_2019_EN_Revised.pdf.

✦✦✦

Chapter Fifteen

A Study over Implementation of District Disaster Management, Guidelines and Evaluation of Capacity Building of Disaster Management in District Kishtwar

Ram Kumar[16]

Abstract

Public Policy study has encompassed all aspects of development, which also includes Disaster Management. The legalized action for Disaster Management in India commenced with The National Disaster Management Act, 2005. This act has created a structure of authority at the grass roots level called District Disaster Management Authority and mentioned several guidelines to consolidate the district disaster management mechanism by enhancing the Capacity Building of the Institutional Machinery and the people of the Community. The present study aims to know about the implementation of the guidelines of the NDM Act, 2005, to assess the Capacity Building of Institutional Machinery and to examine the Community Capacity Building for Disaster Management in District Kishtwar. The nature of the present study is analytical, explorative and evaluative, so, in order to achieve the objectives of the study, both primary and secondary data are used. The primary data is collected from the Institutional Machinery and People of the Community by an Interview Schedule. The collected data is analyzed and interpreted with the help of SPSS software, excel, table graphs etc. to get the adequate conclusion.

Keywords: *Guidelines, Institutional Machinery, Capacity Building, Community, Implementation*

Introduction

Public Policy studies have encompassed all aspects of development, specifically in developing countries, which are more vulnerable for "Disaster" because of

16. Assistant Professor, Public Administration, Government Degree College, Chowari, Himachal Pradesh

multiple hazards that are both natural and man-made. Policy, in simple and broad sense; is a proposed course of action, - which may be of an individual, a group, an institution or government - to achieve some specific objectives or purposes, within the determined environment (Basu, 2004). Policy studies include three central elements in the policy-making process; identifying the problems and resources, evaluating and revising policy production systems and determining policy-making strategies (D. Ravindra Prasad V.S. Prasad P. Satyanarayana, Y. Pardhasaradhi, 2017). Thus, policy is a specific plan of action - to achieve a determined purpose that too in a specific sphere and guidelines.

A Policy or an organised action pertaining to disaster management has been evolved in India of most of the same time when The National Disaster Management Act, 2005, had come into operation. This Act has created a formal structure and a decentralized approach - to efficiently face the impacts of disaster at a different level. The National Disaster Management Authority (NDMA), State Disaster Management Authority (SDMA) and District Disaster Management Authority (DDMA) are the apex bodies entrusted with the task of disaster management at National, State and District levels respectively (NDM Act, 2005).

Now, it is vital to understand the meaning of Disaster before contemplating on the Policy of Disaster Management in India. The NDM Act, 2005 has enshrined the definition of disaster as, - *"Disaster' means a catastrophe, mishap, calamity, adversity or grave occurrence in any area, arising from natural or manmade causes, or by accident or negligence that results in substantial loss of life or human suffering or damage to - and disturbance of, property, or damage to, or degradation of environment, and is - of such a nature or magnitude as to be beyond the coping capacity of the affected area"* (NDMA, 2005). Thus, disaster is such a grave occurrence, that goes beyond the combating abilities of the affected people and they could not recover from that until and unless helped by external source. Therefore, the Act; also elucidated a policy guideline to manage such suffering by Capacity Building in numerous ways and the process is defined as, - "Disaster Management". It means, a continuous and integrated process of planning, organising, co-ordinating and implementing measures, which are necessary or expedient for prevention of danger or threat of any disaster, mitigation or reduction of risk of any disaster or its severity or consequences, capacity-building, prepardeness to deal with any disaster, propmpt response to any threatening disaster situation, assessing the magnitude of effects of any disaster, evacuation rescue and relief and rehabiliation and construction (NDM Act, 2005).

According to the NDM Act, District is the only lower authority which makes a liaison with NDM Authority and the people of the Community to make them resilient for any disaster. Thus, a district is bound to follow the guidelines of The National Disaster Management Plan (NDMP) in its District Disaster Management Plan (DDMA), which provides a framework of guidelines to all government agencies to follow. The guidelines aim that disaster management will be periodically improved, keeping up with the emerging global best practices and knowledge base in disaster management. Therefore, the NDM Plan and DDM Plan are in accordance with the guidelines of the Sendai Framework for Disaster Risk Reduction (DDR) 2015-2030, under the five Thematic Areas for Action (NDM Plan, 2016):-

1. Understanding Risk,
2. Inter-Agency Co-ordination,
3. Investing in DRR – Structural Measures,
4. Investing in DRR – Non-Structural Measures and-
5. Capacity Development.

The above five thematic guidelines cannot work until and unless, they emphasize on the Capacity-Building of disaster management, which is synonymous with Capacity-Development. Capacity-Building means; strengthening of institutions, mechanisms and capacities of all stake-holders at all levels for the prevention and mitigation of risk of hazards, preparedness for response, effective response when disaster occurs and - ability to recover and build back better. The guidelines of the NDM, Act 2005 for better disaster management are incorporated and enumerated in the NDM Plan, 2016 to consolidate the disaster management cycle, not after the happening of a disaster but before any grave occurrence. Therefore, Disaster Management Cycle in NDM Plan and DDM Plan is divided into two phases; (i) Pre-Disaster Management and (ii) Post-Disaster Management. The diagram of the disaster management cycle is illustrated as under:-

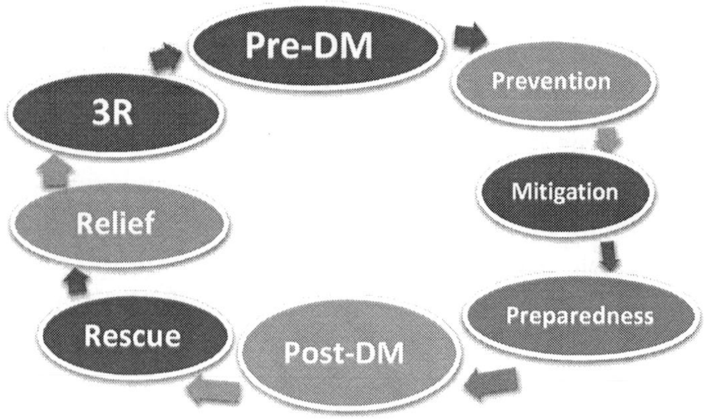

Figure 1: Disaster Management Cycle

Source: (NDM Plan, 2016)

The pre-disaster management lays focus on those initiatives that commence before the happening of any disaster such as - prevention, mitigation and preparedness and - the post-disaster management starts after any disaster occurs as - recue, relief and Recovery (Reconstruction, Rehabilitation and Recovery). In this cycle, the guidelines and provisions elucidated for better disaster management has given more emphasises on the pre-disaster management to prevent and mitigate any disaster by capacity - building of institutional machinery (DDMA) and the community, and if prevention and mitigation is not possible then it is indispensable to prepare those people who are entrusted with the task of disaster management (Institutional Authority) and - the people who are vulnerable to make them resilient.

There are done various studies which has said emphasis on District Disaster Policy, capacity building of institutional machinery and preparedness of community for better disaster management. In the policy framework of India, it is elucidated above that Disaster Management has an indispensable place, that requires a multi-disciplinary and multi-sectoral approach by incorporation of risk reduction measures in the development plans and strategies. These development strategies only can be sustainable, - if the development process lays focus on the mitigation of disasters (Patil, 2012).

The DRR and Sustainable Development rely on adaptive capacity of disaster management which is divided into the themes of governance, policy, leadership, and community engagement. In a policy, a good hierarchical design shows the coping and adaptive potential of a nation for disaster management and to make its community resilient. Coping capacity means - which people or organizations use available resources, skills and opportunities to face adverse consequences of any disaster. The coping capacity can be built, if it has a social character, economic-capital, infrastructure, planning, emergency services, information and community engagement (Melissa Parsons, Sonya Glavac, Peter Hastings, Graham Marshall, James McGregor, Judith McNeill, Phil Morley, Ian Reeve, Richard Stayner,, 2016).

The study of the flood of Ladakh, 2010 is one of the instances which have emphasized on the approach of Disaster Risk Reduction initiatives of central and state governments at district level to address vulnerability and capacity building. It revealed that National and State Policies of disaster management have well integrated the concept of hazards, vulnerability and disaster but the study brought out that, only establishing of policies do not guarantee that appropriate practices will happen at ground level. The study has found that only the formulation of policies are not enough, until and unless the policy framework of DDR will address the socioeconomic causes of disasters, to prepare people, to recover from emergencies and integration of DRR in development projects to achieve sustainable development for the better disaster management and to make the community resilient (Masson, 2015).

The study of Bihar has also asserted that all risks of disaster can be reduced, if we focus on different aspects of the development at district level in disaster management. The study includes the contents: (i) making district disaster management plan pro-poor and local experience; (ii) a human rights-based approach in district disaster management plans; (iii) placing community first; (iv) a change of mind set is needed; (v) to know about the hazards, vulnerability and capacity building to make the community resilient (viii) need of district disaster management approach in disaster management (World Meteorological Organisation).

In this study, it was further, found that the intensity of disasters have increased manifold and even the Government of India has undertaken various measures to mitigate the impact of these disasters. But even after that, there is still unpreparedness and incompetency in disaster management at grass-roots-level. The authority neither has focused on the capacity-building of civil administration, nor on the community-capacity-building (Gautam).

The study has found here that community participation is the most effective element to achieve sustainability in dealing with natural and man-made disaster risks. Unawareness of the community becomes itself a source of risk of disasters by constructing physical infrastructure. For an instance, in the cases of earthquake, where the majority of victims are being killed by collapsing houses. So, an approach is needed for the communities which are at risk to them into pre-disaster management to post-disaster management cycle. They need to be empowered by dissemination of best practices in disaster risk management at the community level and formulation of integrated programs for sustainable development through disaster risk management initiatives (Bhagat).

Objectives

1. To know the implementation of guidelines of National Disaster Management Act, 2005 in District Kishtwar.
2. To assess the Capacity-Building of Institutional Machinery in terms of Human Resources, Finance, Technology for the Disaster Management of District Kishtwar.
3. To examine the Community-Capacity-Building for Disaster Management in District Kishtwar

The Study Area

The study area is District Kishtwar of Jammu and Kashmir Union Territory. It is the land of saffron and sapphire and was an independent hill state during the medieval period of Maharaja Gulab Singh and Dogra Ruler. It is carved out from erstwhile District Doda. Kishtwar is one of the main districts of this Union Territory which is vulnerable for multiple hazards due to its topography and Climatology, along with extreme seasonal changes, that is winter and summer. It is a plateau on the height of 5300 feet or 1631 metres above the sea-level. It lies between the 75 - 25 East longitude & 34-10 North latitude. It is situated at a distance of 234 kms from Jammu and 280 from Kashmir. There are high altitude mountains ranging between 20,000 feet to 21,000 feet like Num Kum, Burmah and Barn. Demographically, the study area is divided into:- (i) Three Sub-Divisions, (ii) 11 Tehsils, (iii) 13 Blocks and (iv) one Town (Divided into 13 Wards) for its administrative set up (DDM Plan, 2018-19).

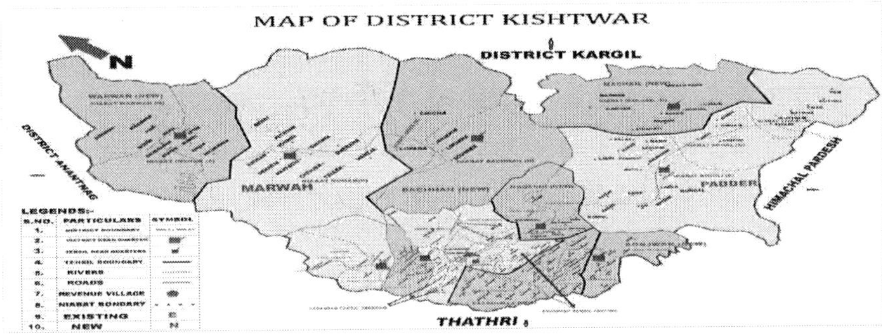

Figure: 1 Map of District Kishtwar

Source: https://kishtwar.nic.in/map-of-district/

The study area is not only vulnerable for natural hazards but also for man-made hazards. The center and surrounding of study area is on its pace of developments. There are a number of development projects which have enhanced the risk of disaster and one of the examples is Dull Hasti Hydro Project. The DDM Plan of District Kishtwar has mentioned following hazards and risks of disaster in the Table No. 1.

Table No. 1: Hazards and Risk of Disaster in District Kishtwar

S.No.	Variables	Hazards					
		Earthquake	**Flood Flash-Flood**	**Drought**	**Land- slides**	**Wind Storms**	**Building Fire**
1	Past History	Yes	Yes	Yes	Yes	Yes	Yes
2	Frequency	Zone- V	April-August (Rainy Seasons)	Likely in Summer Seasons	Very Likely	Very Likely	Summer and in Winter it increases
3	Vulnerability	100% District	½ District	Whole District	N.C.	10% of District	10% of District
4	Likely to Damage Life and Property	Human, Property and Other Living Things	Minimal	NIL	1800 Households	Roofs of Houses, Fruit Trees	Wood and Kachna Houses

Source: DDM Plan-2018-19

The highest Institutional Authority in the District for disaster management according to the guidelines of National Disaster management Act, 2005 is

District Disaster Management Authority (DDMA). The head of DDMA is District Commissioner, who directs co-ordinates and implements all the plans pertaining to disaster management in the district. The district has its own District Disaster Management Plan (DDM Plan) which has followed the guidelines of NDM Act, and NDM Plan to consolidate its capacity building for disaster management. Besides that there is a sole and specialized force in the district for disaster rescue, relief and shelter operation. This district disaster force is composed of State Disaster Response Force (SDRF) along with other temporary forces such as Home Guards (H.G.) and Civil Defence Wardens (C.D.W.) who works from pre-disaster to post-disaster management course of action in the district (DDM Plan, 2018-19).

Research Methodology and Sample Design

The nature of the present study is analytical, explorative and evaluative. So, in order to achieve the objectives of the study, both primary and secondary data are used. With need of objectives, the primary data was collected from Institutional Machinery (District Disaster Management Force) and People of the Community by Interview Scheduled to know about the implementation of the guidelines of NDM Act, 2005 at grass-roots-level. Apart from that it was necessary to examine and assess the capacity building for disaster management of institutional machinery and people of the community. The study with the help of literature reviews and by Purposeful Sampling, the samples were chosen from Institutional Machinery and the Community which had proximity with the Headquarter of District Disaster Force and the Wards of the Town respectively.

Sample Design of Institutional Machinery

The total strength of the disaster management force in the district were 258 members which was distributed as; 13 members of State Disaster Response Force (SDRF), 161 members of Home Guard (HG) and 84 members of Civil Defence Warden (CDW). But the actual strength which was proximate to study area were : 13 members of SRDF, 22 members each from HG and CDW. So, by the Purposeful Sampling, based on proximity and availability of the respondents in the study area, the total sample size was taken '52' which was distributed among these three forces as; 8 members of SDRF and 22 members of both the forces that is HG and CDW.

Table No.2: Distribution of Respondent of Disaster Management Force

S. No.	Name of the Organisation	Frequency	Percentage
1	SDRF	8	15.4
2	HG	22	42.3
3	CDW	22	42.3
Total		52	100

Source: Primary Data

The Table No. 2 above shows the percentage of Sample Size of the Disaster Management Force as 15.4% of SDRF members and HG and CDW both combinedly are 42%.

Sample Design of the Community

At the community level, the universe was Kishtwar Town, which was divided into 13 Wards. And by Purposeful Sampling, the Sample of 5 wards was chosen out of 13 wards by Random Sampling. Further, for these 5 wards the total sample size was 250 respondents by Purposeful and Convenient Sampling. And this sample of 250 respondents was distributed into the five wards according to the total no. of households in one ward and divided by the total no. of households in five wards, which was multiplied by the total sample size that was 250.

The formula is given below and ward wise respondents distribution is shown in Table No. 3. below:-

$$\frac{\text{Total No. of households in one ward}}{\text{Total No. of households in five wards}} \times 250, \text{ e.g. } \frac{250}{1388} \times 250 = 45$$

Table No. 3: Distribution of Respondent at Community Level

Ward No.	Name of Ward	No. of Households in each wards	No of Respondents
1.	Malipath	250	45
2.	Shaheedi Mohalla	252	45
3.	Kripak Mohalla	261	47
4.	Bagwan Mohalla	247	44
5.	Akhyarabad Mohalla	378	68
Total		1388	250

Source: Primary Data

Data Analysis and Interpretation

The secondary and collected data from Institutional Machinery and Community Level is analyzed in accordance with the objectives of the study by entering and analysing the data into SPSS and represented by Table and Graphs. The analysis of the data is done by a statistical tool called Majority of Responses (more than half of total responses e.g.51 out of 100), when comes either as 'Yes' or 'No' and is considered as highest indication of a response.

Table No. 4: Hazards in the District Kishtwar

S.No	Type of Disaster	Responses of D.M.F.		Responses of Community	
		Frequency	Total	Frequency	Percentage
1	Earthquake	52(100)	52(100)	245(98.8)	250(100)
2	Flood	52(100)	52(100)	236(94.4)	250(100)
3	Landslide	52(100)	52(100)	225(90.0)	250(100)
4	Avalanches	21(40)	52(100)	186(74.4)	250(100)
5	Drought	52(100)	52(100)	199(79.6)	250(100)
6	Fire	52(100)	52(100)	233(93.2)	250(100)
7	Accident	52(100)	52(100)	229(91.6)	250(100)
8	Communal Clash	37(71.0)	52(100)	192(76.8)	250(100)
Total		52		250	

Source: Primary data, Parentheses is percentage given in bracket

The Table No.4 above, depicts the responses of Disaster Management Force (D.M.F.) and Community's about the possibility of occurrence of multiple hazards in district Kishtwar. The 'Yes' response of occurrence of Earthquake, Flood, Landslides, Avalanches, Drought, Fire and Accident of D.M.F. is 100%. The 'No" response for Communal Clash of D.M.F. is 71%. The 'Yes' responses of Community's for Earthquake, Flood, Landslides, Avalanches, Drought, Fire and Accident is 98.8%, 94.4%, 90.0% 74.4%, 79.6%, 93.2% and 91.6% respectively. The 'No' responses of Community's for Communal Clash is 76.8%.

Table No.5: Increasing Causes of Hazards and Vulnerability of District Kishtwar

S. No.	Causes of Increasing the Vulnerability of Disasters	Frequency	Percentage
1	Unplanned Construction	217(86.8)	250(100)
2	Uncompleted Construction	225(90.0)	250(100)
3	Development Projects	193(77.2)	250(100)
4	Geographical Conditions	156(62.4)	250(100)
5	Climate Change	228(91.2)	250(100)
6	Communal Clashes	192(76.8)	250(100)
Total		250	52(100)

Source: Primary data, Parentheses is percentage given in bracket

The Table No. 5 above, shows the responses of the Community about the causes which are making the district more hazardous and vulnerable. It represents the 'Yes' responses of Community's for Unplanned Construction, Uncompleted Construction, Development Projects, Geographical Conditions and Climate Change as 86.8%, 90.0%, 77.2%, 62.4% and 91.2% respectively. It further shows 76.8%, 'No' response for Communal Clashes.

Table No.6: Assessment of the Capacity Building of Institutional Machinery

S.No.	Subjects Asked	Frequency	Percentage
1.	Adequacy of Funds	52(100)	52(100)
2.	Adequacy of Human Resource	52(100)	52(100)
3.	Adequacy of Infrastructure, Tools and Equipments	52(100)	52(100)
4.	Availability of Early Warning System	52(100)	52(100)
5.	Providing Tools and Equipments for Community	52(100)	52(100)
6.	Training of Disaster Management	39(75)	52(100)
7.	Providing Awareness, Mock-Drill and Training for Community	44(85)	52(100)
Total		52	52(100)

Source: Primary data, Parentheses is percentage given in bracket

The Table No.6 shows the responses of Institutional Machinery (D.M.F.) about their different Capacity Building processes for Disaster Management in the district. It depicts 100% 'No' responses about the Adequacy of Funds, Human

Resource, Adequate Infrastructure, Tools and Equipments, Availability of Early Warning System and Providing Tools and Equipments for Community. It further shows 75%, 'No' response for getting any Training of Disaster Management. The last question is about the participation of D.M.F. members in any programme of Providing Awareness, Mock-Drill and Training to prepare Community and the response is 85% said 'No'.

Table No.7: Basic Knowledge about Rescue in Disaster Management

S. No	Cases of Disaster Management	Responses	
1	Respondents Case	35(67.4)	52(100)
2	Opening of Air Ways	39(75.0)	52(100)
3	Emergency Moves	34(65.4)	52(100)
4	Whistle Signals	36(69.3)	52(100)
Total		52	52(100)

Source: Primary data, Parentheses is percentage given in bracket

The Table No. 7 above shows the responses of D.M.F. members about their Basic Knowledge of Rescue operation in Disaster Management. The first question asked whether they know about "Respondent Case" or not and 67.4% said 'No'. The second question asked whether they know about the "Opening of Air Ways" of a patient or not and the response was 75.0% who said 'No'. The third question asked pertaining to what "Emergency Moves" they would take in a rescue operation and the response is - 65.4% said that they do not know about the emergency moves. The last question was about "Whistle Signals" in a rescue operation and the response was 69.3% said 'No' that they do not know about the Whistle Signals.

Table No.8: Community Capacity Building for Disaster Management

S.No.	Subjects Asked	Frequency	Percentage
1.	Institutional Initiatives to Mitigate Hazards	247(98.8)	250(100)
2.	Participated in Awareness Programme/Mock Drill/Training	246(98.4)	250(100)
3.	Emergency contact number of D.M.F.	250(100)	250(100)
4.	Houses Constructed in accordance with BIS Code	230(92)	250(100)
Total		52	250(100)

Source: Primary data, Parentheses is percentage given in bracket

The Table No. 8 above represents the responses of Community's Capacity -Building for Disaster Management in the district. The first question was whether there is any initiative run or not by Government to mitigate the hazards and reduces vulnerability in the district. The response is 98.8% said 'No' that there is no initiative or programme run by the government. The second question was the participation of people in any Awareness Programme/Mock-Drill/Training and the response is 98.4% said 'No' that they haven't participated in above such programmes. The third question was whether - the people have any Emergency contact number of D.M.F. (District Management Force) or not and the response is 100% said 'No'. The last question asked whether the people have constructed their houses according to the guidelines of Bureau of Indian Standard (BIS) code or not. The response is 92% said 'No' that they have not followed the BIS code.

Findings

It is found from the interpretation of a majority of responses of Table No. 4 of Disaster Management Force members and the People of the Community that the district is vulnerable for multiple hazards, that is, 7 out of 8 hazards have a probability of occurrence in the district.

It is found from the majority of responses of Table No. 5 of People of the Community that the district is becoming more vulnerable for disaster due to increasing causing of hazards. It found that 5 causes out of 6 are perpetually enhancing vulnerability of the community for multiple hazards.

It is found here from the elucidation of majority of responses (100%) of Disaster Management Force members of Table No.6 that the Institutional Machinery has 0 (Nil) Capacity or Adequacy of Funds, Human Resource, Infrastructure, Tools and Equipments, Availability of Early Warning System and Providing Tools and Equipments to Community for the enhancement of Capacity Building of Disaster Management Force and the Community to aptly face and manage disaster in the district. The Table also found from the majority of responses (75%) of members of Disaster Management Force that they haven't got any Training of Disaster Management. It also found from the majority of responses (85%) that they haven't participated in any programme to Provide Awareness, Mock-Drill and Training for People of the Community suffered.

The Table No. 7 above has found from the majority of responses of members of Disaster Management Force about their Basic Knowledge of Rescue Operation in Disaster Management. It is found here from the majority of response (67.4%) of members that they don't know about Respondents Cases in rescue operation of patients in disaster management. It is also found here from the majority of responses (75%) that - they don't know how to Open the Air Ways of a patient in a rescue operation. The Table further also found from the majority of responses (65.4%) that the members of force don't know about the Emergency Moves in rescue operation. The last finding of this table from the majority of responses (69.3%) is that they do not know about Whistle Signals in the rescue operation of disaster management.

The Table No. 8 has interpreted the responses of people of the Community about their Capacity Building of Disaster Management in the district. It has found from the majority of responses (98.8%) of people that the Government has not taken any Institutional Initiatives to Mitigate Hazards in the district. It also found from a majority of responses (98.4%) that they haven't participated in any Awareness Programme/Mock-Drill/ Training of Capacity-Building for disaster management. It is further found by the majority of responses (100%) that they don't have any Emergency Contact Number of Disaster Management Force (D.M.F.) to contact them in any disaster. The last finding of this table is that the majority of responses (92%) of people have not constructed their Houses in accordance with BIS Code.

Discussion and Conclusion

Discussion

Section 30, Sub-section- 2 and Clause- iii, viii and xxiv of National Disaster Management, Act 2005, directs the following guidelines to district disaster management authority:-

Clause-iii, "*ensure that the areas in the district vulnerable to disasters are identified and measures for the prevention of disasters and the mitigation of its effects are undertaken by the departments of the Government at the district level as well as by the local authorities*" (NDM Act, 2005),

Clause-viii, "*lay down guidelines to be followed by the Department of the Government at the district level for purpose of integration of measures for prevention of disaster and mitigation in their development plans and projects and provide necessary technical assistance therefor*" (NDM Act, 2005) and-

Clause-xxiv, *"examine the construction in any area in the district and, it is of the opinion that the standards for the prevention of disaster or mitigation laid down for such construction is not being or has not been followed - may direct the concerned authority - to take such action as may be necessary to secure compliance of such standards"* (NDM Act, 2005).

It is clear from the above stated guidelines of the National Disaster Management Act, 2005 and the finding of the study (that is 5.1) which has found that the area is vulnerable for 7 hazards (Earthquake, Flood, Landslides, Avalanches, Drought, Fire and Accident) and the possibility of occurrence of these hazards are increasing perpetually according to the finding of 5.2 due to the 5 different causes such as; Unplanned Construction, Uncompleted Construction, Development Projects, Geographical Conditions and Climate Change. It ratifies that the guidelines of NDM, Act, 2005 are not fully implemented in the district and there is a lack of co- ordination of National Disaster Management Plan and the State Disaster Management Plan with the grass-root level that is District Disaster Management Plan.

6.1 Conclusion: It is concluded here from the above discussion that the district disaster management plans need a proper check, control and accountability pertaining to the implementation of national guidelines to consolidate the disaster management mechanisms in the country to save life and property at the district level. The study here also achieved the first objective of the study to know about the implementation of NDM Act, 2005 guidelines in the district.

6.2 Discussion: The following mentioned guidelines of Section 30,Sub-section-2 and Clause- x, xii, xiii, xxv and xiv and Section 31, Sub-section 2, Clause-C of National Disaster Management, Act 2005, direct the following guidelines for district disaster Institutional Machinery to enhance their Capacity-Building of disaster management in their district;

The Section 30,Sub-section-2 and Clause- x has given the guidelines to - *"review the state of capacities for responding to any disaster or threating disaster situation in the district and give directions to the relevant departments or authorities at the district level for their upgradation as may be necessary"* (NDM Act, 2005), and Section 31, Sub-section 2, Clause- C has stated the guidelines to, *"capacity-building and preparedness measures required to be taken...at the district level...to respond to any threatening disaster situation or disaster"* (NDM Act, 2005).

The finding of the study (that is 5.3) about the capacity-building of Institutional Machinery (D.M.F.) has found that the machinery does not have adequate funding and there is also - a scarcity of human resource to manage any disastrous situation in the district.

6.2 Conclusion: It is concluded here from the above discussion of disaster management guidelines and finding of the study that the district does not have adequate source of funds to enhance the capacity of Institutional Machinery (D.M.F.) in terms of human resource, technology, tools and equipments to face the multiple hazards of the district. It is also concluded here that there is no specific allocation of fund for district disaster capacity building. Thus, it is vital after the identification of multiple hazards in the district that there should be a specific and adequate allocation of funds to prevent, mitigate and prepare commensurate human capacity for the effective management of any disaster.

6.3 Discussion: The Section-30, Sub-section-2, Clause- xxv and xiv states the guidelines as to-

"establish stockpiles of relief and rescue materials or ensure preparedness to make such materials available at the short notice" (NDM Act, 2005) and *"set up, maintain, review and -*

upgrade the mechanism for early warning and dissemination of proper information to public"(NDM Act, 2005).

The interpretation of above guidelines elucidate about the capacity-building of district institutional machinery in terms of its infrastructure, stockpile of tools and equipments and early warning system. But the study has found in 5.3 finding that the machinery has not an adequate infrastructure, tools and equipments to aptly manage any disastrous situation in the district. The machinery does not have any forecasting system for Early Warning of any hazards to evacuate the vulnerable people and to save their property before happening of any disaster.

6.3 Conclusion: It is concluded here that the Disaster Management Force does not have a proper place for their human power and along with unavailability of tools and equipments of specific hazards of the respective area; making them more vulnerable. The unavailability of early warning system is a weak mark of district disaster management system of India, where the first hand reactionary of any disaster resides. It has further concluded that the guidelines of NDM Act, 2005 are still on the papers and the process of capacity building of district disaster management is far behind their requisite capacities of disaster management.

6.4 Discussion: The Section- 30, Sub-section-2 and Clause- xii and xiii directs to - *"organise and coordinate specialized training programmes for different levels of officers, employees and voluntary rescue workers in the district"* (NDM Act, 2005) and *"facilitate community training and awareness programmes for prevention of disaster or mitigation with the support of local authorities, government..."* (NDM Act, 2005).

The study has found in its finding 5.3, the majority of 75% members of the force have not got any training of disaster management and majority of 85% members have not participated in any program to provide Awareness, Mock-drill and Training to the people of the district. The study here found a co-relation of finding 5.3 and finding 5.4 that the members of force do not have the Basic Knowledge of Rescue Operation in disaster management because of lack of training of disaster management and participation in awareness program, mock-drill and training to the community.

6.4 Conclusion: The above interpretation of the guidelines and the finding of the study have concluded here that there is a lack of implementation NDM, Act's guidelines at district level and the consequence is there is a lack of adequate training to all the members of disaster management force and subsequently, the members of the force are not competent to do the rescue operation of any disaster in the district. It is also concluded here that the district Institutional Machinery (D.M.F.) is playing a meager role to enhance the Community Capacity Building for disaster management and the people of the district are still vulnerable to get destructed along with their property in case of happening of any disaster.

6.5 Discussion: The National Disaster Management Act, 2005 has given various following guidelines to consolidate Community Capacity-Building of disaster management under the Section 30, Sub-section-2 and Clause- viii, xiii, xiv, xx and xxiii;

Section 30, Sub-section-2 and Clause- xx has stated the guidelines-

to district authority to, *"coordinate with, and give guidelines to, local authorities in the district to ensure that measures for the prevention or mitigation of threatening disaster situation or disaster in the district are carried out promptly and effectively"* (NDM Act, 2005).

The above-mentioned Clause-xx has already been discussed alongwith Clause- viii, xiii and xiv in the 6.2 above.

Discussion gives clear guidelines to the district authority to take prevention and mitigation measures to reduces the threat or impact of disaster, to train all people at local level by organising awareness programmes, mock-drills, training and to provide early warning of disaster to increases and build the community capacity to face disaster efficiently. But the study has found in its finding 5.5 that majority of responses (98.8%) the district authority has not taken any preventive or mitigative measures of disaster management, the majority of people (98.4%) said that they have not participated in any Awareness Programme/Mock-Drill/ Training and lastly the majority of people (100%) said that they do not have any Emergency Contact Number of Disaster Management Force.

Section 30, Sub-section-2 and Clause xxiii has also mentioned guidelines to the district authority to - "*examine the construction in any area in the district and, if it is of the opinion that the standard for the prevention of disaster or mitigation laid down for such construction is not being or has not been followed, may direct the concerned authority to take such action as may be necessary to secure compliance of such standards*" (NDM Act, 2005).

The guidelines direct the district authorities to examine the construction of the area to follow the standards fixed for that area on the bases of their vulnerability of hazards. The study area comes in an Earthquake Seismic Zone- v of very high risk zone (DDM Plan, 2018-19).Thus, authority has to take such actions which are necessary to secure compliance of such standards to prevent or mitigate hazards and which makes a resistance not to convert a hazard into a big disaster. The construction standards for the study area are also passed in the Building ByeLaws Under J&K Municipal Corp. Act 2000 to secure from happening of any construction sort of disasters (DDM Plan, 2018-19). But the study has found in its finding 5.5 that majority of people (92%) have not constructed their houses and other building neither under the Bureau of Indian Standard (BIS) Code nor any state laws.

6.5 Conclusion: It is concluded here from the above discussion of Community Capacity-Building of disaster management that there are a number of guidelines which have been mentioned in the NDM, Act, 2005 to consolidate the district disaster management mechanism. But, even, after the vulnerability of the study area for multiple hazards, no initiative has been taken to prevent or mitigate hazards, which shows a lack of check, co-ordination and accountability of implementation of guidelines of higher authority at community level by district authority. Community is the first hand reactionary for any kind of disaster but the process of community capacity building is negligible and it is also concluded here that there is no co-relation of providing and getting of disaster management awareness/mock-drill/training by disaster management force and the people of the community respectively. It is also concluded that the study area is vulnerable to multiple hazards and comes in a very high risk zone, especially seismic zone- v but inspite of that there is a lack of compliance of BIS standards in construction. Besides that there is no control on anthropogenic activities, consequently, the capacity building of disaster management in the study area is diluting, reducing and becoming negligible in the name of development, by only focusing on the top-down approach rather focusing on bottom-up approach of community capacity building of disaster management.

References

1. *UNISDR*. (2009, May). Retrieved October 13, 2019, from ISDR: https://www.unisdr.org/files /7817_UNISDRTerminologyEnglish.pdf
2. *NDM Plan*. (2016). Retrieved October 13, 2019, from Policy and Plan: https://ndma.gov.in/ images/ guidelines/national-dm-policy2009.pdf
3. *DDM Plan*. (2018-19). Retrieved 10 08, 2019, from District Kishwtwar: https://kishtwar.nic.in/disaster- management/
4. Basu, R. (2004). *Public Administration concepts and theories.* New Delhi: Sterling Publishers Pvt. Ltd.
5. Bhagat, S. N. (n.d.). Retrieved 12 12, 2019, from http://www.pdpu.ac.in/downloads/1%20 Community-Based-Disaster-Management.pdf
6. D. Ravindra Prasad V.S. Prasad P. Satyanarayana, Y. Pardhasaradhi. (2017). *Administrative Thinkers.* D. R. Prasad, V. S. Prasad, P. Satyanarayana, & Y. Pardhasaradhi, Eds. New Delhi: Sterling Publishers(P) LTD.
7. *District Kishtwar*. (n.d.). Retrieved 12 09, 2019, from https://kishtwar.nic.in/administrative-setup/ Gautam,
8. S. H. (n.d.). Retrieved 12 10, 2019, from https://idsa.in/system/files/jds_6_1_Shivanandah.Gautam.pdf
9. Masson, V. L. (2015). *BioOne*. Retrieved 12 08, 2019, from https://doi.org/10.1659/MRD-JOURNAL-D-14-00086.1
10. Melissa Parsons, Sonya Glavac, Peter Hastings, Graham Marshall, James McGregor, Judith McNeill, Phil Morley, Ian Reeve, Richard Stayner,. (2016, 10). *International Journal of Disaster Risk Reduction*. Retrieved 11 25, 2019, from ScienceDirect: https://www.sciencedirect.com/science/article/pii/S2212420916300887
11. *NDM Act, 2005.* (n.d.). Retrieved October 13, 2005, from NDMA: https://ndma.gov.in/images/ndma-pdf/DM_act2005.pdf
12. *NDM Plan*. (n.d.). Retrieved 12 10, 2019, from NDMA: https://ndma.gov.in/images/ndma-pdf/DM_act2005.pdf

13. Patil, P. (2012), *Research Gate.* Retrieved 12 10, 2019, from ResearchGate: https://www.researchgate.net/publication/314216553_Disas ter_Management_in_India
14. *World Meteorological Organisation.* (n.d.). Retrieved 12 10, 2019, from World Meteorological Organisation:http://www.preventionweb.net/files/28558_2855886snetdistrictdisaster manageme.pdf

Chapter Sixteen

Impact of E-Governance Initiatives in Grievance Redressal A Study of CM Window System in Haryana

Mohit Bishnoi[17] *& Vidya Bhaskar Shukla*[18]

Abstract

The success of democracy and development depends to a great extent on the efficiency of the government machinery. However, in the exercise of administrative powers, there is always a possibility of malpractices. These malpractices result in public grievances towards the administration. This paper is an effort to determine how E-Governance initiatives are playing a pivotal role in Grievance Redressal. The paper positively concludes that the multiplier effect of e-Governance initiative such as CM Window system will ensure good governance fostering digital democracy and inclusive growth and will revolutionize the Grievance Redressal system in India.

Keywords: *Grievance Redressal, E-Governance, Good Governance, CM window system*

Introduction

The orientation of public administration has undergone a paradigm shift with the advent of the 21st century. The success of administration and development depends to a great extent on the efficiency of the government machinery. However, in the exercise of administrative powers, there is always a possibility of malpractices. These malpractices result in public grievances towards the administration. Instead of good government, governance has become the buzz word. It has become citizen-centric from bring state-centric. Therefore, the provision of a variety of public services to its citizenry has become the primary mandate of governance.These changes led to such virtues as transparency, responsiveness and accountability which in-turn ensured good governance. Today e-governance is the most significant theme in the development discourse.E-Governance has

17. Guest Faculty, Department of Political Science, Jamia Millia Islamia, New Delhi
18. PhD (Research Scholar), Department of Political Science, Jamia Millia Islamia, New Delhi

made a profound impact on every aspect of human life, including work and business, and contributed tremendously to the competitiveness of our nation through social and economic development (Kalsi, Kiran & Vaidya 2009). Today, connectivity, convergence, internet and networks are the new mantras for the success of any government policy and programme.

To ensure the success of service delivery, the administration must address grievances which arise during the delivery of these services. The traditional Grievance Redressal Mechanisms may not be useful in the era of technology and digitalization. Hence using e-governance in the sphere of grievance redressal has become significant to realize the goals of good governance and citizen-centric delivery of services.

Concept of Grievance Redressal Mechanism

According to the Cambridge dictionary, grievance means 'a complaint or a strong feeling that one has been treated unfairly' In a democracy people should have the opportunities to ventilate their grievances and a system of redressal is required to address those grievances. Grievance Redressal Mechanism is a part and parcel of the machinery of any administration. No administration can claim to be answerable, responsive, and user-friendly unless it has established a proficient and effective grievance redressal mechanism. The grievance redressal mechanism of an organization is an approximation to scrutinize its efficiency and effectiveness as it provides meaningful feedback on the working of its administration. The gap between the performance of the administration and the expectations of the people also created a negative image of the administration. The democratic -aspirations of the people and the authoritarian attitude of administrators produced tensions between the two. The contradictions in the social situation have resulted in inequalities. There is discrimination in the treatment of citizens by the administration. There are the chronic delays in getting things done, and many rules and regulations that are not easily comprehensible to ordinary citizens. The cumulative effect of all these factors is the piling up of public grievances against the administration. Some of the common grievances against administration may include- Corruption, Nepotism, Neglect of Duty, Delays and Inadequate Redressal Machinery.

Simplification of rules & procedures has been suggested and carried on in practice to deal with the redressal of citizens' grievances. Besides these, new institutions have also been recommended and set up in many countries.

Created for the redressal of public grievances, the institution of "Ombudsman" is typically Scandinavian. The office of Ombudsman has been in existence in Sweden since 1809 and in Finland since 1919. Denmark introduced the system in 1955. Norway and New Zealand adopted it in 1962, and the United Kingdom appointed the Parliamentary Commissioner for Administration in 1967. Several countries in the world have since adopted the Ombudsman-like institution.

In India, it has been observed by many committees and commissions that special machinery should be set up to deal with public complaints against the administration. The government has also created the Department of Administrative Reforms and Public Grievances. It is the nodal agency of the government for Administrative Reforms as well as redressal of public grievances. The public grievance redress mechanism functions in India on a decentralized basis. An officer of the level of joint secretary is designated as director of grievances of the Ministry/Department/Organization. The enactment of Administrative Tribunal Act 1985 opened a new chapter in the sphere of administrating justice to the aggrieved government servant and in some cases, public members. However, the factors such as lack of awareness and lack of relevant information make this process even more tedious.

Sevottam framework was created by the Department of Administrative Reforms and Public Grievances, Government of India in 2005, after study of the best international practices such as the Charter Mark of United Kingdom and the Malcolm model of United States of America. It is a framework for bringing continual improvements in service delivery by government organizations until excellence is achieved. The framework has a total of 3 modules with three criteria and 11 elements in each. The first module is the *Citizen's Charter* that specifies the standards for service delivery, the second is the *Grievance Redress Mechanism* to get redress if service is not provided as per standards, and the third is the *Capability Building* for building the capability and capacity of the organization to deliver its services as per standards included in its Charter. With three criteria and 11 elements in each module, the QMS *Sevottam* has a total of 9 criteria and 33 elements that comprehensively cover all aspects of service delivery to monitor gaps as well as improvement.

Concept of Good Governance and E-Governance

As explained by World Bank in its 1992 Report on Governance and Development; Good Governance is central to creating and sustaining an environment which fosters strong and equitable development, and it is an essential complement to sound economic policies. (World Bank, 1992). Good governance aims at providing an environment in which all citizens irrespective of class, caste and gender can develop to their full potential. In addition, good governance also aims at providing public services effectively, efficiently and equitably to the citizens. Citizens are thus at the core of good governance. Therefore, good governance and citizen centric administration are inextricably linked.

In October 1995 by a policy paper called "Governance: Sound Development Management", the ADB (Asian Development Bank) outlined its policy on Good Governance. The ADB has identified four basic elements of good governance - *a) Accountability:* Public officials should be answerable for government behavior and responsive to the entity from which they derive authority. The accountability of public sector institutions is facilitated by evaluation of their economic performance. The suggested specific areas of action would be in the building of government capacity through, for example, public-sector management, public-enterprise management and reform, public financial management and civil-service reform. b) *Participation:* Government structures should be flexible enough to offer beneficiaries and others affected the opportunity to improve the design and implementation of public programmes and projects. The specific areas of action would be in the development of participatory development processes through, for example, participation of beneficiaries, a public/private-sector interface, decentralization/empowerment of local government and cooperation with non-governmental organizations (NGOs)c) *Predictability:* Laws and policies should exist that regulate society and that are applied fairly and consistently. Predictability requires the state and its subsidiary agencies to be bound by and answerable to the legal system in the same way as private enterprises and individuals. The specific area of action could be the development of predictable legal frameworks for private-sector development. d) *Transparency.* Information should be made available to the general public and there should be clarity as to rules and regulations. Access to timely information on the economy can be vital to economic decision-making by the private sector and can also serve to inhibit corruption.

The absence of good governance has proved to be particularly damaging to the "corrective intervention" role of government. Any Programme aiming for delivery of services to citizens, poverty alleviation and economic development, for example, can be totally undermined by a lack of public accountability, corruption, and the "capture" of public services by elites. In twenty first century the equitable delivery of services with proper accountability cannot be imagined without using the Information and Communication (ICT) technology in delivery of services to the citizens of any nation.

Concept of E-Governance

Reinventing government has been a dominant theme since the 1990s, wherein governments world over are attempting to improve the systems of public service delivery. Rapid strides made in the field of Information and Communication Technology (ICT) have facilitated the reinvention of governments and prepared them to serve the needs of a diverse society. In other words, the information age has redefined the fundamentals and transformed the institutions and mechanisms of service delivery forever. The vision is the articulation of a desire to transform the way government functions and the way it relates to its constituents. The concept of electronic governance, popularly called e-governance, is derived from this concern. Democracies in the world share a vision of the day when e-governance will become a way of life.

Technology is transforming governments, especially in the performance of their functions. It is the sole reason for governments all over the world, embracing technology and becoming electronically viable. ICT enables and facilitates good governance agenda of transparency, accountability, empowerment, decentralization and fiscal reforms. It is this agenda that governments of today are aspiring to achieve. Governments are using ICTs in restructuring their traditional organizational setup, re-engineering the work processes, interacting with citizens and stakeholders, rendering services and information, and efficient human resources management, financial management and decision-making.

E-governance is the application of ICT to the processes of government functioning for good governance. In other words, e-governance is the public sector's use of ICTs to improve information and service delivery, encourage citizen participation in decision-making and make government more accountable, transparent and efficient.

The Ministry of Information and Technology states that e-governance mechanism goes far beyond mere computerization of stand alone back-office operations. It also implies fundamental changes in government operations; and new set of responsibilities for the legislature, executive, judiciary and citizens. According to the Comptroller and Auditor General, UK, e-governance means providing public access to information via the internet by government departments and their agencies. The rapid diffusion of ICTs has transformed governance for good. Government's ability to execute and deliver on its roles and functions has certainly been enhanced significantly by the digital revolution; and, people are now more able to participate in public decision-making processes, to connect and mobilize, to influence government, and to hold government to account.

So in essence, e-governance is the application of ICT in government functioning to bring in SMART governance, implying: simple, moral, accountable, responsive and transparent governance. Hence, ICTs are playing a significant role in enabling governments to pursue the agenda of good governance.

E-Governance in India

Dr. APJ Abdul Kalam, former President of India, had visualized e-Governance in the Indian context to mean: *"A transparent, smart e-Governance with seamless access, secure and authentic flow of information crossing the interdepartmental barrier and providing a fair and unbiased service to the citizen."* E-Governance in India has been designed and developed to take care of all such problems of the people without stepping in to the offices of ministries and government organizations. In the majority of cases, citizens do not even know who is accountable to listen to their problems. Therefore, the significance of such e-government systems is felt even more for smooth, transparent, and impartial running of the governments. Thus, the OPGRS has emerged as such an e-government system, which is primarily meant for addressing the grievances, issues, and problems of citizen's everyday life and gets them resolved online by the high-level government officials designated for it (Rana, Dwivedi, & Williams, 2013).The success of this system can be measured only when a large section of the society adopts this system to register complaints and the government responses properly to their issues leading to the citizens' satisfaction

In order to unify the e-Governance initiatives under a common objective, the National e-Governance Plan (NeGP) was launched in 2006 with an attempt to push e-Governance as an integral part of the functioning as to how government services will be delivered. NeGP comprises 27 Mission Mode Projects (MMPs) and eight-core/support components. Despite the success of NeGP, there was a need to revolutionize e-Governance by bringing further transformation in the government's functioning and society's involvement in a digitally empowered knowledge society. Hence, a plan for Digital India was conceptualized and approved subsequently in 2015. The span and vision of Digital India is wider than NeGP since Digital India incorporates electronic delivery of services with several other key strategic areas such as broad band highways, ICT manufacturing, access to mobile connectivity, employment creation along with e-Governance, etc.

E-Governance and Grievance Redressal in India

The traditional approach of addressing grievances of the citizens did not have desired results hence the use of ICT or e-governance strategies have been advocated. In the context of Grievance Redressal e-governance strategies play a pivotal role and the recommendations of the Second ARC's Fourth Report, 'Ethics in Governance', Eleventh Report, 'Promoting e-Governance: The SMART Way Forward' and Twelfth Report, 'Citizen-Centric Administration' highlights this changing paradigm. The recommendations were focused not only on creating such a robust mechanism of service delivery but also to address the grievances after the service delivery. With changing times, the concentration of government has moved past the service delivery and is also focusing on addressing the grievances so that the real intent of policies can be achieved in more efficient as well as effective manner.

In this context, many state governments came out with different e-governance strategies to address the evolving problem of un-addressed grievances. On April 24th 2003,Gujrat became the first State to introduce a combination of digital and communication technology in the form of a programme for addressing grievances using e-governance platform naming, State Wide Attention on Grievances by Application of Technology (SWAGAT) with an objective of giving attention on grievances to strengthen *good governance*, analyzing the nature of grievances submitted to Government, bringing attention on the quality of Redressal at all levels and activate administration to solve public grievances at State, District and Sub District levels.

On July 31st 2014, the CM Helpline, a good governance initiative by Madhya Pradesh (MP) government was inaugurated which is envisioned as a bridge connecting citizens to the state. It is a public-private partnership between the

State Agency for Public Services of the state government of MP and a private business process outsourcing (BPO) services firm. In the CM Helpline, phone operators record the complaints of callers. The operators work from inside the government to route the complaint to the appropriate official. Complaints automatically escalate until they are deemed to be resolved.

CM Window System in Haryana: An Analysis

A majority of Haryana's population still live in the villages; almost 65.12 % of the population is rural and only 34.88% is urban with the rural literacy rate being 71.42%. In recent decades, Haryana has experienced rapid economic growth, making it one of the most affluent states of the country but public services delivery is not as effective as it should be. Citizens in rural areas still face difficulties in accessing public services and poor awareness levels prevent them from realizing their rights and entitlements. Moreover the grievance redressal at district and block level is slow and required a revamp.

The lack of awareness among the citizens regarding the competent authority for filling the complaints and also involvement of multiple administrative offices in the traditional grievance redressal mechanism system plays a hindrance in addressing the complaints in quick time. Besides, the attitude and willingness of the government functionaries also becomes crucial in this respect. Citizen-friendly officers are required to attend the complaints in time-bound manner to make the grievance redressal apparatus work.

Keeping these circumstances, in December 2014, on National Good Governance Day, the Haryana Chief Minister launched the CM Web Portal and a CM Window in all districts of the State to bring transparency in governance and ensure prompt redressal of people's grievances. It is a simple and user friendly one stop complaint cell exclusively for citizens' grievance redressal located in all district headquarters of the state. This kind of pro-active approach will bring more transparency and accountability in the administrative system.

It is clear from the data that in the first year of its setting, CM Window at Director General of Police Office, Out of a total of 24198 complaints 11,188 had been disposed and over 9323 complaints even Action Taken Report had been submitted in the first year itself. If we talk about the year 2017, a total of 264302 complaints have been received and 225355 have been disposed off and 8946 are in action and 2199 Action Taken Reports have been submitted. Applications submitted are scanned and updated to the office of the Chief Minister and thereafter are routed back to the concerned government departments. Within 30 days of lodging the complaint, the respective government department should either redress the grievance or reply to the complainant why the request cannot be approved.

Since the launch of this mechanism on December 25, 2014, the Haryana government and several nongovernmental organizations working in the state have been encouraging and assisting the communities to make effective use of the same. The objective is to address the complaints related to poor delivery of food items in the Public Distribution System, pendency of pensions, teachers' poor attendance in schools, and many more that are reported and resolved at this one-stop window more or less within the stipulated time limit.

In the present paper the data from 2015 -17 has been analysed for understanding the functioning of C.M. Window System and bring out the advantages of e-governance system and also showing how administration is using "data manipulation" in addressing the grievances of the citizens.

Period- Jan-July 2015

89228 (Total Registrations- Grievances, Demands, Suggestions)

- 1195 Fresh (Grievances /Demands /Suggestions)
- 7891 In Action (Grievances)
- 43978 ATR Received (Grievances /Demands /Suggestions)
- 19886 Disposed Off (Grievances /Demands /Suggestions)
- 3022 (No Action Required)
- 175 In Action (Demand)
- 78 In Action (Suggestion)
- 13003 Overdue (Grievances /Demands /Suggestions)

0 Complaints Registered as Others

In the 2nd August 2015 meeting of C.M. Window System the data presented shows total 89228 fresh complaints were filed from January 2015 – July 2015 period. Out of this ATR has been submitted for 43978 complaints and 7,891 complaints were in action and 19,886 (22.26% only) complaints have been disposed off. But on carefully examining the data it can be concluded that nearly 73% complaints are yet to be disposed off. In the meeting it was also disclosed that there were complaints of vague replies, non compliance or non joining of the complainant, disposed off citing non availability of record or persons and non action even though complaints were disposed off were found, showing that the administration is manipulating the data and grievances are still unheard at the grass root level.

Period- January - April 2016

CM Window Dashboard

155531 (Total Registrations- Grievances, Demands, Suggestions)		
910 Fresh (Grievances /Demands /Suggestions)	7588 In Action (Grievances)	4890 ATR Received (Grievances /Demands /Suggestions)
115291 Disposed Off (Grievances /Demands /Suggestions)	7624 (No Action Required)	68 In Action (Demand)
14 In Action (Suggestion)	9604 Overdue	9542 Clarification sought

Receipt-Wise

Departments	Total Receipt	Overdue	Disposed	Clarification
Police	32327	2144	27249	1234
Panchayats	12975	2326	9294	1333
Power	7098	560	5897	279
Revenue	6730	690	5438	353
School Education	6727	1148	5054	550
Urban local Bodies	6208	1377	4057	633
T&CP HUDA	4357	1386	2563	631
Social Justice	3814	231	3039	176
PHE	3200	118	2783	70
F & S	3081	388	2524	115
Health	2830	654	1915	414

In the C.M. Grievances Cell Meeting held on 18th May 2016, it was mentioned that a total of 1, 55,531 complaints were registered and out of which 1,15,291 complaints were disposed off showing nearly 73% complaints were disposed but on carefully analyzing the data of Receipt wise break up it can be said that the disposed off complaints number came down drastically. It is also understood that disposed off data also incorporated the trailing demands and suggestions over the abovementioned complaints and again it may be concluded that the discrepancies were found in the data presented and claims made by the administration.

Period January – June 2017

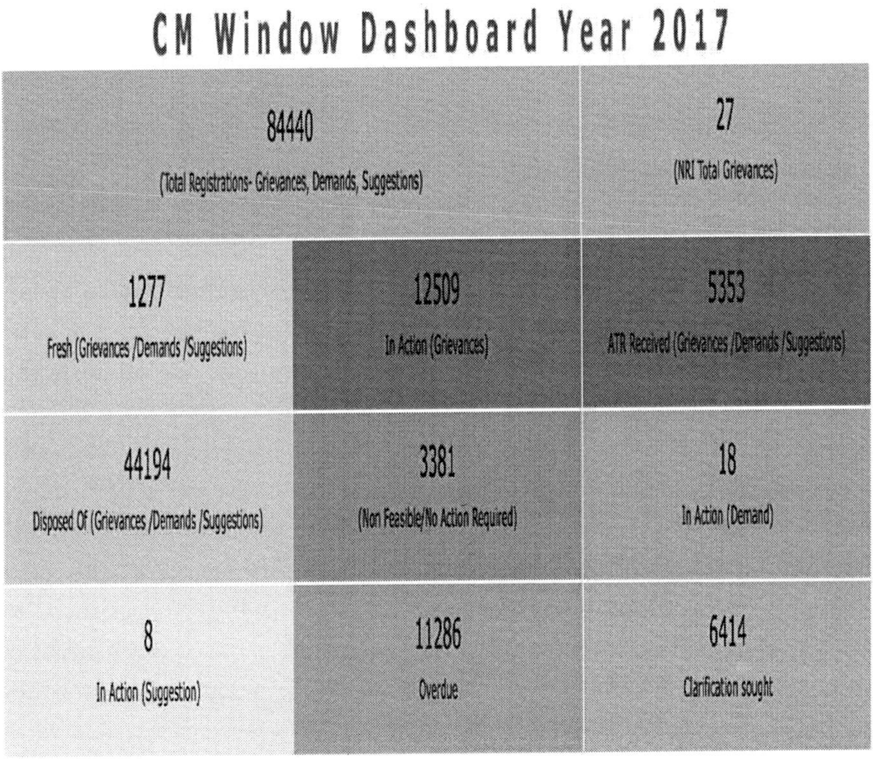

In the C.M. Grievances Cell Meeting held on 24th July 2017, it was disclosed that total complaints registered were 84440 and disposed off complaints were 44,194 complaints comprising only 52% of the complaints and the ATR (Action Taken Report) number was 5353, if we include these numbers in the pending number the pending percentage may shoot up to nearly 62%. The number of overdue complaints have shown an upwards trend in all these years, showing that the complaints are not held in the prescribed time of 30 days. Hence the goal of this e-governance initiative lies unrealized and still grievances of thousands of citizens lay un-addressed.

Special Cases

Two special cases pertaining to C.M.Window system have also been included in the present paper. In the first case (CMOFF/N/2015/65253) belonging to the Panchayati Raj Department of Gadhiwali village of district Sonipat, Haryana the complainant faced undue pressure from the administration to withdraw the case. But even after the inquiry got completed and Panchayat secretary was charge sheeted, there was no action taken against the Sarpanch till date. In the second case (CMOFF/N/2018/017325) belonging to forest department the same officer was made the in-charge of the inquiry who was one of the accused in the case related with falsely tempering of the Annual Confidential Report (ACR) of a tainted officer.

On carefully examining the data of the abovementioned periods and two special cases, it can be concluded that there plenty of qualitative defects in the ATR submitted by grass root level offices to the C.M. office because main concentration of any concerned department is not to address the complaint but file the ATR in stipulated time and maintaining the high percentage in the C.M. Grievance Cell meetings. The only concern is not the late submission of ATRs but the qualitative defects in the ATRs being received from different departments. Now that the majority of the ATRs are being received within the stipulated time frame, another problem regarding qualitative aspect of the action taken is a cause of concerned. But Government is also keeping a close watch over the functioning of the administration at lower levels and recently seven officers of various departments were suspended for negligence over the C.M. Window complaints. Government has also launched feedback mechanisms on the C.M.Window System portal. Overall, government seriousness and these numbers reflect the increased confidence in the new governance system which incorporates the new reformative way of handling the grievances of the citizens and paving a futuristic course for effective administration.

Conclusion

The interaction between citizens and administration in a democracy is a very complicated process. The conflict in society and the values of the society are reflected in this interaction. The capable machinery for the redressal of citizen's grievances makes the administration more human and civilized. This paper was an attempt made to study the nature of public grievances with particular reference to the new e-governance initiative by Haryana government. E-Government is not just "electronic" government. It is "enabled" government, the government that delivers different and better programs and services. E-Governance is that the discrepancies were found in the data presented and claims made by the administration.

Period January – June 2017

CM Window Dashboard Year 2017

84440 (Total Registrations- Grievances, Demands, Suggestions)		27 (NRI Total Grievances)
1277 Fresh (Grievances /Demands /Suggestions)	12509 In Action (Grievances)	5353 ATR Received (Grievances /Demands /Suggestions)
44194 Disposed Of (Grievances /Demands /Suggestions)	3381 (Non Feasible/No Action Required)	18 In Action (Demand)
8 In Action (Suggestion)	11286 Overdue	6414 Clarification sought

In the C.M. Grievances Cell Meeting held on 24th July 2017, it was disclosed that total complaints registered were 84440 and disposed off complaints were 44,194 complaints comprising only 52% of the complaints and the ATR (Action Taken Report) number was 5353, if we include these numbers in the pending number the pending percentage may shoot up to nearly 62%. The number of overdue complaints have shown an upwards trend in all these years, showing that the complaints are not held in the prescribed time of 30 days. Hence the goal of this e-governance initiative lies unrealized and still grievances of thousands of citizens lay un-addressed.

Special Cases

Two special cases pertaining to C.M.Window system have also been included in the present paper. In the first case (CMOFF/N/2015/65253) belonging to the Panchayati Raj Department of Gadhiwali village of district Sonipat, Haryana the complainant faced undue pressure from the administration to withdraw the case. But even after the inquiry got completed and Panchayat secretary was charge sheeted, there was no action taken against the Sarpanch till date. In the second case (CMOFF/N/2018/017325) belonging to forest department the same officer was made the in-charge of the inquiry who was one of the accused in the case related with falsely tempering of the Annual Confidential Report (ACR) of a tainted officer.

On carefully examining the data of the abovementioned periods and two special cases, it can be concluded that there plenty of qualitative defects in the ATR submitted by grass root level offices to the C.M. office because main concentration of any concerned department is not to address the complaint but file the ATR in stipulated time and maintaining the high percentage in the C.M. Grievance Cell meetings. The only concern is not the late submission of ATRs but the qualitative defects in the ATRs being received from different departments. Now that the majority of the ATRs are being received within the stipulated time frame, another problem regarding qualitative aspect of the action taken is a cause of concerned. But Government is also keeping a close watch over the functioning of the administration at lower levels and recently seven officers of various departments were suspended for negligence over the C.M. Window complaints. Government has also launched feedback mechanisms on the C.M.Window System portal. Overall, government seriousness and these numbers reflect the increased confidence in the new governance system which incorporates the new reformative way of handling the grievances of the citizens and paving a futuristic course for effective administration.

Conclusion

The interaction between citizens and administration in a democracy is a very complicated process. The conflict in society and the values of the society are reflected in this interaction. The capable machinery for the redressal of citizen's grievances makes the administration more human and civilized. This paper was an attempt made to study the nature of public grievances with particular reference to the new e-governance initiative by Haryana government. E-Government is not just "electronic" government. It is "enabled" government, the government that delivers different and better programs and services. E-Governance is about people; new skill sets, mindsets and leadership approaches. (Santosh & Teene, 2017).The e-governance initiatives and the e-governance strategies also face multiple challenges. The challenges in e-Governance have been described as centered around 4 key areas viz. people, process, technology and resources. Some of the challenges being faced by government in successfully implementing e-governance initiatives to achieve the goals of good governance are:-*Local Language Support-* The e-Governance project should be in local language because a large part of Indian society lives in rural areas. India is a multi-linguistic nation and before implementing E-Governance project software must be developed in local languages. *Transparency is needed in both workflow and content*; the notion of transparency is typically limited to making content publicly available, but in the context of grievance resolution, it is crucial to adopt transparency in both workflow and content. *Easy Access for users-* The vehicle for E-Governance is computer but in most villages of India computers are not available until and unless government ensures availability of computers in rural areas the fruits of e-Governance can't reach the masses. Even with C.M. Window System it was found that the tracking of complaint after filing is really a tedious task and can only be operated by a SMART phone only. This has also made the complainant discouraged to pursue their complaints after undue delays.

Therefore, designers, developers, and policy makers for the e-government system should focus more on minimizing the complexities associated with exploration and use of the system, if there is any, and usefulness of the system such that acceptance and use of such systems may be managed more successfully. Possible ways of achieving these objectives may include wider and more accurate representation of user requirements to systems analysts, designers, and developers or selection and use of those e-government systems (i.e., as a benchmark) that are more consistent with user requirements and having wide acceptance, and effective communication of the system's capabilities through product brochures, live demonstrations, and success stories. An alternative way to develop widely acceptable and easy to use system can also be developed in consultation with the experienced designers, systems analysts, and software developers who possess a good experience of developing such systems and understand user's anguish and expectations from such system. We also found that social influence had direct impacts on attitude and facilitating conditions on behavioral intention. This suggests that individuals may associate importance to the facilitating conditions such as help desks and training programs as well as to the experiences of other individuals in using the e-government system in question. Hence, the concerned government organization or department should consider providing adequate infrastructural facilities and proper training to users through the established CSCs across the country so that they can be positively inclined to use relatively new e-governance system like C.M.Window system Concerned government departments and/or officials may proactively manage social influence that could be exerted on individuals by organizing forums for sharing best use practices, instituting champions who are enthused about diffusing awareness and benefits of the new e-governance system like C.M.Window system and can generate positive word-of-mouth, and planning counter-measures for any negative feedback.

A state-run initiative serves as the first point of contact for citizen grievances and information-seeking, and a citizen-led initiative serves as watchdog and avenue for escalation for longer-term grievances affecting a large number of people. Such a combination has the potential to foster increased participation, transparency and accountability in governance.

Ultimately, the success of any e-Governance initiative lies in how efficiently it has enhanced citizen's participation in government functioning through wide ICT access, bringing government and the services it offers closer to its citizens, promoting accountability, transparency and responsiveness in government functioning and ensuring that government, not only delivers its services efficiently but also addresses the grievances thereon . These are the sine qua non for *good governance* in a vibrant democracy like India.

References

Ahmad, Furqan and Bishnoi, Mohit, 2019 "Good Governance & Administrative Reforms - An Analysis of Indian System in Contemporary Times. *Think India Journal,* Vol. 22, No. 13, December-2019, pp. 8429-8439.

Alathur, Sreejith, Ilavarasan, P. Vigneswara and Gupta, M.P. 2016, "Determinants of E-participation in the citizens and the government initiatives: Insights from India" *Socio-Economic Planning Sciences*, Vol. 55, September 2016, pp. 36-46

Bhatnagar Subhash, 2004, *E Government from Vision to Implantation*, New Delhi, Sage Publications.

CM window of no use, (2019) The Tribune, Accessed on December 10, 2019, https://www.tribuneindia.com/news/archive/cm-window-of-no-use-870905.

Debika Goswami, 2017, CM Window Spreads its Roots in Haryana Subdivisions, Accessed on 15 December 2019, http://www.smsfoundation.org/wpcontent/uploads/OpeningofBlockWindows_Final1.pdf.

Except Graft, India Didn't Improve on any WB Governance Indicator in 10 years, (2017) Business Standard, Accessed on January 02, 2020

https://www.business-standard.com/article/economy-policy/except-graft-india-didn-t-improve-on-any-wb-governance-indicator-in-10-yrs-117120500163_1.html.

E-Governance Empowering India, (2019) Business Line, Accessed on January 06, 2020, https://www.thehindubusinessline.com/brandhub/e-governance-empowering-india/article26457213.ece?utm_campaign=amp_article_share&utm_medium=referral&utm_source=whatsapp.com.

Government of Haryana, 2017, CM Window Haryana Online Grievance Redressal System, Accessed on December 27, 2019, https://cmharyanacell.nic.in/office/docs/ONLINE%20GRIEVANCES%202017.06.22%20AS%20.pdf.

Kalsisingh, Nirmaljeet, Kiran, Ravi and Vaidya, S. C. 2009 "Changing perspectives and pragmatics of good governance and e-governance in India: a shared vision of citizens" *Int. J. Electronic Governance,* Vol. 2, Nos. 2/3, 2009, pp. 251- 271.

Khurana, Reema, Subramaniam, Sharada and Routry Susmi, 2014, "E-governance initiatives in India – critique and challenges" *Int. J. Procurement Management,* Vol. 7, No. 1, 2014, pp. 85-102.

Monitor Grievances About Undue Delay: Haryana CM Manohar Lal Khattar to Officials, (2015) The Economic Times, Accessed on January 4, 2020, https://economictimes.indiatimes.com/news/politics-and-nation/monitor-grievances-about-undue-delay-haryana-cm-manohar-lal-khattar-to-officials/articleshow/49802561.cms?utm_source=whatsapp_pwa&utm_medium=social&utm_campaign=socialsharebuttons&from=mdr

Seven Suspended in Haryana for Neglecting Complaints on 'CM Window' (2017) The Times of India, Accessed on January 10, 2020, https://timesofindia.indiatimes.com/city/chandigarh/7-suspended-in-haryana-for-neglecting-complaints-on-cm-window/articleshow/58250106.cms

Rana, Nripendra, Dwivedi, Yogesh, Williams, Michael and Lal, Banita, 2015, "Examining the Success of the Online Public Grievance Redressal Systems: An Extension of the IS Success Model", *Information Systems Management,* Vol, 32, No. 01, pp. 39-59.

Rana, Nripendra, Dwivedi, Yogesh, Williams, Michael and Weerakkodi, Vishanth, 2016, "Adaption of Online Public Grievance Redressal System in India: Toward Developing Unified View" *Computer in Human Behavior,* Vol. 59, 2016, pp. 265-282.

Rana, Nripendra, Dwivedi, Yogesh and Williams, Michael, 2013 "Evaluating the Validity of IS Success Models for the Electronic Government Research: An Empirical Test and Integrated Model" *International Journal of Electronic Government Research,* Vol. 9 No. 3, 1-22, July-September, pp, 2013, 01-04.

Rajak, Kumar Santosh and Dhariwal, Teena, 2017, "A Study of E-Governance Initiatives in State of Madhya Pradesh", *International Journal of Educational Planning & Administration*, Vol. 7, Number 1, 2017, pp. 23-29.

World Bank, 1994, Governance the World Bank Experience, Accessed on January 12, 2020, http://documents.worldbank.org/curated/en/711471468765285964/pdf/multi0page.pdf

World Bank, 1992, Governance and Development, Accessed on January 20, 2020. http://documents.worldbank.org/curated/en/604951468739447676/pdf/multi-page.pdf.